Write for a Reason

WRITE FOR A REASON

Patricia Teel Bates
Louisiana State University in Shreveport

ST. MARTIN'S PRESS   NEW YORK

Senior editor: Mark Gallaher
Managing editor: Patricia Mansfield
Associate editor: Edward Mitchell-Hutchinson
Production supervisor: Katherine Battiste
Text design: Leon Bolognese & Associates
Graphics: G&H Soho, Elise Bauman
Cover art and design: Nadia Furlan-Lorbek

Library of Congress Catalog Card Number: 89-63884
Copyright © 1991 by St. Martin's Press, Inc.
All rights reserved. No part of this book may be reproduced, stored in a retrieval system, or transmitted by any form or by any means, electronic, mechanical, photocopying, recording, or otherwise, except as may be expressly permitted by the applicable copyright statutes or in writing by the Publisher. Manufactured in the United States of America.
5 4 3 2 1
f e d c b a

For information, write:
St. Martin's Press, Inc.
175 Fifth Avenue
New York, NY 10010

ISBN: 0-312-00397-8

ACKNOWLEDGMENTS

Angelou, Maya. Selected excerpts from *I Know Why the Caged Bird Sings*. Copyright © 1969 by Maya Angelou. Reprinted by permission of Random House, Inc.

Deener, Bill. "Keeping the Covenant" from *The Dallas Morning News*, August 15, 1987. Reprinted with permission of *The Dallas Morning News*.

Frankl, Viktor. Selected excerpts from *Man's Search for Meaning*. Copyright © 1959, 1963, and 1984 by Viktor Frankl. Reprinted by permission of Beacon Press.

Lopez, Enrique "Hank." "Back to Bachimba" from *Horizon*, volume 9, number 1, 1967. Copyright 1967 by American Heritage, a Division of Forbes, Inc.

Newman, Ruth. "Imagination Helps Communications" from *Communicating in Business Today*. Excerpted by permission of the Royal Bank of Canada Monthly Newsletter.

Peck, Scott. Excerpt from *The Road Less Traveled*. Copyright © 1978 by M. Scott Peck, M.D. Reprinted by permission of Simon and Schuster, Inc.

Schlafly, Phyllis. "The Power of the Positive Woman" reprinted from *The Power of the Positive Woman*. Copyright © 1977 by Phyllis Schlafly. Reprinted by permission of Phyllis Schlafly and Crown Publishers, Inc.

Steinem, Gloria. "Words and Change" excerpted from *Outrageous Acts and Everyday Rebellions*. Copyright © 1983 by East Toledo Productions, Inc. Reprinted by permission of Henry Holt and Company, Inc.

**For Jimmy, Scott, and Catherine—
always with memory**

Preface

Write for a Reason is an interactive writing text appropriate for basic composition classes in community and two-year colleges and the more traditional four-year colleges and universities. It includes ample material for students of varying levels of ability.

Each chapter includes a substantial reading selection, along with preview and review questions, which serves as a springboard for the writing instruction. Step-by-step suggestions for completing each chapter's writing assignment, in addition to student-written examples and revision checklists, guide students through the process of planning, drafting, and revising. Following James Britton's model of discourse, assignments are arranged to emphasize personal, or expressive, writing (Part I) and public, or transactional, writing (Part II). Part III, the Handbook, focuses on matters of language.

Unlike grammar-oriented texts that promote little more than "correct" academic prose written for the teacher, *Write for a Reason* asks students to write informally as well as formally; to write for themselves, for peers, and for others; and to write for the real world as well as the classroom. They are asked to write letters, journal entries, and other forms in addition to informal and formal essays. As they write, they will practice a range of strategies in order to develop skill in planning, drafting, and revising.

Principles and assumptions that guided the development of *Write for a Reason* include the following:

- ❑ An effective basic writing course motivates and encourages students, enables them to experience success, and demonstrates the practical value of effective writing.
- ❑ Students are more motivated to develop abilities they find personally beneficial.
- ❑ Basic writers have a wealth of knowledge, talents, and interests that can be tapped in order to help them develop more skill in writing.
- ❑ Class members are vital resources for one another. Thinking, listening, talking, and reading together can help them learn to write.

- Reading is not simply a mirror image of writing; it is a productive act comparable to the productive act of writing. Learning to read more effectively helps one develop skill in writing.
- Errors and problems with writing should be viewed positively—as an opportunity to learn rather than an invitation to avoid taking risks.
- Different varieties and levels of language serve different purposes and are effective in different situations with different audiences. That is, a particular dialect or form of language is neither good nor bad in and of itself; only within a rhetorical context is one dialect or form of language more or less effective than another.
- Achieving a variety of writing aims requires a variety of planning, drafting, and revising strategies.

Abstracts of related research appear throughout the Instructor's Manual and provide rationale for the methods and materials used in the text.

Acknowledgments

I am indebted to the thousands of students I have worked with over the last twenty-five years, especially those who have allowed me to use their writing for the purposes of this book. These include Scott Brown, Wes Browning, Randy Cooksey, Chuck Fisher, Robert Ford, Kim Hough, Gwin Johnson, Bonnie Lowe, Aneatha Mack, Julia Moore, Tam Nhan, Bill Rice, Tim Spohrer, Tammy Stevens, Nghia Troung, John Watson, and Steve Witte. Rose Van Thyn also permitted me to use her work. Graduate students Jon Barnes, Nancy Victory, and Kristina Nemec worked with me most closely on the book and the Instructor's Manual; I thank them for their sensitivity to language, the careful way they listened to my ideas, and all they taught me. Reviewers who helped me refine my work at various stages of its development include Josephine Koster Tarvers, Rutgers University; Stuart Greene, University of Wyoming; Thomas Franke, Lansing Community College; John Dick, University of Texas at El Paso; Jerry Olson, Middlesex Community College; Marti Singer, Georgia State University; Barbara Henning, Long Island University; Judy Hathcock, Amarillo College; Beth Daniels, Clemson University; Reese Carleton, Lander College; and Linda Harris, University of Maryland at Baltimore City.

For the theoretical grounding they gave to my study of rhetoric and composition, linguistics, and reading, I am grateful to my former professors at the University of Texas at Austin, especially James Kinneavy, Maxine Hairston, John Roueche, Stephen Witte, Lester Faigley, John Daly, and Robert Kline. And I thank them for the importance they gave to the work of Linda Flower, John Hayes, David Bartholemae, Mike Rose, Diane Schallert, James Britton, Robert Tierney, and M. A. K. Halliday, among others. My colleagues at LSU in Shreveport, some of whom I have taught with for more than two decades, have been a constant source of knowledge and encouragement. In particular, I appreciate Evelyn Herring for her extensive assistance with the Handbook, Mary McBride for her unfailing belief in me and for her administrative support that allowed me to finish the book, and Robert Benefield and Leroy Musselman for points of view from other disciplines. Thanks also to colleagues in the Dallas County Community College District for making an array of resources available to me.

St. Martin's has a talented group of editors and staff, who know how to have fun after work. In the order I've come to know them, I thank Kenny Nassau, now national sales manager, who introduced me to the others; Susan Anker who had the vision to see where I was going and the faith to believe I would get there; Andrea Guidoboni; and especially assistant editor Edward Mitchell-Hutchinson and senior editor Mark Gallaher for guiding the editing process with patience and skill. Also, thanks to managing editor Patricia Mansfield for seeing the project through. My secretarial assistants Elizabeth Scalf and Debra Davis were far more than typists; they helped me with my ideas, made a number of valuable suggestions, and just generally kept me going.

Finally I am grateful to my family for the countless personal sacrifices they made so that I could accomplish my goals—my mother and father Maizie and Albert Teel, my husband Jimmy, my son Scott, and my daughter Catherine.

Patricia Teel Bates

Contents

Preface vii

Introduction / Getting Started 1
About this Book 1
A Note from the Author 2
Write It Out: A Letter to Your Instructor 3
Overcoming Negative Writing Attitudes 5
    Strategy 1: Examine Your Feelings 6
    Strategy 2: Study the Writing Process 6
    Strategy 3: Change Self-Defeating Habits 7

Personal Summary 9
Additional Writing 10
Additional Reading 10

Part One — WRITING FOR PERSONAL REASONS 13

Chapter One / Writing: A Problem-Solving Process 15

Reading 15
    Preparing to Read 15
    M. Scott Peck, from *The Road Less Traveled* 16
    Thinking about Your Reading 19

Writing Assignment 21
    A Writing Process 21
        Planning *21*
        Drafting *23*
        Revising *24*

    Write It Out: A Class Newsletter 26
        Planning *27*
        Drafting *28*
        Revising *29*
        A Sample Freshman Class Newsletter *30*

Personal Summary 36
Additional Writing 37
Additional Reading 37

Chapter Two / Personal Writing: From Memory to Insight 38

Reading 38

    Preparing to Read 38
    Maya Angelou, from *I Know Why the Caged Bird Sings* 39
    Thinking about Your Reading 43
    A Reading Process 46
        Planning *47*
        Drafting *48*
        Revising *49*

Writing Assignment 52

    Keeping a Journal 52
    Write It Out: From Journal Entry to Essay 53
        Record a Memory *53*
        Ask a Question *55*
        Answer the Question *55*
        Read before You Write *55*
        Draft Your Narrative *56*
            Sample Rough Draft: "Children's Day" by Gwin Johnson *56*
        Share Your Draft *58*
            Sample Reader Commentary on Gwin's Draft *58*
        Revise Your Draft *59*
            Sample Revised Draft: "Children's Day" by Gwin Johnson *60*

Personal Summary 62
Additional Writing 62
Additional Reading 63

Chapter Three / Voices from the Past 64

Reading 64

    Preparing to Read 65
    Enrique "Hank" Lopez, "Back to Bachimba" 65
    Thinking about Your Reading 69

Writing Assignment 72

    Language, Dialect, and Standard English 72
    Write It Out: An Essay on Family or Culture 75
        Stimulate Your Thinking *75*
        Choose an Interview Subject *75*
        Conduct the Interview *76*
            Sample Interview Transcript: "New Ramah Primitive Baptist Church, Yesterday and Today" by Bonnie Lowe *78*
        Draft Your Essay *81*
            Sample Rough Draft: "Life on 'The Rock'" by John Watson *81*

Share Your Draft *83*
  Sample Group Feedback on John Watson's Draft 83
Revise Your Draft *84*
  Sample Revised Drafts: "Life on 'The Rock'" by John Watson and "New Ramah Primitive Baptist Church, Yesterday and Today" by Bonnie Lowe 84

Personal Summary 88
Additional Writing 89
Additional Reading 90

Part Two   WRITING FOR PUBLIC REASONS 91

Chapter Four / Public Writing from Personal Opinion 93

Readings 94
  Preparing to Read *95*
  Gloria Steinem, from "Words and Change" *96*
  Thinking about Your Reading *98*
  Preparing to Read *100*
  Phyllis Schlafly, from *The Power of the Positive Woman* *101*
  Thinking about Your Reading *103*

Writing Assignment 106
  Writing and Critical Thinking *106*
    Using Evidence *107*
    Evaluating Evidence *111*
  Write It Out: An Opinion Essay *119*
    Freewrite *121*
    Discuss Your Freewriting *122*
    Use the Staircase Method of Freewriting *122*
    Question Your Freewriting *122*
    Find the Main Point and Key Subpoints *124*
    Diagram Your Points *124*
    Find the Lead (Introduction) and the End (Conclusion) *125*
    Get Feedback *125*
    Create a Bare-Bones Outline *125*
    Find Your Evidence *126*
    Write a Rough Draft *126*
    Share Your Draft *126*
    Revise Your Rough Draft *126*
      Sample Student Essay: "It's Still Tough to Be a Woman" by Tammy Stevens 127

Personal Summary 129
Additional Writing 130
Additional Reading 130

Chapter Five / Public Writing from Sources 131
Reading 131
    Preparing to Read 132
    Viktor Frankl, from *Man's Search for Meaning* 133
    Thinking about Your Reading 139

Writing Assignment 143
    Write It Out: An Essay Using Sources 144
        Select a Topic *144*
        Explore Sources *145*
        Summarize the Problem *146*
        Collect Your Information (Summarize, Paraphrase, and Quote) *148*
        Develop Your Thesis, or Main Point *151*
        Organize Your Material *154*
        Draft Your Essay *156*
        Evaluate Your Draft *158*
        Rework Your Draft to Make Your Point Convincing *159*
        Refine Your Draft *162*
            Sample Student Essay: "Drinking, Driving, Dying" by Bill Rice 162

Personal Summary 164
Additional Writing 166
Additional Reading 166

Chapter Six / Writing for the Workplace 167
Reading 169
    Preparing to Read 170
    The Royal Bank of Canada, from "Imagination Helps Communication" 170
    Thinking about Your Reading 172

Writing Assignment 174
    The Conventions of Professional Writing 174
    Write It Out: A Job Application Letter and Résumé 178
        Set Career Goals *178*
        Assess Your Strengths *178*
        Write a "Nutshell" Biography *179*
        Prepare to Draft *180*
        Draft Your Letter *181*
            Sample Plan for a Job Application Letter: Job Application Letter (Rough Draft) by Scott Brown 181
        Get Feedback on Your Draft *183*
            Sample Feedback 183
        Revise Your Draft *183*
            Job Application Letter (Final Draft) by Scott Brown 184

Write Your Résumé *185*
Sample Résumé 186
Personal Summary 187
Additional Writing 188
Additional Reading 188

Part Three HANDBOOK 189

Sentence Structure 192
Subjects and Predicates 192
Sentence Fragments 194
Run-ons and Comma Splices 199

Coordination and Subordination 208
Coordination 208
Subordination 209

Verb Forms 216
Base Form 217
S Form 217
Ed Form 218
En Form 219
Ing Form 221
Regular and Irregular Verbs 222

Subject-Verb Agreement 233
Singular and Plural Subjects 233
Compound Subjects 235
Alternative Subjects 235
Words between the Subject and the Verb 236

Pronouns 240
Pronoun Reference 241
Using Standard Pronoun Forms: Case, Number, Gender, and Person 242
Choosing the Correct Number and Gender 245
Choosing the Correct Person 246

Punctuation 249
End Marks: Period, Question Mark, Exclamation Point 250
Turn Mark: Semicolon 251
Pause Mark: Comma 251
Colon 255
Quotation Marks 256

Capitalization 260

Spelling 268
    Spelling Demons 268
    Spelling Hints 269
    Rules of Thumb 270
    Memory Devices 272
    Noun Plurals 273
    Noun Possessives 274
    Look-alikes and Sound-alikes 275

Index 279

Introduction: Getting Started

In this introduction you will:

✔ Become familiar with the format of this text so that you can use it for maximum benefit

✔ Share information about yourself so that your instructor can give you the help you need

✔ Set some writing-related goals so that you can begin work on becoming a better writer

ABOUT THIS BOOK

Write for a Reason contains three major parts:

1. Three chapters that teach you to write for personal reasons
2. Three chapters that emphasize more public kinds of writing
3. A handbook that focuses on the language you use as you write

Each chapter in Part One and Part Two contains these sections:

❑ An introduction of the chapter's goals and theme
❑ A reading section that includes preview questions, a passage to read, and review questions
❑ A writing section that offers specific instruction and problems for practice
❑ A summary section with questions for personal review and suggestions for additional writing and reading

For Further Thought

To get a better understanding of how *Write for a Reason* can help you, skim the contents at the beginning of the book and list here the topics that you think you need the most help with.

_____   _____

_____   _____

_____   _____

_____

  Now review the goals listed at the beginning of Chapters One through Six, and list those that you think will benefit you the most.

_____

_____

_____

_____

A NOTE FROM THE AUTHOR

When you need to write, do you get a strange, uncontrollable urge to wash your car or scrub the bathroom floor instead—*anything* to justify putting off the task of writing?

When you finally pick up pen and paper or sit down at the typewriter or computer, does your mind go stubbornly blank? After you've managed to squeeze out a few words, do you usually dislike the results? Or perhaps you like to write but feel that the writing process is a mystery you'll never fully understand.

Whatever your attitude toward writing, if you're like most beginning writers, there is good news:

- ❑ You likely already know more about the writing process than you realize.
- ❑ You have the ability to learn to write successfully.
- ❑ You have more resources to draw on than you may be aware of.

A major aim of *Write for a Reason* is to help you build on the knowledge, ability, and resources you already have so that you can become a better, more confident writer.

Another important aim of this text is to help you learn to write effectively for a variety of purposes and audiences and give you practice in writing for a variety of reasons. You will gain personal insight and find creative solutions to problems through writing. You will learn how to make your writing more convincing and appealing to different types of readers. In short, you will learn that effective writing can serve you well both in and out of the classroom.

You may not always find the act of writing to be easy or pain-free. But through learning and practice, you will find it to be a valuable tool you can successfully use.

WRITE IT OUT: A LETTER TO YOUR INSTRUCTOR

Write a letter to your instructor (one to two pages long) to provide insight into the kind of writing help you need.

You don't have to be formal or fancy; just "talk" on paper, speaking honestly about yourself as a beginning writer, describing any or all of the following:

1. Your past successes and frustrations with writing
2. Your writing hopes and concerns
3. Any other information about you that your instructor could use to help you as much as possible

A good way of creating ideas to write about for a particular reader is to imagine yourself being that reader and then to decide what such a reader might want or need to know. In other words, to come up with good points to make in your letter, imagine that you are the instructor, think about what he or she might want or need to know in order to help you most, and then write about these points.

Also remember that when describing your attitudes, feelings, thoughts, or background, you are the expert; there is no need to worry about having "nothing to say."

STUDENT EXAMPLE

Here is a portion of a letter that a former student agreed to share as a way of stimulating your thoughts. Use examples of other students' writing to jog your thinking but not to limit you.

> Dear Dr. Bates:
>
> You asked me to describe my past successes and frustrations as a writer. Believe it or not, I used to like to write, but in my junior year of high school, I had a teacher who brought my "writing career" to a screeching halt. He seemed to have a lot of anger in him. When the students did not do what he asked, he would get very frustrated and scream, "I can't believe I went to college four years for this. I get paid peanuts for trying to train you monkeys."
>
> One day, after having suffered through the traumas of a high school romance, I wrote a poem about love and turned it in. The assignment had been open and I had chosen to write about my "broken heart."
>
> I can remember this like it was yesterday, instead of nearly five years ago; as we got settled in our seats, he began to read our papers out loud. When he came to mine, his voice became sarcastic and he began to make faces. As I felt the blood rush to my face, I held my breath and wanted to die. Finally, I could not sit and endure the punishment

> any more. I picked up my book and ran from the room, crying.
> After that, I was so ashamed and embarrassed; I hated the class, the teacher, and the assignments. I never really tried any more; when I turned in an assignment, I did just enough to get by with a passing grade. After that year I quit writing.
>
> Sincerely,
> Tam

For Further Thought

Despite her high school experience, Tam overcame her negative attitude toward writing and went on to become a successful writer. How do you think sharing her experiences helped?

_____

_____

OVERCOMING NEGATIVE WRITING ATTITUDES

"Negative writing attitudes," as the phrase is used here, refers to any of your feelings, beliefs, or ways of acting that interfere with your writing success. Examples of negative writing attitudes include feelings of anxiety, frustration, and hopelessness and the tendency to procrastinate, or put off, writing until the last possible minute.

To overcome such problems, you can use three strategies:

1. Examine your feelings.
2. Study the writing process.
3. Change self-defeating habits.

Strategy 1: Examine Your Feelings

To illustrate the point, let's say you become overly anxious when you try to write. How do you cope? You can take a first step by admitting how you feel. Are you afraid you will get a negative reaction to your work? If so, it's important to realize that criticism of your writing is not a criticism of you as a person, even though it may feel personal.

If you don't get rid of your anxiety completely, you are in good company; many professional writers suffer at one time or another from such fear. Following their example, you may learn to value the results of the writing process enough to tolerate some pain during the process. As one writer put it, "I like having written." Other pros turn their anxiety into an asset by using it to motivate themselves to do their best work.

Ask Yourself

What are some negative feelings I have about writing (frustration, anxiety, worry, anger, disgust, and so forth)?

_____

_____

Strategy 2: Study the Writing Process

To cope with negative attitudes, you will also need to learn more about writing processes (the subject of Chapter One). Writing is a problem-solving process, just as working a long-division problem in mathematics is. But whereas math problems are usually solved according to set formulas, writing problems require a more flexible approach.

The more you learn about the choices that are available to you throughout the writing process, the more confidence you will have. Confidence leads to success, and success leads to more confidence.

Ask Yourself

What aspects of writing do I need to learn more about in order to cope with my negative attitudes (for example, how to organize my thoughts, how to correct my errors)?

_____

_____

Strategy 3: Change Self-Defeating Habits

Finally, you may need to change old habits that keep you from being as good a writer as you are able to become. Let's say that you have the tendency to procrastinate. Changing old habits, you would begin work on a writing project as soon as you knew about your task rather than wait until 10 P.M. the night before the paper was due.

Maintaining a schedule, you would divide your work into manageable units of time in order to keep a fresh outlook. Also, you would write several drafts rather than try to create a perfect paper the first time you sat down to work.

Ask Yourself

What old habits do I need to change (for example, procrastination, writing only one draft, neglecting to get help)?

_____

_____

Your instructor, tutor, or counselor may have other suggestions for overcoming negative attitudes toward writing. If you need more help, let someone know.

For Further Thought

Now is the time to make plans and set goals for the writing program you are in. By planning your work and working your plan, you will soon start to feel, think, and behave like the successful writer you can become.

Complete the following statements, being as specific as possible. You will probably refine these goals along the way, but for the time being they will serve as your guide.

1. When I write, I want to experience feelings of

   a. _____

   b. _____

   c. _____

   (Sample response: "being satisfied with my work")

2. Also, I want to learn more about

   a. _____

   b. _____

   c. _____

   (Sample response: "how to find something to say")

3. When writing, I want to stop

   a. _____

    b. _____

    c. _____

    (Sample response: "telling myself I'm stupid")

4. When writing, I want to start

    a. _____

    b. _____

    c. _____

    (Sample response: "making my writing more interesting")

5. Other writing goals I hope to achieve include

    a. _____

    b. _____

    c. _____

PERSONAL SUMMARY

1. Review the goals on page 1, and check off each one that you have successfully accomplished.

2. Summarize the main lessons you have learned by working through this introduction.

_____

_____

3. List the subjects covered in this introduction that you still need more work on.

ADDITIONAL WRITING

Earlier you wrote a letter to your instructor, talking on paper about yourself as a beginning writer. Now write a note to yourself to be sealed in an envelope and reopened toward the end of the semester. In your personal note, describe what you hope to accomplish during the coming weeks in your writing course, and explain the changes you will have to make in your study and work habits in order to reach your goals. This note will make up your writing plan. Later you will receive instructions for opening the envelope and reacting to your plan.

ADDITIONAL READING

Goldberg, Natalie. *Writing Down the Bones, Freeing the Writer Within*. Boston: Shambhala Publications, 1986. For anyone who wants to write but is having trouble getting started, this book is a practical and delightful guide.

May, Rollo. *The Courage to Create*. New York: Norton, 1975. A challenging, thought-provoking book that explains, from a psychoanalytic point of view, why creativity is naturally accompanied by anxiety.

Minninger, Joan. *Free Yourself to Write*. 2nd ed. San Francisco: Workshops for Innovative Teaching, 1980. Helps writers overcome writing anxiety through a series of simple exercises designed to make writing more enjoyable.

Part One

WRITING FOR PERSONAL REASONS

Writing: A Problem-Solving Process

> *In this chapter you will:*
>
> ✔ Learn more about problem solving in order to solve writing problems more effectively
>
> ✔ Analyze the main parts and subparts of the writing process so that you can improve your own approach to writing
>
> ✔ Practice writing with a group in order to profit more from the help of others

READING

As you begin to study the writing process, a rewarding journey lies before you. But expect some discomfort on your way to success, because writing is a problem-solving process, and problems sometimes bring pain.

M. Scott Peck, well-known psychiatrist and author of *The Road Less Traveled*, reassures us that along with the uncomfortable feelings problems bring, they also give our lives meaning, helping us to become our best. Peck goes on to say that the key to successful problem solving is discipline. Like a basic tool kit, it equips us to solve life's problems and, in the process, promotes learning and growth. Taken from *The Road Less Traveled*, the following passage explains and demonstrates how the disciplined approach to problem solving works.

Preparing to Read

Before you read, ask yourself: How would I generally rate myself as a problem solver—superior, average, or poor? **As you read**, think about the following:

1. What happens when I follow the motto "Play now and pay later"?
2. How can Peck's suggestions for becoming a better problem solver help me become a better writer?

From
The Road Less Traveled
by M. Scott Peck

transcend: rise above

Life is difficult.

This is a great truth, one of the greatest truths.* It is a great truth because once we truly see this truth, we transcend it. Once we truly know that life is difficult—once we truly understand and accept it—then life is no longer difficult. Because once it is accepted, the fact that life is difficult no longer matters. . . .

Life is a series of problems. Do we want to moan about them or solve them? Do we want to teach our children to solve them?

Discipline is the basic set of tools we require to solve life's problems. Without discipline we can solve nothing. With only some discipline we can solve only some problems. With total discipline we can solve all problems [within our control].

What makes life difficult is that the process of confronting and solving problems is a painful one. Problems, depending upon their nature, evoke in us frustration or grief or sadness or loneliness or guilt or regret or anger or fear or anxiety or anguish or despair. These are uncomfortable feelings, often very uncomfortable, often as painful as any kind of physical pain, sometimes equaling the very worst kind of physical pain. Indeed, it is *because* of the pain that events or conflicts engender in us that we call them problems. And since life poses an endless series of problems, life is always difficult and is full of pain as well as joy.

Yet it is in this whole process of meeting and solving problems that life has its meaning. Problems are the cutting edge that distinguishes between success and failure. Problems call forth our courage and wisdom; indeed, they create our courage and wisdom. It is only because of problems that we grow mentally and spiritually. When we desire to encourage the growth of the human spirit, we

---

*The first of the "Four Noble Truths" that Buddha taught was "Life is suffering."

challenge and encourage the human capacity to solve problems, just as in school we deliberately set problems for our children to solve. It is through the pain of confronting and resolving problems that we learn. As Benjamin Franklin said, "Those things that hurt, instruct." It is for this reason that wise people learn not to dread but actually to welcome problems and actually to welcome the pain of problems.

Most of us are not so wise. Fearing the pain involved, almost all of us, to a greater or lesser degree, attempt to avoid problems. We procrastinate, hoping that they will go away. We ignore them, forget them, pretend they do not exist. We even take drugs to assist us in ignoring them, so that by deadening ourselves to the pain we can forget the problems that cause the pain. We attempt to skirt around problems rather than meet them head on. We attempt to get out of them rather than suffer through them. . . .

gratification: pleasure

Delaying Gratification. Delaying gratification [one of the tools of discipline] is a process of scheduling the pain and pleasure of life in such a way as to enhance the pleasure by meeting and experiencing the pain first and getting it over with. It is the only decent way to live.

This tool or process of scheduling is learned by most children quite early in life, sometimes as early as age five. For instance, occasionally a five-year-old child when playing a game with a companion will suggest that the companion take the first turn, so that the child might enjoy his or her turn later. At age six children may start eating their cake first and the frosting last. Throughout grammar school this early capacity to delay gratification is daily exercised, particularly through the performance of homework. By the age of twelve some children are already able to sit down on occasion without any parental prompting and complete their homework before they watch television. By the age of fifteen or sixteen such behavior is expected of the adolescent and is considered normal.

It becomes clear to their educators at this age, however, that a substantial number of adolescents fall far short of this norm. While many have a well-developed capacity to delay gratification, some fifteen- or sixteen-year-olds seem to have hardly developed this capacity at all; indeed, some seem even to lack the capacity entirely. These are the problem students. Despite average or better intelligence, their grades are poor simply because they do not work. They skip classes or skip school entirely on the whim of the moment. They are impulsive, and their impulsiveness spills over into their social life as well. They get into frequent fights, they become involved with drugs, they begin to get in trouble with police. Play now, pay later, is their motto. . . .

The feeling of being valuable—"I am a valuable person"—is essential to mental health and is a cornerstone of self-discipline . . . because when one considers oneself valuable, one will take care of oneself in all ways that are necessary. Self-discipline is self-caring. For instance—since we are discussing the process of delaying gratification, of scheduling and ordering time—let us examine the matter of time. If we feel ourselves valuable, then we will feel our time to be valuable, and if we feel our time to be valuable, then we will want to use it well. . . .

Problem-solving and Time. Let us examine some of the more subtle yet quite devastating ways in which difficulties in delaying gratification affect the lives of most adults. For while most of us, fortunately, develop sufficient capacity to delay gratification to make it through high school or college and embark upon adulthood without landing in jail, our development nonetheless tends to be imperfect and incomplete, with the result that our ability to solve life's problems is still imperfect and incomplete.

At the age of thirty-seven I learned how to fix things. Prior to that time almost all my attempts to make minor plumbing repairs, mend toys or assemble furniture according to the accompanying hieroglyphical instruction sheet ended in confusion, failure and frustration. Despite having managed to make it through medical school and support a family as a more or less successful executive and psychiatrist, I considered myself to be a mechanical idiot. I was convinced I was deficient in some gene, or by curse of nature lacking some mystical quality responsible for mechanical ability. Then one day at the end of my thirty-seventh year, while taking a spring Sunday walk, I happened upon a neighbor in the process of repairing a lawn mower. After greeting him I remarked, "Boy, I sure admire you. I've never been able to fix [such] things or do anything like that." My neighbor, without a moment's hesitation, shot back, "That's because you don't take the time." I resumed my walk, somehow disquieted by the gurulike simplicity, spontaneity and definitiveness of his response. "You don't suppose he could be right, do you?" I asked myself. Somehow it registered, and the next time the opportunity presented itself to make a minor repair I was able to remind myself to take my time. The parking brake was stuck on a patient's car, and she knew that there was something one could do under the dashboard to release it, but she didn't know what. I lay down on the floor below the front of her car. Then I took the time to make myself comfortable. Once I was comfortable, I then took the time to look at the situation. I looked for several minutes. At first all I saw was a confusing jumble of wires and tubes and rods, whose meaning I did not know. But gradually, in no hurry, I was able to focus my sight on the brake apparatus and trace its course. And then it became clear to me that there was a little latch

hieroglyph: hard-to-understand symbol

guru: spiritual leader
definitiveness: authority

preventing the brake from being released. I slowly studied this latch until it became clear to me that if I were to push it upward with the tip of my finger it would move easily and would release the brake. And so I did this. One single motion, one ounce of pressure from a fingertip and the problem was solved. I was a master mechanic!

Actually, I don't begin to have the knowledge or the time to gain that knowledge to be able to fix most mechanical failures, given the fact that I choose to concentrate my time on nonmechanical matters. So I still usually go running to the nearest repairman. But I now know that this is a choice I make, and I am not cursed or genetically deficient or otherwise incapacitated or impotent. And I know that I and anyone else who is not mentally defective can solve any problem if we are willing to take the time.

impotent: weak

The issue is important, because many people simply do not take the time necessary to solve many of life's intellectual, social or spiritual problems, just as I did not take the time to solve mechanical problems. Before my mechanical enlightenment I would have awkwardly stuck my head under the dashboard of my patient's car, immediately yanked at a few wires without having the foggiest idea of what I was doing, and then, when nothing constructive resulted, would have thrown up my hands and proclaimed, "It's beyond me." And this is precisely the way that so many of us approach other dilemmas of day-to-day living.

Thinking about Your Reading

If you have found the passage helpful, you may want to read Peck's entire book, *The Road Less Traveled*, which offers many insights into successful living.

For now, answer the following questions in order to improve your understanding of the key points the author makes and to apply them to your own experience, especially with writing.

1. In a word, what is the basic set of tools required to solve life's problems?

   _____

2. Why does Peck say we should welcome problems?

3. What do you as an individual do to avoid problems?

4. What is meant by delaying gratification?

5. Give an example of when delaying gratification helped you to grow or become more successful.

6. What important lesson did Peck learn from his neighbor who was repairing a lawn mower?

7. How can this lesson help you become a better writer?

8. The next time you feel some discomfort when writing, what helpful points from Peck can you call to mind?

___

___

WRITING ASSIGNMENT

A Writing Process

Self-discipline and practice are essential to becoming a good writer. The more disciplined your work habits and the more you practice those habits, the more successful you will be in solving your writing problems. The more successful you are, the more satisfaction you will gain from writing and the more you will want to write.

If you believe that the kind of thinking required of a good writer is more advanced than the mental processes you currently use, keep in mind that skilled writers rely on common steps like planning and goal setting to solve the writing problems they face. You routinely practice these same steps, not only when you write but also when you solve the problems of daily life.

As you note the main parts and subparts of the writing process in the diagram on page 22, you can see which ones you need to pay more attention to or learn more about. You will want to be sure to use all parts of the process. Learning by doing, you'll be on your way to writing well.

Note that the three main parts of the writing process—planning, drafting, and revising—each include three subparts. Arrows pointing back and forth between the parts and subparts indicate that writers move back and forth among the elements as the need arises instead of proceeding in a rigid 1-2-3 order. Further, the amount of time needed on any one part will vary from one writing situation to another.

Planning

Planning as you write is more or less like the planning you do almost anytime you make something, whether simple or complex: you *create*, you *set*

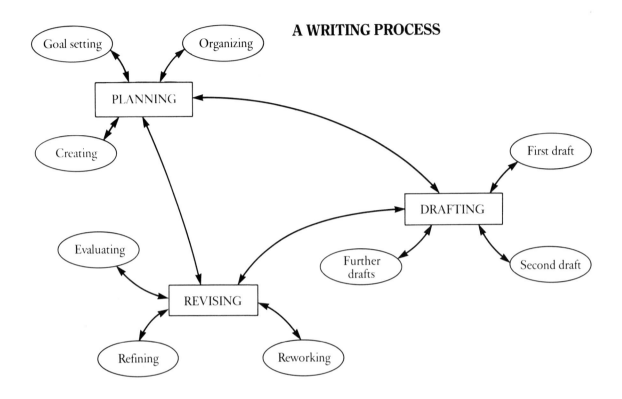

A WRITING PROCESS

goals, and you *organize*. Take something as ordinary as preparing a meal for friends. Planning ahead, you create a menu based on recipes you already know, or perhaps you look through cookbooks for new ideas; you decide how many guests to invite and let them know your plans; and you organize everything you will need in order to follow through with your plan.

Compare this planning process to one that you might use while writing. Through preliminary thinking, reading, and talking, you will call to mind prior knowledge and create some ideas to write about, decide what writing goals you want to accomplish, and organize your thoughts into an overall plan. The bigger and more significant the project, the more important good planning becomes.

The subparts of the planning process—creating, goal setting, and organizing—don't necessarily have to occur in any given order. Creative thinking and background reading may lead to goal setting, or vice versa. *When you're thinking creatively, it's important not to worry about spelling, punctuation, or grammar rules or to be critical of yourself; play with ideas—even if some of them seem "off the wall."*

Ask Yourself

1. When beginning a writing project, how much time do I allow myself for planning?

_____

2. Which subparts of the planning process do I need to learn more about—creating ideas, setting goals, or organizing my thoughts?

_____

_____

3. Do I allow myself the freedom and flexibility I need in order to think creatively? _____

Drafting

Drafting involves putting your ideas into a visible, more or less finished form, whether you're preparing a meal or writing a paper. If you're experimenting with a new recipe, you may want to try it out a couple of times for yourself before serving it to company. Similarly, when writing, you will probably need to produce several versions, or *drafts*, before you have a finished product that will accomplish your goal. Between drafts, it's a good idea to give yourself a break, if possible, so that you can come back to your work with a fresh outlook.

Ask Yourself

1. When writing, do I usually take the time to produce more than one draft?

_____

2. Do I take needed breaks between drafts? _____

3. Am I more likely to accomplish my writing goals by producing multiple drafts? _____

Revising

Revising means "seeing again" and refers, in part, to the act of looking at a piece of writing in order to *evaluate* the strengths and weaknesses of what you have produced.

Just as in the planning process you *pre-view* your work and in the drafting process you *view* it, in the revising process you *re-view* it. *This is the ideal time to bring a critical eye to your efforts, calling up the useful writing rules and guidelines you know.* You may do all of the evaluating yourself, or you may ask others to give you helpful feedback.

As a result of such evaluation, you will usually discover the need to do some *reworking* and *refining*. Looking at your work as a whole in light of your purpose for writing and the audience you are writing for will tell you whether you need to make any big changes (reworking). Looking at it in a more detailed way will help you notice the small but important adjustments you need to make (refining). Both reworking and refining are vital elements of the revising process, and neither should be neglected.

It's a good idea to make big changes, such as improving an introduction or eliminating an ineffective example, before making smaller ones, such as correcting spelling and punctuation. Doing the refining and polishing first may discourage you from wanting to make any big changes, even though your better judgment tells you they're needed.

Ask Yourself

1. When I evaluate my work, do I look for big problems, such as poor organization, along with smaller details, such as grammatical errors? _____

2. When revising, do I try to rework and refine my work at the same time?
   _____

3. Why is it better to *rework* my writing before I *refine* it?

   _____

   ———————

As you practice the writing process, *be sure not to neglect any of the main parts or subparts.* You will probably notice that some aspects of the process are easier for you than other aspects, depending on such matters as your general attitude toward writing and the way you tend to approach problem solving. Further, the task at hand can be easier or more difficult, depending on your situation at the particular time. But normally you will find that the more you practice, the more confidence and skill you will develop and the more effective your writing will become.

For Further Thought

1. When you begin to write, do you find yourself getting stuck on the first few sentences because you are trying to be sure the spelling and grammar are perfect? _____ If so, which subpart do you need to concentrate on for the time being, and which subpart do you need to postpone working on?

   _____

2. Have you told yourself in the past that you are not a creative person? _____ What effect is such negative "self-talk" likely to have?

   _____

   _____

3. Do you try to produce only one draft of what you write—planning, drafting, and revising all at the same time—instead of going through the entire

process, as described here? _____ Why do you think such a "one-shot" approach may actually require more time but lead to less effective results? _____

4. Look back at the model of the writing process on page 22, and circle each main part and subpart that you think you need more practice on.

Write It Out: A Class Newsletter

In your writing class, other students as well as the instructor are important resources to learn from as you set out to become a more skilled writer.

- ❏ They may give you ideas to think and write about as they discuss their writing projects.
- ❏ They will listen as you share your creative thoughts, identifying what they find to be most interesting or significant.
- ❏ They can give you the encouragement and feedback you need, enhancing your strengths and helping you watch for potential pitfalls.

To begin to know the members of your writing class and to begin your work as a writer in this course, get into small groups and take turns introducing yourselves.

Next, form pairs within your group, and introduce your partner to the rest of the class, telling what you found to be most interesting or unique. Describe something positive you learned about your partner that the rest of the class is likely to remember.

Your assignment is to write one or more paragraphs (at least five or six sentences long) describing an *interest*, *success*, or *accomplishment* of your partner. Once your work has been revised, it can be put together with everyone else's to form a class newsletter. Suggestions in these pages can help guide you through the various parts and subparts of the writing process. For some examples of the kind of paragraph you might write, look at the sample newsletter on pages 30–32.

Planning

GOAL SETTING. The main goals of your writing the newsletter are for you to get to know the members of your class, to learn to give and receive help in writing, and to practice all parts and subparts of the writing process so that you can develop more self-confidence and skill in order to write successfully. Take a few minutes to think about what else you might hope to achieve in completing this project.

The audience for the newsletter will be your class members.

CREATING. To guide your collection of information, ask your partner *who, what, when, where, how,* and *why* questions, as journalists do when they gather the daily news. Notice that in some instances the student writers who created the sample paragraphs quoted the exact words of the partner they were interviewing. You might try doing the same. (For help with quotations, see page 256.)

The two sets of questions given here are intended as general guides. Feel free to use some, all, or none of the questions or variations of them.

Sample questions on an *interest*

- *What* is your main interest?
- *When* and *where* did you develop it?
- *How* did you become interested in it?
- *Who* helped you or was interested with you?
- *Why* were you interested in it? (Are you still interested?)

Sample questions on a *success* or an *accomplishment*

- *What* success or accomplishment are you especially proud of?
- *When* and *where* did it happen?
- *How* did you achieve it?
- *Who* helped you?
- *Why* were you interested in achieving it?

ORGANIZING. After gathering your information, decide how the details should be arranged. Probably, time (chronological) order will work best; this means that you relate events in the order in which they happened, telling what occurred first, second, third, and so on.

Drafting

Once you have organized your information, write it out in complete sentences. (For help with sentence structure, see pages 192–207.)

Looking at the sample newsletter on pages 30–32, you will notice that each entry is a group of sentences organized as a paragraph. Here are some basic principles for writing effective paragraphs.

Basic Paragraph Principles

1. Often the first sentence of a paragraph—called the *topic*, or *lead*, sentence or *main idea* statement—will tell what the other sentences in the paragraph are about or give the main idea. Sometimes such a sentence will appear at the end of the paragraph rather than the beginning, and occasionally a main idea will be implied rather than stated directly.

   The main idea statement, or topic sentence, functions like a directional signal for both writer and reader. It sets them on a course of thought and keeps them on course throughout the paragraph. Even when a paragraph doesn't have a specific topic sentence, it should focus on only one subject or idea.

   EXAMPLES:
   a. Robert Ford is a guitar enthusiast.
   b. Leonard Fontenot has an unusual hobby—collecting animal skulls.
   c. Jeannette Wynne is very determined to obtain a degree in the medical field even though it will require hard work.

2. A topic sentence contains *key words* to indicate how the paragraph will be developed—that is, what facts it will contain. Together, the topic sentence and the supporting factual sentences make up the paragraph. The key words in the sentences in principle 1 are these:

   a. Robert Ford, **guitar enthusiast**
   b. Leonard Fontenot, **unusual hobby, collecting animal skulls**

Jeannette Wynne

There she was, a graduate of Southwood High School. Anxious about her future career, she reviewed her options and decided to enroll in college. She began to develop an interest in the medical profession because of her course in biology. After much consideration and observing medical technologists at work, she has decided to study medical technology. Jeannette Wynne is very determined to obtain a degree in the medical field even though it will require hard work.

Trenton Redstone

Trenton Redstone has always liked to draw and create things on paper as far back as he can remember. At the age of ten, he often drew pictures of ships, boats, cars, and even a few comic strips. When he entered junior high, his mother enrolled him in private art lessons. He would ride his bicycle a block or two to an old garage in his neighborhood that had been converted into an art studio. "That garage," he said, "was the perfect place to take art lessons. It wasn't too crowded, the temperature was always comfortable, and it even smelled like an art class because of all the paint and fresh clay in the room. On the walls there were paintings of animals, people, and trees that the students had created." Perhaps these childhood experiences, in addition to his natural ability, help explain why Trenton is now enrolled in college as an art major and hopes to be a commercial artist some day.

Errol Smith

Errol Keith Smith is proud to be in the United States Army. In the spring of 1988, he entered boot camp at Ft. Jackson, South Carolina, where he received eight weeks of basic training and learned the value of self-discipline. After completing this training, he attended Ft. Benning Jump School in

North Carolina for four weeks. Here he was taught the rudiments of proper parachuting. The biggest challenge he faced was jumping at night, when all he could see were the stars above and pitch black darkness below. On July 4, Independence Day, Errol graduated as an Army Reserve jump specialist and celebrated the holiday with new-found pride.

Kim Dang

Kim Dang is accomplishing what she once thought was impossible, supporting herself and paying her way through college. Earlier she had found it difficult just supporting herself without attempting college work as well. "I thought that going to college and working wouldn't blend together, but I have found that with a lot of determination, it can be done," Kim said. Now she goes to college, where she is making passing grades, and fully supports herself by driving a city bus.

For Further Thought

1. Underline the topic sentence of each paragraph in the sample newsletter.
2. Circle the key words in each of the sentences you have underlined.
3. Here is the first draft of the paragraph on Robert Ford. Read it and compare it to the final draft appearing in the sample newsletter.

Robert Ford is interested in music, and he is also a sports fan. He started playing the guitar last Christmas. The guitar was a present from his mother. He said that his first love is rock 'n' roll. He also teaches himself theory and music out of books. He wants to pursue his interest in the classical guitar. When he has time, he watches football on television and plays basketball with neighborhood kids after school.

Now answer the following questions.

a. Why is the topic sentence of the final draft more effective than the one in the first draft?

_____

_____

_____

b. How many different topics are discussed in the first draft?

_____ In the final draft? _____

4. Here is the first draft of the paragraph on Jeannette Wynne. Read and compare the first and final drafts.

```
     Jeannette Wynne wants to obtain a degree in medical
technology. She has taken a course in biology and has ob-
served the work of medical technologists. She is a gradu-
ate of Southwood High School. When she graduated, she was
undecided about what she wanted to do.
```

a. Write a paragraph explaining why you think the final draft is more interesting and effective than the first.

_____

_____

_____

_____

_____

b. What two functions does the last sentence in the final draft serve?

_____

_____

_____

5. Compare this first draft of the paragraph on Trenton Redstone to the final draft.

> Trenton Redstone has always been a pretty creative person as far as art is concerned. Today on the way to work he heard a song that reminded him of his childhood, when he took art lessons. The song itself has a lot of meaning, but it is not only the words but the blend of the singer's voice and the musical instrument combined with the smell of moist clay in his hands or the smell of the paint he used. It was like the song drew life into the small art room, which was an old garage in his neighborhood that had been converted into an art studio. "This garage," he says, "was the perfect place to take art lessons. It wasn't too crowded, the temperature was always comfortable, and it even smelled like an art class because of all the paint and fresh clay in the room. There were tall shelves against one of the walls, and on the other walls were paintings of animals, people, and trees that the students had created." It doesn't even have to be the whole song but just the words "blinded by the light" that will always remind him of that underground garage.

a. What do you notice about the first and last sentences?

_____

_____

_____

b. Why was it appropriate to omit from the final draft all sentences related to his hearing a song on the radio?

_____

_____

_____

c. Identify the unrelated sentences in the first draft, and draw a line through them.

d. Do you think the material would be more enjoyable to read if it were broken into several paragraphs? _____ Why or why not?

_____

_____

_____

6. Reread the newsletter item written about you that describes some interest, success, or accomplishment of yours. What personality traits helped you achieve this success?

_____

_____

_____

7. Suggest possible ways in which these traits can help you become a more accomplished writer.

_____

◆◆◆

PERSONAL SUMMARY

1. Review the goals at the beginning of this chapter, and check off each one that you have successfully accomplished.

2. Summarize the main lessons you have learned by working through this chapter.

3. List the subjects covered in this chapter that you still need more work on.

ADDITIONAL WRITING

1. Compose an additional paragraph or more about yourself and one of your interests, successes, or accomplishments, following all the instructions already provided. In this case, however, you will "interview" yourself rather than a partner. If necessary, this paragraph can serve as a substitute paragraph about you in the class newsletter.
2. If you had to choose three of your possessions that best demonstrate what you like most about yourself, what would they be? Write a paragraph about each, explaining what these possessions reveal about your personality and ability.

ADDITIONAL READING

Ellis, David. *Becoming a Master Student.* 5th ed. Rapid City, S.D.: College Survival Inc., 1985. A basic text designed to help students succeed in college.

James, Muriel, and Dorothy Jongeward. *Born to Win.* Reading, Mass.: Addison-Wesley, 1976. Helps readers understand common behavior patterns in order to live more successfully.

Peck, M. Scott. *The Road Less Traveled.* New York: Simon & Schuster, 1978. A challenging and inspirational book that helps readers overcome negative habits and attitudes.

Personal Writing: From Memory to Insight

In this chapter, you will:

✔ Compare reading and writing processes in order to read and write more effectively

✔ Practice keeping a journal as a source of material to use in your writing

✔ Write from past experience to build on valuable knowledge you already have

✔ Develop creative insights by examining memories

READING

Memories of your past, whether positive or negative, are a powerful resource you can draw on as you write. Learning to use your memory in a creative way, you will gain valuable insights that can enrich your work.

In the moving autobiography *I Know Why the Caged Bird Sings*, author Maya Angelou transformed her memories and insights into a widely respected and much-read work of literature. Looking back through adult eyes, Angelou re-creates the joy and pain of her childhood through vivid recollection of people, places, and events. In the process, helpful insights and understanding emerge.

In the following excerpt, Angelou tells about growing up with her brother Bailey and their grandmother and uncle in a small southern town, where they lived in the rear of the family store. Drawing on the knowledge gained through her experience, she concludes the passage by providing insights into the needs of a lonely child.

Preparing to Read

Before you read, recall important periods of your life that you can still learn from by reflecting on them. **As you read**, think about the following:

1. What personal memories of your own does the passage help you recall?
2. As Angelou looks back on her childhood, what understanding, or insight, does she reveal?
3. How does she appeal to the five senses—touch, taste, smell, hearing, and sight—in order to make a portion of her childhood come alive in words?

From
I Know Why the Caged Bird Sings
by Maya Angelou

When I was three and Bailey four, we had arrived [at our grandmother's] wearing tags on our wrists which instructed—"To Whom It May Concern"—that we were Marguerite and Bailey Johnson Jr., from Long Beach, California, en route to Stamps, Arkansas, c/o Mrs. Annie Henderson.

calamitous: disastrous

Our parents had decided to put an end to their calamitous marriage, and Father shipped us home to his mother. A porter had been charged with our welfare—he got off the train the next day in Arizona—and our tickets were pinned to my brother's inside coat pocket. . . .

The town reacted to us as its inhabitants had reacted to all things new before our coming. It regarded us awhile without curiosity but with caution, and after we were seen to be harmless (and children) it closed in around us, as a real mother embraces a stranger's child. Warmly, but not too familiarly.

We lived with our grandmother and uncle in the rear of the Store (it was always spoken of with a capital *s*), which she had owned some twenty-five years.

Early in the century, Momma (we soon stopped calling her Grandmother) sold lunches to the sawmen in the lumberyard (east Stamps) and the seedmen at the cotton gin (west Stamps). Her crisp meat pies and cool lemonade, when joined to her miraculous ability to be in two places at the same time, assured her business success. From being a mobile lunch counter, she set up a stand between the two points of fiscal interest and supplied the workers' needs for a few years. Then she had the Store built in the heart of the Negro area. . . .

fiscal: financial

staples: basic items

The formal name of the Store was the Wm. Johnson General Merchandise Store. Customers could find food staples, a good variety of colored thread, mash for hogs, corn for chickens, coal oil for lamps, light bulbs for the wealthy, shoestrings, hair dressing, balloons, and flower seeds. Anything not visible had only to be ordered. . . .

Each year I watched the field across from the Store turn caterpillar green, then gradually frosty white. I knew exactly how long it would be before the big wagons would pull into the front yard and load on the cotton pickers at daybreak to carry them to the remains of slavery's plantations.

During the picking season my grandmother would get out of bed at four o'clock (she never used an alarm clock) and creak down to her knees and chant in a sleep-filled voice, "Our Father, thank you for letting me see this New Day. Thank you that you didn't allow the bed I lay on last night to be my **cooling board**, nor my blanket my **winding sheet**. Guide my feet this day along the straight and narrow, and help me to put a bridle on my tongue. Bless this house, and everybody in it. Thank you, in the name of your Son, Jesus Christ, Amen."

cooling board: board on which a dead body was laid

winding sheet: cloth in which a corpse was wrapped

Before she had quite arisen, she called our names and issued orders, and pushed her large feet into homemade slippers and across the bare lye-washed wooden floor to light the coal-oil lamp.

The lamplight in the Store gave a soft make-believe feeling to our world which made me want to whisper and walk about on tiptoe. The odors of onions and oranges and kerosene had been mixing all night and wouldn't be disturbed until the wooden slat was removed from the door and the early morning air forced its way in with the bodies of people who had walked miles to reach the pickup place.

"Sister, I'll have two cans of sardines."

"I'm gonna work so fast today I'm gonna make you look like you standing still."

"Lemme have a hunk uh cheese and some sody crackers."

"Just gimme a coupla them fat peanut paddies." That would be from a picker who was taking his lunch. The greasy brown paper sack was stuck behind the bib of his overalls. He'd use the candy as a snack before the noon sun called the workers to rest.

In those tender mornings the Store was full of laughing, joking, boasting and bragging. One man was going to pick two hundred pounds of cotton, and another three hundred. Even the children were promising to bring home fo' bits and six bits.

four bits: fifty cents

boll: cotton seed pod

The champion picker of the day before was the hero of the dawn. If he prophesied that the cotton in today's field was going to be sparse and stick to the **bolls** like glue, every listener would grunt a hearty agreement.

The sound of the empty cotton sacks dragging over the floor and the murmurs of waking people were sliced by the cash register as we rang up the five-cent sales. . . .

Weighing the half-pounds of flour, excluding the scoop, and depositing them dust-free into the thin paper sacks held a simple kind of adventure for me. I developed an eye for measuring how full a silver-looking ladle of flour, mash, meal, sugar or corn had to be to push the scale indicator over to eight ounces or one pound. When I was absolutely accurate our appreciative customers used to admire: "Sister Henderson sure got some smart grandchildrens." If I was off in the Store's favor, the eagle-eyed women would say, "Put some more in that sack, child. Don't you try to make your profit offa me."

Then I would quietly but persistently punish myself. For every bad judgment, the fine was no silver-wrapped Kisses, the sweet chocolate drops that I loved more than anything in the world, except Bailey. And maybe canned pineapples. My obsession with pineapples nearly drove me mad. I dreamt of the days when I would be grown and able to buy a whole carton for myself alone.

Although the syrupy golden rings sat in their exotic cans on our shelves year round, we only tasted them during Christmas. Momma used the juice to make almost-black fruit cakes. Then she lined heavy, soot-encrusted iron skillets with the pineapple rings for rich upside-down cakes. Bailey and I received one slice each, and I carried mine around for hours, shredding off the fruit until nothing was left except the perfume on my fingers. I'd like to think that my desire for pineapples was so sacred that I wouldn't allow myself to steal a can (which was possible) and eat it alone out in the garden, but I'm certain that I must have weighed the possibility of the scent exposing me and didn't have the nerve to attempt it.

Until I was thirteen and left Arkansas for good, the Store was my favorite place to be. Alone and empty in the mornings, it looked like an unopened present from a stranger. Opening the front doors was pulling the ribbon off the unexpected gifts. The light would come in softly (we faced north), easing itself over the shelves of mackerel, salmon, tobacco, thread. It fell flat on the big vat of lard and by noontime during the summer the grease had softened to a thick soup. Whenever I walked into the Store in the afternoon, I sensed that it was tired. I alone could hear the slow pulse of its job half done. But just before bedtime, after numerous people had walked in and out, and argued over their bills, or joked about their neighbors, or just dropped in "to give Sister Henderson a 'Hi y'all,'" the promise of magic mornings returned to the Store and spread itself over the family in washed life waves.

Momma opened boxes of crispy crackers and we sat around the meat block at the rear of the Store. I sliced onions, and Bailey opened two or even three cans of sardines and allowed their juice of oil and fishing boats to ooze down and around the sides. That was supper. . . .

Bailey was the greatest person in my world. And the fact that he was my brother, my only brother, and I had no sisters to share him with, was such good fortune that it made me want to live a Christian life just to show God that I was grateful. Where I was big, elbowy and grating, he was small, graceful and smooth. . . .

When our elders said unkind things about my features (my family was handsome to a point of pain for me), Bailey would wink at me from across the room, and I knew that it was a matter of time before he would take revenge. He would allow the old ladies to finish wondering how on earth I came about, then he would ask, in a voice like cooling bacon grease, "Oh Mizeriz Coleman, how is your son? I saw him the other day, and he looked sick enough to die."

Aghast, the ladies would ask, "Die? From what? He ain't sick."

And in a voice oilier than the one before, he'd answer with a straight face, "From the Uglies."

I would hold my laugh, bite my tongue, grit my teeth and very seriously erase even the touch of a smile from my face. Later, behind the house by the black-walnut tree, we'd laugh and laugh and howl.

Bailey could count on very few punishments for his consistently outrageous behavior, for he was the pride of the Henderson/Johnson family.

His movements, as he was later to describe those of an acquaintance, were activated with oiled precision. He was also able to find more hours in the day than I thought existed. He finished chores, homework, read more books than I and played the group games on the side of the hill with the best of them. He could even pray out loud in church, and was apt at stealing pickles from the barrel that sat under the fruit counter and Uncle Willie's nose.

Once when the Store was full of lunchtime customers, he dipped the strainer, which we also used to sift weevils from meal and flour, into the barrel and fished for two fat pickles. He caught them and hooked the strainer onto the side of the barrel where they dripped until he was ready for them. When the last school bell rang, he picked the nearly dry pickles out of the strainer, jammed them into his pockets and threw the strainer behind the oranges. We ran out of the Store. It was summer and his pants were short, so the pickle juice made clean streams down his ashy legs, and he jumped with his pockets full of loot and his eyes laughing a "How about that?" He smelled like a vinegar barrel or a sour angel.

After our early chores were done, while Uncle Willie or Momma minded the Store, we were free to play the children's games as long as we stayed within yelling distance. Playing hide-and-seek, his voice was easily identified singing, "Last night, night before, twenty-four robbers at my door. Who all is hid? Ask me to let them in, hit 'em in the head with a rolling pin. Who all is hid?" In follow the leader, naturally he was the one who created the most daring and interesting things to do. And when he was on the tail of pop the whip, he would twirl off the end like a top, spinning, falling, laughing, finally stopping just before my heart beat its last, and then he was back in the game, still laughing.

Of all the needs (there are none imaginary) a lonely child has, the one that must be satisfied, if there is going to be hope and a hope of wholeness, is the unshaking need for an unshakable God. My pretty Black brother was my Kingdom Come.

Thinking about Your Reading

If you enjoyed reading the passage, you may want to read the entire book *I Know Why the Caged Bird Sings*, which tells the story of Angelou's life from age 3 to age 16 with great beauty and power. For now, answer the following questions in order to improve your understanding of Angelou's story and the qualities that make her writing effective.

1. Without looking back through the reading selection, write down as much as you can remember of Angelou's story on a separate sheet of paper. Afterward, think about what made these particular scenes or passages stand out in your memory.

2. You may find, as you go back to the parts you remembered, that Angelou has filled them with details that appeal to your senses: sight, hearing, taste, smell, and touch. We call such details concrete sensory language. It is the kind of language that makes writing "come alive," and it is one sure way of making your personal writing more memorable. Here are some examples and the number of the paragraph in which each occurs.

> SIGHT: **"Each year I watched the field across from the Store turn caterpillar green, then gradually frosty white."** (7)

HEARING: "the Store was full of laughing, joking, boasting and bragging" (15)
TASTE: "crisp meat pies" (5); "sweet chocolate drops" (19); "syrupy golden rings" (20)
SMELL: "The odors of onions and oranges and kerosene had been mixing all night" (10)
TOUCH: "pickle juice made clean streams down his ashy legs" (30)

Go back to the reading and try to find more examples of language that appeals to the senses.

3. a. Put into your own words why you think her grandmother's store was an important place to Angelou.

_____

_____

_____

b. Describe a place that was important to you as a child, a place that you were perhaps reminded of as you read the selection. Use concrete sensory details in your description.

_____

_____

_____

_____

c. How did you feel as you recalled the memory?

_____

_____

4. a. Describe the feelings young Maya had for her brother.

___

b. Make a list of the words and phrases she used that help you understand her feelings.

___

c. Why did she look upon Bailey as "an unshakable God" and her "Kingdom Come"?

___

d. Describe someone who was important to you as a child, perhaps a person whom you were reminded of as you read the selection.

___

5. As M. Scott Peck suggests in *The Road Less Traveled* (Chapter One), we may find conflict painful, but we can get valuable insights by using conflict rather than avoiding or ignoring it. What conflict do you think Angelou must have felt or experienced that gave her insight, or understanding, into the needs of a lonely child? You might think about her parents' calamitous marriage, how the townspeople reacted to her appearance, and her emotional needs that Bailey satisfied.

_____

_____

_____

_____

6. What humorous insight does she reveal about herself when she explains why she probably didn't steal pineapples?

_____

_____

_____

7. Imagine that you are Maya Angelou as a child. On a separate sheet of paper, write a letter to Bailey explaining why he is so important to you. In order to help him understand his importance to you, tell him what your life would be like without him.

A Reading Process

While reading the passage from *Caged Bird*, you engaged in a number of the same mental activities used in writing—for example, "planning," "drafting," and "revising." In fact, if you analyze the reading process by breaking it into its main parts and subparts (as the accompanying diagram does), you may note that it is quite similar to the writing process presented in Chapter One.

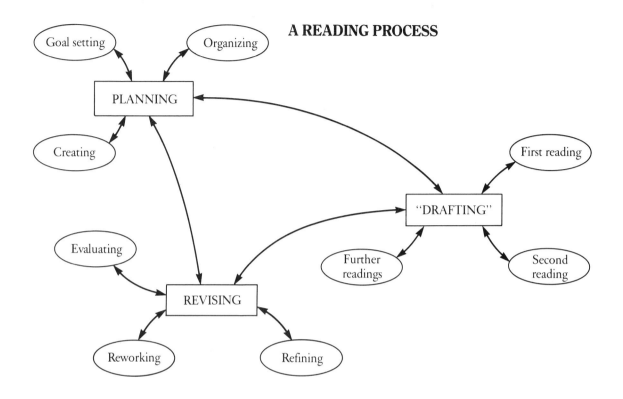

The value of such analysis is that it can help you discover whether you are omitting any important parts as you read.

As you come to understand what these elements involve and to use them all, you will be on your way to becoming a better reader as well as a better writer. Not only does reading give you facts and ideas to interact with and write about, but also, because the reading and writing processes use interrelated skills, learning about one process teaches you about the other.

Planning

Planning to read is like planning to write: you *create*, you *set goals*, and you *organize*. Thinking *creatively* about a reading selection, you make an educated guess about its content based on your prior knowledge of the subject, the title of the material, and any other clues to its content; you set reading *goals* based on your purpose for reading and any questions you need to answer; and you *organize* your thoughts into a kind of mental framework, or outline, by skimming (or running your eyes quickly over) the passage to get the main ideas.

Contrast this process to the approach that ineffective readers use. They simply pick up their reading material and expect the author to do their thinking for them. They do no preliminary planning. They don't bring to mind prior knowledge of the subject, nor do they anticipate what the passage will say. They have no conscious purpose for reading nor questions in mind to answer, and they rarely preview material to get a general understanding of the content.

Ask Yourself

1. When beginning to read, do I take time to plan my work? _____

2. Is my mind active as I begin to read, or do I expect the author of the passage to do all the thinking for me?

_____

3. Which subparts of the planning process do I need to concentrate more on—creating, goal setting, or organizing?

_____

_____

Drafting

Once you've skimmed a passage and organized your thoughts into a mental outline, you are ready to read it more closely and produce a more complete mental "*draft*." As you read, you will blend what you already know and believe with what you read; in the process, you will create new ideas. For instance, you might combine your prior knowledge and beliefs with what you learn from your reading in order to interpret a set of facts or draw an original conclusion. In a real sense, you and the author produce something new. If you use all the parts and subparts of the reading process, you may produce several mental versions of the material before your reading goals are fully satisified.

In contrast to this approach, less skilled readers rarely read a passage more than once or produce more than one mental draft of it. Or if they do, they plod through their reading task with little active questioning or concentration or awareness of their prior knowledge of the subject they are reading about.

Ask Yourself

1. When reading, do I usually take time to read a passage more than once? _____

2. Am I more likely to accomplish my reading goals by producing several mental drafts of the material? _____

3. Do I allow myself enough time to develop a thorough understanding of what I read? _____

4. Do I read in a mentally alert and active way? _____

Revising

At some point in the reading process, you may begin revising your understanding of the material—perhaps through rereading and answering challenging questions. As you do so, you will *evaluate* whether your first thoughts were accurate, then *rework* or expand your overall understanding, and finally *refine* your ideas. This is the kind of reading you do when you study. Not only are you getting the facts, but you are also interpreting what you read on the basis of what you already know, and you are reading critically, mentally challenging the author to prove a point.

Just as in the planning process you *pre-view* what you are reading and in the drafting process you *view* it more closely to fill in the details, in the revising process you *re-view* it and finalize your thoughts.

Once more, think about the approach less able readers use. Chances are, they accept everything they see in print, never stopping to interpret what is said or evaluate how worthy or well-supported the author's ideas are. Rarely do they challenge their original understanding of the material.

> **Ask Yourself**
>
> 1. When I evaluate what I read, do I review the overall organization and main ideas of the passage? _____
>
> 2. Do I read in an active way, interpreting the facts for myself? _____
>
> 3. When revising my understanding of what I have read, do I mentally challenge the author to prove all points with supporting details? _____

As with writing, the order of the parts and subparts will vary from time to time, depending on your purpose for reading. For example, if your purpose is to prepare for an exam, you might first *evaluate* the usefulness of a reading selection by skimming the material in order to identify the main points. Or near the end of your reading, you might *read creatively*, generating new ideas of your own as a result of mentally interacting with the text. At different times you will do different amounts of *revising*, depending on your goals and the difficulty of what you are reading.

Also as with writing, you may repeat different steps in the process as often as needed. Let's say that you're reading a very interesting but challenging passage that is hard to understand; you may have to produce two or three mental drafts before you are confident that you fully understand the material. *The main point to remember when reading (as well as when writing) is not to neglect any of the parts or subparts.*

As you follow the guided practice provided in this text, you should improve your ability to read, along with your ability to write.

For Further Thought

1. Why would improving your reading tend to improve your writing?

   _____

2. When you begin to read, do you plunge immediately into a word-by-word reading of the material without establishing an overall strategy, or plan, for understanding what you are about to read? _____ If so, which main part and subparts do you need to concentrate on at first? _____

   _____

3. Do you sometimes make an educated guess about what you are going to read but then fail to modify your initial guess as you read in more depth? _____ If so, which main part and subparts do you need to pay more attention to? _____

4. Do you automatically accept everything an author says without evaluating the supporting details he or she provides? _____ If so, which subpart would be most helpful to you? _____

5. Look back at the diagram of the reading process on page 47, and circle each main part and subpart that you need more practice with.

   _____

Now reread the passage from *Caged Bird*, applying what you have learned about the reading process and its main parts and subparts.

◆◆◆

WRITING ASSIGNMENT

Keeping a Journal

Personal experience is one of a writer's most valuable resources, and recording it for your personal use is an important reason for writing. You might try collecting those personal writings in a journal, or writer's notebook, as some professionals do.

The journal is a place where you can save memories, observations, and ideas in order to develop important insights, or understanding, or to work through a problem. It is a place to collect the raw energy of your thoughts before deciding whether to put them into a form for others to read. There is no right or wrong in keeping a journal, so you should find it the ideal place to practice and experiment with your writing—to write as freely as you want. Once collected, journal entries become a kind of gold mine, where you can go to get the nugget of an idea to be fashioned into a polished piece for others to read.

Your journal can take any physical form you want. Whether you use old-fashioned pen and ink or a computer is up to you. Colored paper in a decorative binder may catch your fancy, or you may like a spiral notebook or loose sheets of notepaper collected in a folder. Whatever its form, the journal is yours to use and adapt as you wish. You can use it for any type of writing you want or need to do, not only the personal memories in this assignment. In fact, you may want to continue your journal as a place to keep notes on the subjects you will write about in later chapters.

General Guidelines for Keeping a Journal

1. Try to write for a set period of time each day; ten or fifteen minutes will be a good start.
2. Don't worry about "correctness" as you write.
3. If some of the material is very personal, you may want to keep it in a private place, remembering that it is yours to share with others only as you see fit.

For Further Thought

To get you started, here are several approaches you might take. (You or your instructor may want to modify an approach to suit your needs.)

1. Each day for a week, record a vivid memory of an earlier time in your life, being sure to describe the concrete sensory details, feelings, and thoughts that you still remember. Here are some subjects you might write about:
    a. A place that was important in your past
    b. A person who has meant a great deal to you
    c. An important scene or event from earlier days
    d. Any combination of places, persons, or events in your past

    If vivid memories don't come to mind, try listening to a favorite piece of music, looking at a picture that you like, or rereading a story you enjoyed as a child and see what you are reminded of.

2. If you prefer to write about more recent experiences, you might describe some observations, along with related thoughts, that you have each day for a week.
    a. Your observations might occur at a place that is special to you—say, a favorite restaurant or place where you like to go to relax.
    b. You might observe a person who makes a vivid impression on you, one whom you may or may not know.
    c. It could be an important scene or event you observe.
    d. You could combine observations of people, places, and events.

Pay attention to the sights, sounds, textures, odors, and tastes associated with whatever you experience, along with your related thoughts and feelings, and record them as accurately as possible.

Write It Out: From Journal Entry to Essay

1 **RECORD A MEMORY.** Write at least three journal entries from different stages of your life, each describing an important memory of a time when you experienced or observed some kind of conflict that you are willing to share with others. You might have been in a conflict with someone else, or perhaps you felt a conflict within yourself, or you might have seen other people in some kind of conflict. (As Maya Angelou demonstrates in the excerpt from *I Know Why the Caged Bird Sings*, creative thinking, in the form of understanding or insight, can emerge from reflecting on such conflict.)

In the first entry you might describe your very earliest significant memory involving a conflict. Another memory might come from your early teenage years and another from your first days in college. These are just some of the possibilities.

Before starting to write each entry, you might want to shut your eyes, carrying yourself back in time, and recollect as many details as you can. Some may be vivid, others hazy: What is happening? What do you see? Who is there? Is anyone talking? What is being said? Do you hear anything else? What conflict do you notice? How do you feel? As you begin to write, you will likely recall more details. Describe the scene as completely and as vividly as you can.

Consider the following sample journal entry by student writer Gwin Johnson.

> I'm supposed to think about a memory that has some kind of conflict. This morning as I left for school, I noticed the mimosa tree across the street. A guy was washing off dead blossoms that had covered his car. All of a sudden I was remembering when I was seven and playing in my grandmother's yard and got in trouble because of my big-mouth brother.
>
> We called it Children's Day. A Sunday in June when all of the cousins were at my grandmother's to "meet and eat." All us little hellions ran around and saw what kind of mischief we could find.
>
> I remember the favorite game was seeing how high you could climb in the mimosas. The older kids took their turns; then it was mine. I climbed up the tree until I got to a limb that was no bigger around than my arm. Then a crack and a crash. I was on the ground and the limb was on top of me.
>
> What to do with the limb? I was pretty devious for a seven-year old — I hid the evidence out past the fence and hoped my grandmother wouldn't find out.

Chapter Two / Personal Writing: From Memory to Insight

> *Vernon ratted on me, but while Grandma let me sweat a little, she got over it pretty fast. It was Children's Day and she was always very good to me. I could have killed my brother.*

2 ASK A QUESTION. After recording several memories, reread each of your journal entries, imagining that you are the same age you were when the event actually occurred. As a child or a young person, what did you *not* understand about the experience?

At the end of each entry, write out a question regarding what you did not understand. If you need help wording your questions, study the following example; then ask your instructor or tutor to help you.

SAMPLE QUESTION: **Why didn't Grandma spank me?**

3 ANSWER THE QUESTION. Thinking like the older, more mature person you are today, answer the question that you wrote at the end of each journal entry. The idea is to look at an experience from different points of view (through a child's eyes and through an adult's eyes) in order to "shift mental gears" and thereby stimulate your creative thinking. The answers you come up with are the insights you have gained from thinking creatively about an experience you have stored in memory.

Try to state the insight as a significant truth or lesson that others could learn from, using either your own wording or a popular saying such as "Look before you leap" or "You can't judge a book by its cover." Ask for help if you need it; this is a crucial step.

SAMPLE INSIGHT: **There's a time to forgive and forget.**

4 READ BEFORE YOU WRITE. Read over your journal entries, the questions you have asked, and the answers you have given in the form of sayings or lessons that others could learn from. Then select the experience that seems most meaningful to put into narrative, or story, form as Maya Angelou did. You may want to reread the Angelou passage or check one of her books out of the library and read more before you write.

5 **DRAFT YOUR NARRATIVE.** As you write,

1. Check to be sure you have selected a significant memory that will be of interest to others.
2. Be sure that a conflict is involved, even if it is only hinted at, as Maya Angelou's was.
3. Begin with a sentence or a paragraph that will arouse your readers' interest in the story you have to tell. Consider the following example:

   A telephone ring that could have awakened the dead at 2 A.M. on a Tuesday morning began what was probably the worst day of my life. I was only eight years old at the time, but I was about to learn a lot.

4. Tell all the details of the story, and make the description vivid and colorful like a television drama or movie, complete with setting, characters, action, and dialogue, so that a reader can "relive" the experience and understand its significance for you.
5. Somewhere in the narrative, probably near the beginning or near the end, clearly state the insight you gained as a result of shifting from the child's to the adult's point of view and answering the child's question.
6. Conclude with a lesson that others could profit from, using these examples:

   From this experience I learned a very important lesson that I think others could profit from: . . .

   I've learned from this experience that . . .

Sample Rough Draft

As you read the following example, notice that the student author drew on her original journal writing to compose a rough draft and then reworked and refined it in order to produce a better version. Also notice the significance of the experience, the details, the conflict, and the insight, or lesson, that make her writing memorable.

CHILDREN'S DAY
by Gwin Johnson
(rough draft)

It was a Sunday afternoon in June. All the families were to meet at Grandma's house for Children's Day. It really wasn't too much from the norm. We usually met every Sunday at her house, but this Sunday there was added excitement. Family get-togethers were always at Grandma's house. She loved to cook and have all her children around. She had soft-brown eyes and was small in statue. A tough-spoken brown-skinned woman about 130 pounds. And when she spoke it was like E. F. Hutton, we listened! We had eaten our fill and the grown ups were settling down to talk. And Grandma decided to visit Uncle Nelson in the hospital. She told us she would be back shortly and to mind our manners.

No sooner was she out of sight, someone suggest we see who could climb the highest in the mimosa trees. And there were plenty of trees just ripe for the climbing. The game was to see who could go the highest and farthest to the end of the tree limb. I scooted to the end of the limb and heard a loud crack! The limb and I fell to the ground. Everyone scattered from the area. Well, I figured no evidence, no conviction. I dragged the limb to the very end of the yard where the fence was. And somehow got the limb over the fence into the underbrushes on the other side. I figured the removal of the evidence would ensure at least a delay in punishment. I warned my cousins don't talk and I won't tell anything on any of them. After all I wasn't the only one in the trees. I was the unfortunately creation that the stupid limb broke on.

On Grandma's return we all were a little afraid of her discovering the broken tree limb. You see Grandma likes to work in her yard and she would know if something was amiss. Later on that night we had a wiener roast. The fire was going down and Grandma had just came out with some more wieners. Vernon, my big-mouth brother, told her he knew where more wood was. And promptly asked her if we could use the limb that I broke earlier today while she was away. I tell you there was the largest space around me as if each of them had taken ten paces back. My eyes widen with fear that I was now exposed for my deed. She called me over and stared into my eyes and ask that dreaded question. "Did you break my limb?" I could not speak, only nod my head in affirmation.

Well my Grandma was shrewd. She knew to spank me would break the spirit of the day. So she took the time to give a "fire and brimstone sermon" to all of us and let the games continue. After all it was Children's Day. My Grandma was a sweet old lady. But my mother says if they had done anything like break a limb or not have chores done she would have flogged them like a seafaring captain!

It's amazing how they mellow over the years and learn to forgive and forget. I just glad she's my Grandma and I loved her very much.

6 **SHARE YOUR DRAFT.** Once you've finished drafting, let someone else—a classmate, a tutor, or your instructor—read and comment on it. You may also want to step back and read your draft as though for the first time to determine for yourself how it might be improved.

Sample Reader Commentary on Gwin's Draft

Gwin Johnson's writing lab tutor read her draft of "Children's Day" and made the following comments. Notice how many times the tutor has pointed out places where Gwin's writing could be improved by the addition of specific details.

Paragraph 1

--Describe "Children's Day" in greater detail. What was it all about? What went on? Remember to use concrete details that appeal to the senses.
--Could you at least give a hint as to the significance of this memory?
--Great "E. F. Hutton" line! You might save the description of your grandmother for the later scene when she discovers your "crime."

```
Paragraph 2
--Try to describe the mimosa trees in greater detail. What
did they look like? How did the bark feel?
--To make your work more interesting, create a vivid pic-
ture of the child's clever efforts to get out of a jam.
For added interest, show the humor of the situation.

Paragraph 3
--Here go into greater detail to show your grandmother's
authoritative and shrewd character. Continue to show the
humor of the situation created by your brother's betrayal
and your fear of being caught.

Paragraph 4
--Say more about why your grandmother didn't spank you.
Remember that you're looking for some kind of insight,
some kind of meaning, in this memory.
--How does your memory of your grandmother affect your
life now? What did this incident teach you?
```

7 **REVISE YOUR DRAFT.** Taking into account the comments of your reader or readers and your own critical reading of your first draft, rewrite your narrative. Add new material where it will be useful, and delete any material that seems to wander from the main point. You may wish to rearrange material as well.

After you've reworked your essay, remember to make any corrections in spelling, punctuation, grammar, and word choice that need to be made. If you have any questions or want any more help, be sure to ask.

For Further Thought

Notice how Gwin Johnson reworked and refined her draft to produce a better version. What differences can you see between the two drafts?

Sample Revised Draft

```
      CHILDREN'S DAY
       (final draft)
      by Gwin Johnson
```

When I was a child, my family would spend almost every Sunday at my grandma's house. But I remember one Sunday afternoon in June when there was added excitement. That day was Children's Day: there were more cousins to play with, more varieties of food to plunder, more fun to be had. But while this was a day for children, I learned something about my grandma's judgment that remains with me still.

We had eaten our fill of fried chicken and mashed potatoes and gravy, and the older people were sitting down to talk when Grandma announced that she had decided to visit Uncle Nelson in the hospital. She told us she would be back shortly. "Mind your manners," she said as she left the house. But no sooner was she out of sight than someone suggested we see who could climb the highest in the mimosa trees. (My grandma's yard had several trees that just begged to be climbed.)

The object of the game was to see who could go the highest in the mimosa's sprawling branches, with extra points awarded to those who could crawl out onto the slender brown limbs away from the thick main trunk. When it was my turn, I climbed up high and then scooted across cool smooth bark to the end of a branch. Just as I reached the end, I heard a loud "crack"! The next thing I knew, the limb and I were on the ground, and my cousins had scattered like a covey of quail.

Dazed by the fall, I got up, dusted myself off, and tried to figure out what to do next. "Well," I thought, "no evidence, no conviction." So I dragged the splintered limb to the very end of the yard where the fence was and, even though I was only seven years old at the time, heaved it across the fence into the underbrush on the other side. Removal of the evidence should ensure at least a delay in punishment, I reasoned. I then warned my cousins to keep quiet unless they wanted to get in trouble with me. At age seven I had learned a basic rule: "Never go down alone on the ship, not if you can take a couple of first mates with you." After all, I wasn't the only one in the trees, I told myself. I was merely the unfortunate creature who broke the stupid limb.

On Grandma's return we all were a little afraid of her discovering the broken tree limb. While Grandma didn't look or act like an ogre--in fact she was small in stature and had soft brown eyes and wispy gray hair--when she spoke it was like E. F. Hutton--we listened! And while we all walked around trying to look like angels, we were really dreading the inevitable, for all of us were in awe of Grandma's shrewd investigative powers.

Later on that night we had a wiener roast, complete with toasted marshmallows. We straightened out clothes hangers and stuck the red wieners on the end and roasted them to a dark brown over a barrel of fire. The fire was going down and Grandma had just brought out more wieners when Vernon, my big-mouthed brother, "happened" to mention to her that he knew where more wood was. "Could we," he asked in his most innocent voice, "use the limb that Gwin had broken off and hidden?" My eyes widened; I was exposed. My grandma called me over to her and stared into my eyes and asked that dreaded question--"Did you break my tree limb?" I couldn't speak; I only nodded my head in affirmation.

Today my mother says that if she and her playmates had done anything half as bad as breaking a limb from one of my grandma's mimosas, the woman would have flogged them like a seafaring captain disciplining a mutinous crew. But my grandma was shrewd. She knew that to spank me would break the spirit of the day. She took the time to give a half-hearted "fire and brimstone" sermon to all of us and let the games continue. After all, it was Children's Day.

More than several years have passed since that June afternoon, but I look back now and see my grandmother's wisdom. When she looked at us, she had somehow remembered what it means to be a child. To know there's a time to forgive and forget--that may be a hard lesson to remember. But for <u>my</u> grandchildren's sake, I hope I will.

PERSONAL SUMMARY

1. Review the goals at the beginning of this chapter, and check off each one that you have successfully accomplished.

2. Summarize the main lessons you have learned by working through this chapter.

_____

_____

_____

_____

_____

3. List the subjects covered in this chapter that you still need more work on.

_____

_____

_____

_____

ADDITIONAL WRITING

Without giving much thought, quickly list in your journal the ten events in your life that you consider to be the most significant. Then go back and describe each event in detail. Do these events have anything in common? What do you learn about yourself from your recollection and recording of these events? Write down your insights as they come to you.

Using the steps outlined in this chapter, write an essay about one of these experiences.

ADDITIONAL READING

Angelou, Maya. *I Know Why the Caged Bird Sings*. New York: Random House, 1969. An autobiography, both humorous and inspiring, that recounts the early years of a well-known African-American writer and activist.

———. *Just Give Me a Cool Drink of Water 'fore I Diiie*. New York: Random House, 1971. A book of poetry by Maya Angelou.

A Portrait of Maya Angelou (videotape). Washington, DC: PBS Video, 1982. Television journalist Bill Moyers accompanies Angelou back to her small Arkansas hometown to discover how her passion for expression and achievement was shaped.

Progoff, Ira. *At a Journal Workshop*. New York: Dialogue House Library, 1975. A basic text and guide for using the journal as a means of personal growth.

Chapter Three
Voices from the Past

> *In this chapter, you will:*
> ✔ Learn interview techniques for collecting material to write about
> ✔ Use writing as a means of learning
> ✔ Preserve information about a people or a culture for others to read about

READING

Just as writing can capture a memory of your personal past and help you learn from it, you can also use writing to record a glimpse of the family traditions or culture which you have grown up in and which, in part, makes you the unique person you are. Or you can use writing as a means of exploring the heritage of others.

Enrique "Hank" Lopez wrote "Back to Bachimba" as a personal, family, and cultural story all in one. The passage you are about to read describes the "cultural tug-of-war" and personal conflicts Lopez, who was born in Mexico and grew up in this country, experienced as a young Chicano. Although Lopez worked hard to master English, he said the "hard core" of him remained stubbornly Mexican. And despite his success in school, he and his Chicano friends were looked upon as inferior by their teachers. What he doesn't tell you in this passage is that later he earned distinction as the first Hispanic graduate of Harvard Law School.

By preserving information about his family's background, Lopez helps us understand the powerful effect one's culture can have on one's development and one's use of language. Similarly, as you write about some important aspect of your own cultural or family traditions for others to read about, you can better understand the impact your heritage has had on you. Or if you choose to write about some aspect of the cultural or family traditions of other people, you can learn by comparing their heritage to yours.

Chapter Three / Voices from the Past

Preparing to Read

Before you read, ask yourself: Why is the language of a culture such a vital part of its identity?

As you read, think about the following:

1. How did the trip back to Bachimba affect Lopez?
2. What aspects of his culture were a source of pride for Lopez?
3. How did the racial prejudice Lopez experienced in school affect his education?

Back to Bachimba
by Enrique "Hank" Lopez

I am a *pocho* from Bachimba, a rather small Mexican village in the state of Chihuahua, where my father fought with the army of Pancho Villa (Mexican revolutionary and folk hero [1878–1923] who led guerrilla raids into U.S. territory in 1915). *Pocho* is ordinarily a derogatory term in Mexico (to define it succinctly, a *pocho* is a Mexican slob who has pretensions of being a gringo sonofabitch), but I use it in a very special sense. To me that word has come to mean "uprooted Mexican," and that's what I have been all my life. Though my entire upbringing and education took place in the United States, I have never felt completely American, and when I am in Mexico, I sometimes feel like a displaced gringo with a curiously Mexican name—Enrique Preciliano Lopez y Martinez de Sepulveda de Sapien de Quien-sabe-quien. One might conclude that I'm either a schizo-cultural Mexican or a cultured schizoid American.

In any event, the schizo-ing began a long time ago, when my father and many of Pancho Villa's troops fled across the border to escape the oncoming *federales* who eventually defeated Villa. My mother and I, traveling across the hot desert plains in a buckboard wagon, joined my father in El Paso, Texas, a few days after his hurried departure. With more and more Villistas swarming into El Paso every day, it was quickly apparent that jobs would be exceedingly scarce and insecure; so my parents packed our belongings and we took the first available bus to Denver. My father had hoped to move to Chicago because the name sounded so Mexican, but my mother's meager savings were hardly enough to buy tickets for Colorado.

schizoid: divided personality

federales: U.S. troops

There we moved into a ghetto of Spanish-speaking residents who chose to call themselves Spanish Americans and resented the sudden migration of their brethren from Mexico, whom they sneeringly called *surumatos* (slang for "southerners"). These so-called Spanish Americans claimed direct descent from the original *conquistadores*. They also insisted that they had never been Mexicans, since their region of New Spain (later annexed to the United States) was never a part of Mexico. But what they claimed most vociferously—and erroneously—was an absence of Indian ancestry. It made no difference that any objective observer could see by merely looking at them the results of considerable fraternization between the conquering Spaniards and the Comanche and Navaho women who crossed their paths. Still, these *manitos*, as they were snidely labeled by the *surumatos*, stubbornly refused to be identified with Mexico, and would actually fight anyone who called them Mexican. So intense was this intergroup rivalry that the bitterest "race riots" I have ever witnessed—and engaged in—were between the look-alike, talk-alike *surumatos* and *manitos* who lived near Denver's Curtis Park. In retrospect the harsh conflicts between us were all the more silly and self-defeating when one recalls that we were all lumped together as "spiks" and "greasers" by the Anglo-Saxon community.

Predictably enough, we *surumatos* began huddling together in a sub-neighborhood within the larger ghetto, and it was there that I became painfully aware that my father had been the only private in Pancho Villa's army. Most of my friends were the sons of captains, colonels, majors, and even generals, though a few fathers were admittedly mere sergeants and corporals. My father alone had been a lowly private in that famous Divison del Norte. Naturally, I developed a most painful complex, which led me to all sorts of compensatory fibs. During one brief spell I fancied my father as a member of the dreaded *los dorados*, the "golden ones," who were Villa's favorite henchmen. (Later I was to learn that my father's cousin, Martin Lopez, was a genuine and quite notorious *dorado*.) But all my inventions were quickly un-invented by my very own father, who seemed to take a perverse delight in being Pancho's only private.

No doubt my chagrin was accentuated by the fact that Pancho Villa's exploits were a constant topic of conversation in our household. My entire childhood seemed to be shadowed by his presence. At our dinner table, almost every night, we would listen to endlessly repeated accounts of this battle, that stratagem, or some great act of Robin Hood kindness by *el centauro del norte*. . . .

As if to deepen our sense of *Villismo*, my parents also taught us "Adelita" and "Se llevaron el canon para Bachimba" ("they took the cannons to Ba-

Chapter Three / Voices from the Past

poignant: moving

Lewis Carroll: pen name of English writer best known for *Alice's Adventures in Wonderland*

nondescript: plain

vintage: period of time

chimba"), the two most famous songs of the Mexican revolution. Some twenty years later (during my stint at Harvard Law School), while strolling along the Charles River, I would find myself softly singing "Se llevaron el canon para Bachimba, para Bachimba, para Bachimba" over and over again. That's all I could remember of that poignant rebel song. Though I had been born there, I had regarded "Bachimba" as a fictitious, made up, Lewis Carroll kind of word. So that eight years ago, when I first returned to Mexico, I was literally stunned when I came to a crossroad south of Chihuahua and saw an old road marker: "Bachimba 18 km." Then it really exists—I shouted inwardly—Bachimba is a real town! Swinging onto the narrow, poorly paved road, I gunned the motor and sped toward the town I'd been singing about since infancy. It turned out to be a quiet, dusty village with a bleak worn-down plaza that was surrounded by nondescript buildings of uncertain vintage.

chauvinistic: excessively patriotic

Aside from the songs about Bachimba and Adelita and all the folk tales about Villa's guerrilla fighters, my early years were strongly influenced by our neighborhood celebrations of Mexico's two most important patriotic events: Mexican Independence Day on September 16 and the anniversary of the battle of Puebla on May 5. On those two dates Mexicans all over the world are likely to become extremely chauvinistic. In Denver we would stage annual parades that included three or four floats skimpily decorated with crepe paper streamers, a small band, several adults in threadbare battle dress, and hundreds of kids marching in wild disorder. It was during one of these parades—I was ten years old then—that I was seized with acute appendicitis and had to be rushed to a hospital. The doctor subsequently told my mother that I had made a long impassioned speech about the early revolutionist Miguel Hidalgo while the anesthetic was taking hold, and she explained with pardonable pride that it was the speech I was to make at Turner Hall that evening. Mine was one of the twenty-three *discursos* scheduled on the postparade program, a copy of which my mother still retains. My only regret was missing the annual *discurso* of Don Miguel Gomez, my godfather, a deep-throated orator who would always climax his speech by falling to his knees and dramatically kissing the floor, almost weeping as he loudly proclaimed: *"Ay, Mexico! Beso tu tierra, tu mero corazon"* ("Ah, Mexico! I kiss your sacred soil, the very heart of you"). He gave the same oration for seventeen years, word for word and gesture for gesture, and it never failed to bring tears to his eyes. But not once did he return to Chihuahua, even for a brief visit.

discursos: orations

My personal Mexican-ness eventually produced serious problems for me. Upon entering grade school I learned English rapidly, and rather well, always ranking either first or second in my class; yet the hard core of me remained stubbornly Mexican. This chauvinism may have been a reaction to the constant racial prejudice we encountered on all sides. The neighborhood cops were always running us off the streets and calling us "dirty greasers," and most of our teachers frankly regarded us as totally inferior. I still remember the galling disdain of my sixth-grade teacher, whose constant mimicking of our heavily accented speech drove me to a desperate study of Webster's Dictionary in the hope of acquiring a vocabulary larger than hers. Sadly enough, I succeeded only too well and for the next few years I spoke the most ridiculous high-flown rhetoric in the Denver public schools. One of my favorite words was "indubitably," and it must have driven everyone mad. I finally got rid of my accent by constantly reciting "Peter Piper picked a peck of pickled peppers" with little round pebbles in my mouth. Somewhere I had read about Demosthenes.

disdain: contempt

indubitably: undoubtedly

Demosthenes: famous orator of ancient Greece who was said to have improved the clarity of his speech by talking with pebbles in his mouth

During this phase of my childhood the cultural tug of war known as "Americanization" almost pulled me apart. There were moments when I would identify completely with the gringo world (what could have been more American than my earnest high-voiced portrayal of George Washington, however ridiculous the cotton wig my mother had fashioned for me?); then quite suddenly I would feel so acutely Mexican that I would stammer over the simplest English phrase. I was so ready to take offense at the slightest slur against Mexicans that I would imagine prejudice where none existed. But on other occasions, in full confidence of my belonging, I would venture forth into social areas that I should have realized were clearly forbidden to little Chicanos from Curtis Park. The inevitable rebuffs would leave me floundering in self-pity; it was small comfort to know that other minority groups suffered even worse rebuffs than we did. . . .

rebuffs: rejections

My own Mexican-ness, after years of decline at Harvard University, suddenly burst forth again when I returned to Chihuahua and stumbled on the town of Bachimba. I had long conversations with an uncle I'd never met before, my father's younger brother, Ramon. It was Tio Ramon who chilled my spine with eyewitness stories about Pancho Villa's legendary *dorados*, one of whom was Martin Lopez. "He was your second cousin. The bravest young buck in Villa's army. And he became a *dorado* when he was scarcely seventeen years old because he dared to defy Pancho Villa himself. As your papa may have told you, Villa had a bad habit of burying treasure up in the mountains and also burying the man he took with him to dig the hole for it. Well, one day he chose Martin Lopez to go with him. Deep in the mountains they went, near Parral. And when they got to a suitably lonely place, Pancho Villa told him to dig a hole with pick and shovel. Then when Martin had dug down to his waist, Villa leveled a gun at the boy. "Say your prayers, *muchacho*. You shall stay here with the gold—forever." But Martin had come prepared. In his large right boot he had a gun, and when he rose from his bent position, he was pointing that gun at Villa. They stood there, both ready to fire, for several seconds, and finally Don Pancho started to laugh in that wonderful way of his. "*Bravo, bravo, muchacho*! You've got more guts than a man. Get out of that hole, boy. I need you for my *dorados*."

Tio Ramon's eyes were wet with pride. "But what is more important, he died with great valor. Two years later, after he had terrorized the *federales* and Pershing's gringo soldiers, he was finally wounded and captured here in Bachimba. It was a bad wound in his leg, finally turning to gangrene. Then one Sunday morning they hauled Martin Lopez and three other prisoners to the plaza. One by one they executed the three lesser prisoners against that wall. I was up on the church tower watching it all. Finally it was our uncle's turn. They dragged him off the buckboard wagon and handed him his crutches. Slowly, painfully, he hobbled to the wall and stood there. Very straight he stood. Do you have any last words? asked the captain of the firing squad. With great pride Martin tossed his crutches aside and stood very tall on his one good leg. 'Give me, you yellow bastards, give me a gun—and I'll show you who is the man among . . .' Eight bullets crashed into his chest and face, and I never heard that final word. That was your second cousin. You would have been proud to know him."

As I listened to Tio Ramon's soft nostalgic voice that evening, there in the sputtering light of the kerosene lamp on his back patio, I felt as intensely Mexican as I shall ever feel.

Pershing: American general who led troops against Pancho Villa in 1916

nostalgic: yearning for the past

Thinking about Your Reading

Answer the following questions to improve your understanding of Lopez's story and to discover more of its significance for you.

1. What does Lopez mean when he says "I'm either a schizo-cultural Mexican or a cultured schizoid American" (1)? In what way does the name "Hank" Lopez illustrate the truth of his statement?

_____

_____

_____

2. Lopez says that "the bitterest 'race riots' I have ever witnessed—and engaged in" (3) were among two groups of his own people in Denver. What do you think caused these groups to clash?

_____

_____

_____

3. During his growing-up years in Denver, what cultural experiences served to remind Lopez of his Mexican heritage?

_____

_____

4. As a child why was Lopez motivated to develop a large vocabulary and to eliminate an accent from his speech?

_____

_____

_____

5. What insight did Lopez arrive at that explains why the "hard core" of him "remained stubbornly Mexican" (8)? Why did he find it sad that he "succeeded only too well" (8) in developing a larger vocabulary than his teacher?

_____

_____

_____

_____

6. Why was the trip back to Bachimba an important cultural and personal experience for Lopez?

_____

_____

_____

7. When a family or individual moves from one culture to another as the Lopez family did, why might the move create emotional conflict, as it did for Hank Lopez?

_____

_____

8. How are cultural differences sometimes used as weapons among people?

_____

_____

_____

9. Is your home culture very different from the public culture around you?

_____ If it is, what problems has the difference caused for you?

_____

_____

_____

WRITING ASSIGNMENT

Language, Dialect, and Standard English

One of the most important features of a culture or a community is the language used by its people. Of course, the language in use will vary from one nationality to another. And the dialects, or forms, of that language will vary from one region or community to another. You probably noticed the different dialects and languages that appear in the autobiographical writings of Maya Angelou and Enrique "Hank" Lopez.

When writing in their present voices, they use what is known as *standard English*. Sometimes referred to as the "language of wider communication," it is the form of language, or dialect, commonly expected in schools and businesses throughout the United States.

When reflecting the cultural background from which they come, the two writers shift to a different language or to a community dialect—a dialect acceptable in one's home community but different from the standard form of language taught in school and used in the professional world. Sometimes community dialects are referred to as "nonstandard" dialects because the vocabulary, pronunciation, and grammar vary, if even slightly, from one community to another and therefore are not "standard."

In showing how persons in her community spoke informally to one another, Angelou shifts from standard English to nonstandard English. For example, *lemme* is used in place of *let me*. In "Back to Bachimba," Lopez occasionally shifts dialects *and* languages—from standard English to nonstandard Spanish. For example, *pocho* is used as a nonstandard, slang expression to refer to a Mexican who has come to the United States.

For further understanding of the point being made here, consider the word *ain't*. Though it is a popular word in the vocabulary of some nonstandard dialects, it is not considered appropriate in the vocabulary of standard English and would not be evaluated as correct if used in school or business settings.

Although many people may think of one dialect as always good or superior and another as always bad or inferior, many language experts would argue that the "goodness" of any form of language depends on the user's purpose and audience. In the words of an old saying, the experts would advise us: "When in Rome, do as the Romans do." Put another way, they would tell us that when we're in Rome, we should speak and write as the Romans speak and write—that is, if we want to communicate with the Romans.

Let me give a personal example. When I go home to visit my father, who has spent most of his life in a small rural community, I use a dialect that is similar to his. Why? Because I want to maintain a bond with him, and the language I have heard him speak all my life allows me to do so. In this case, I consider a nonstandard dialect more effective than the standard one I would use if I were talking to you in a classroom setting.

On the other hand, when I visit my mother, who for thirty years or so worked in the business world and communicated with people across the country, I use a form of language much closer to what I am writing here. In both cases I am using the most effective form for a given purpose and audience.

You may think this sounds complicated, but experienced users of multiple dialects make such shifts rather easily as they feel the need, just as people who are fluent in two or more languages do. It requires some thought and practice, though, to speak or write a dialect or a language that differs from one that we use most of the time. It was for this reason, in fact, that Lopez had to work hard to master English.

As you work to improve your writing skill, remember that the main reason you need standard English is so that you can communicate more effectively in school and at work no matter what part of the country you live in. But as you learn and practice standard usage, don't forget the value of your community dialect, especially when you go back home.

For Further Thought

To compare differences in standard and nonstandard English and to appreciate the value of community dialect, read the following passage. When the incident originally took place, the speakers were using the dialect most appropriate for the situation.

*A Family Story**
as told to Chuck Fisher

I entered the kitchen where my mother was cooking. Our conversation started with her suggesting that I join a youth fraternity.

"The youth fraternity," I retorted; "Mama, I ain't gon join no youth fraternity. I don't wanna be no Mason."

"Son, ya jest twelve years old," Mama said; "betta shut up talkin' to me like dat. I'm gon whup ya."

"Ya ain't gon whup me. I'll run away from home."

"Ya betta git on in dare and clean up yo' room, 'cause ya ain't gon go nowhere."

"Ah now, Mama, ya said I could go somewhere when I finish cleanin up my room."

"Yeah, right out dare and hep yo daddy work on da car."

So I left the house and walked out to the garage, where Dad was working.

Finding him under the hood of the car, I asked, "Whatcha doin', Daddy?"

"I'm workin' on da carbrator," Daddy replied.

"What's a carbrator for?" I asked.

Dad stopped what he was doing and turned around. With a smiling face he answered, "Now da carbrator is da thing that reglates da gas to da motor."

He went on to explain to me a lot of things about the car. At this point I was very excited, for I had my dad's attention and this was the first time, up to that day, that I had felt comfortable with him.

"Daddy, Mama say I gotta join the youth fraternity—I don't wanna be in no youth fraternity."

Dad responded, "Clyde, me and yo mama love ya. All we want is for ya to make sumpin outta yo self. See, me and yo mama never had a chance to finish school and we want all our chi'ren to finish school. When we tell ya sumpin, it's for ya own good. Me and ya mama think da youth fraternity will be good for ya. Ya can make some new friends and ya can go off to camp doin' da summer."

"Daddy, if I tell Mama I'm gon be in the youth fraternity, then kin I go ova to cuttin Mattie's house?"

cuttin: cousin

"Yeah, and tell ya mama I said ya kin."

"Thank ya, Daddy."

*I want to express my appreciation to language expert Geneva Smitherman-Donaldson for her assistance in editing this passage so that the spelling appropriately reflects the community dialect.

> **For Further Thought**

1. You may want to try your hand at translating the dialogue from community dialect to standard English. If you do, you may notice that the story loses much of its authentic sound and interest when the nonstandard language is eliminated. But once the dialogue is written in standard English, it is easier for a larger number of people to understand.
2. When you read the passage, did the community dialect seem inappropriate to you? If so, you may want to reconsider the points made earlier in this section and discuss them in class.

Write It Out: An Essay on Family or Culture

1 **STIMULATE YOUR THINKING.** To stimulate your thinking about a family or cultural tradition, you might go through old photo albums, mementos, and personal or family "treasures" that you or your family have collected over a period of time. Rummaging through old materials, you may find a family Bible or other religious book with birth and death records, handmade cards, or dried flowers preserved inside. Or perhaps there's an antique jewelry box stuffed with unusual jewelry or family letters.

If you want to investigate a heritage different from your own, you might visit the home or neighborhood of someone from that background. Or you might go to a local museum that collects materials from times past in order to preserve the heritage of the region.

Old books filled with interesting, if outdated, lore (like my grandparents' "sex manual," which I found while digging in my mother's attic) can teach you about ways of the past. Other works like "Back to Bachimba" and *Caged Bird* capture the flavor of a particular culture through the personal stories their authors tell.

2 **CHOOSE AN INTERVIEW SUBJECT.** To preserve some unique, interesting, or unusual aspect of your family history or your own culture, select someone to interview who knows a great deal about your family's past or the background from which you come. This person may or may not be a relative of yours.

Together the two of you might settle on the topic that you want to preserve a record of. This could be a memorable event or incident, an important institution or place, a significant person or object, or a combination of any of these. An old family recipe or special ethnic food, a popular holiday celebration, someone who has an unusual ability—all are possibilities for you to write about.

You might also choose to interview someone from a different cultural background. This might be a person whom you don't know well but who is very familiar with the heritage you want to learn more about. Choose one particular aspect of your subject's culture or tradition to study in detail—celebrations, religious customs, family traditions, history, values, or something else.

3 **CONDUCT THE INTERVIEW.** Ask your interviewee questions that will rekindle old memories, and record the answers on a tape recorder or perhaps in your journal. You can adapt the sample interview questions that follow or make up your own questions. Either way, you will want to use *who*, *what*, *when*, *where*, *how*, and *why* questions as journalists do when they gather the daily news.

SAMPLE INTERVIEW QUESTIONS

Person

1. Who is the person?
2. What was or is this person like?
3. What kind of work did this person do?
4. When and where did this person live?
5. How did you know each other?
6. How does this person affect your present feelings or life?
7. Why is this person important in your life?

Tradition or institution

1. What is it like?
2. Who is associated with it?
3. When and where did it exist?

4. How did it get started?
5. How did it affect you?
6. Why is it still important?

Incident

1. When and where did it happen?
2. Who was there?
3. What occurred?
4. What made it memorable?
5. Why were people doing what they were doing?
6. How did the incident affect you?
7. If you could relive the incident, how would you change it and why?

Place

1. Where was it located?
2. Who went there?
3. What did they do there?
4. When did they go there?
5. How did they go there?
6. When was the first time you went there?
7. What were your first and lasting impressions of the place?
8. Why is it still important to you or others?

ADDITIONAL INTERVIEW TIPS

1. Modify the guide to suit your topic and your purpose for writing. You might use only some of these sample questions, combine the questions in any way you like, add questions, or change the tense of the questions.
2. Be considerate of your interviewee: Put him or her at ease, explaining the purpose of your project and how the information will be used. Be as natural as possible. Be sure all information is accurately recorded, going for a follow-up interview if necessary. Thank the person for his or her time. Share a copy of the final results.

Whether you take notes or record your interview, you'll want to write a clear transcript, or record, of the questions and answers that you can use as the basis for your first draft. You might also provide a brief introduction at this point so that you can share your interview with others for comments and suggestions.

The sample interview transcript that follows was written by Bonnie Lowe, a student who decided to focus on a cultural heritage different from her own. Her final draft begins on page 85.

Sample Interview Transcript

```
              NEW RAMAH PRIMITIVE BAPTIST CHURCH,
                    YESTERDAY AND TODAY
                      (interview notes)
                       by Bonnie Lowe
```

My husband's grandfather, Lynn Z. Benefield, belongs to a small country church known as New Ramah Primitive Baptist Church. Being from California, I had never attended a church quite like this before moving to Louisiana. Four times a year we go to church with Granddaddy. Primitive Baptists of New Ramah Church meet on the first and third Sunday of the month. The pastor preaches for about an hour, and when he preaches, it is like an auctioneer--at one tone level and very, very fast. There is no set salary for the pastor. The members donate what they feel he needs. The Primitive Baptists don't believe in any music being played in church. Most of the members are seventy years old or older, and they are the great-grandchildren of the original church members. I feel very lucky being able to see and enjoy this unique congregation firsthand.

In the following interview Granddaddy tells me more about his religious background and gives me a brief glance at the lifestyle of his childhood. I have tried to record his words exactly as he spoke them rather than in standard English.

BL: Has your family always been Primitive Baptist, Granddaddy?

LZB: There wasn't no church in this country hardly, hardly. Till my mama's mama ordained the New Ramah Church. My granddaddy never did join no church. The Primitive Baptists don't believe going to church has any to do with going to heaven 'cause the Bible says going to church while you're living is for your pleasure.

BL: The New Ramah Church was the first around here?

LZB: It was the first of any kind.

BL: Has the church changed any over the years?

LZB: Yes, credit!

BL: Credit?

LZB: If you'd just rode to town and they'd found out you'd belong to Primitive Baptist, you'd have credit anyway. 'Cause they'd turn you out if you didn't pay your bills. But now they don't do it. Back then you'd be Primitive Baptist, you'd have credit. I know old Evan borrowed a load of corn from Old Man Jones, who'd loan you corn, and he wouldn't pay it back and they had him up in the church for it. They made him pay it. Then they still turned him out for it. We'd use to borrow corn every year from Mr. Jones, but we'd always pay it back.

BL: What was church Sunday like?

LZB: We'd get up early the morning and eat a big breakfast. All of us would get dressed in our Sunday best. We'd get in the wagons and head for church. We'd sing for about forty-five minutes and then the preaching would start. I had an uncle who was a Primitive Baptist preacher. When you sat down, you'd know he'd be going hard and fast an hour or so. It always tired him. Now the church socialization would start Friday and wasn't over till Sunday evening.

BL: What was a church socialization?

LZB: Some people had to come from far away to go to church, and they'd start coming in on Friday. They would start gathering at one house or another and they'd socialize.

BL: Did many people come to the church socializations?

LZB: Used to be when it was socialization you could likely have up to thirty spend the night with you. My mama had a big family. They'd all come in wagons. That's how you got around then. She'd send some boys into the corn field to cut bunches of corn and they'd pile it up in the yard. They'd cook it in her big black kettle. Mama had some pans as big across as her oven and she'd fill one with 'taters, the other with biscuits, not little ones, but as big as your hand. There wasn't no place you could buy meat out of a deep freeze. You'd just kill a cow and hog and divide 'em around. That's the way it was back then. All were friends. There weren't no strangers at supper time. All's welcome.

'taters: potatoes

BL: It must have taken a lot of food. How did you feed all those people?

LZB: During the summer it wasn't bad; everything was fresh. During the winter you had to can 'em or either dry 'em. Sweet 'taters, we'd put 'em in the garden. Make you a bed, and put down pine straw or pine droppings and put your 'taters on it and take corn stalks and stack 'em all over 'em. Take your shovel and just bury the whole thing. You need to leave a place to get the 'taters out. They keep until next spring and you'd can up what's left. I done it with my sweet 'taters every fall. Used to can lots of stuff. Dry your apples and peaches. You could slice 'em up and put 'em in the hot sun and dry 'em. It was just a lot of work to it. You had to take 'em in every night if you didn't want the deer to get in 'em.

pine droppings: pieces of pine cones chewed off by squirrels

BL: Is there any special church socialization that stands out in your memory?

LZB: I remember one big socialization right at Christmas. The menfolk got heavy-handed with the eggnog, and the womenfolk got mad. Well they snuck in the room while's the men slept and took all their pants. They sewed the legs shut at the bottom and then put 'em back. Then they made loud noises to startle the men. Boy, you'd never seen anything funnier. Those men were still feeling the drink and were trying to put on them pants that the legs were sewed shut.

4 **DRAFT YOUR ESSAY.** Once you've collected as much information as you think you need, you will want to think about how best to organize your material: in *chronological*, or time, order, telling what happened first, then second, and so on; in *spatial* order, moving clearly from one part of the setting to another and then another; or in *climactic* order, from least important or interesting detail to most important or interesting.

You might want to record it in the first person (*I*), complete with dialect, as Maya Angelou did. Or you may prefer to use the third person (*he* or *she*), as student writer John Watson did in his essay about his mother titled "Life on 'The Rock,'" the first draft of which follows. Remember, though, to practice pronoun consistency so that your readers won't be confused. (Related information can be found in the Handbook.)

Sample Rough Draft

The following draft is based on an interview John Watson conducted with his mother about a particular place she remembered from her childhood. As you read, notice how John has used both direct quotation and indirect quotation. (For more about quotations, see pages 256–258 in the Handbook.)

```
          LIFE ON "THE ROCK"
             (rough draft)
              by John Watson
```

Alcatraz Federal Penitentiary sounds like a foreboding place, but for three years, from 1935 to 1938, my mother lived on "The Rock." She was "incarcerated" at the young age of four. At that time Alcatraz Island was her home, where she lived with her uncle Royal Cline, who was a prison guard. All guards' families were required to live on the island. Because it was the top security prison in the country at that time, there were some differences in life style on the island. In telling me about the years she lived there my mother said, "The water boat from San Francisco was the only way on or off the island. It brought water and food twice a day. It also took prisoners to and from the island. The guards were everywhere; there were walkways on the walls where guards were stationed. Some guards walked the grounds, and others were stationed in the different shops where prisoners worked."

At the time my mother lived on Alcatraz, some of the biggest criminals of the depression era were imprisoned there. In fact, my mother has a jewelry box made by Al Capone. I asked her how she got it, and she replied, "That's an interesting story. I took Uncle Royal's lunch to him every day, and sometimes I would see Capone being exercised alone in the yard, although I didn't know who he was at the time. I would wave at him through the fence, and he would wave back. Uncle Royal ran the furniture shop where Capone worked, and he asked Uncle Royal who the little girl was that he saw every day. When my uncle said I was his niece, Capone asked him to give a jewelry box he'd finished to "the little girl." My mother still has the jewelry box, and it has become a small family treasure.

In May 1938, Royal Cline was killed in a prison escape attempt. With his death he became the first prison officer to be killed at Alcatraz. In those days there was little justice in prison. The murderer, in addition to receiving another life sentence on top of his original sentence, received a cruel and unusual punishment from the guards. He was put in solitary confinement and was never allowed to visit or talk to any of the other prisoners. The guards never spoke a word to him and never acknowledged his presence. Set apart and forgotten, he remained in solitary confinement for ten years. Due to a later prison riot which brought about prison reform, Royal Cline's killer was found to be receiving cruel punishment and was released from solitary. The years of confinement and total separation from others had driven him insane. He was then transferred to a mental institution for treatment.

Shortly after Royal Cline's death, his family and my mother left Alcatraz Island. Looking back on this unusual period of her life, she remembers it as a happy time in her childhood except for the death of her uncle.

5 **SHARE YOUR DRAFT.** Bring your interview notes and rough draft to class. In small groups, review each person's draft, checking the following aspects of it:

1. *Unity.* Does your draft treat only one main topic? Does each paragraph treat only one aspect, or part, of that topic?
2. *Completeness of information.* Where are the gaps that need to be filled in? Are all people and places adequately identified so that readers can understand and appreciate your work?
3. *Use of concrete sensory details.* Does the draft show how things look, sound, feel, smell, and taste?
4. *Order of details.* Are details appropriately arranged in chronological (according to time), spatial (according to space), or climactic (according to importance) order?

Sample Group Feedback on John Watson's Draft

Here are the comments John Watson's group made on his rough draft of "Life on 'The Rock.'"

```
Paragraph 1

--Attention-getting opener; effective concrete detail.
Would you have better paragraph unity if you broke the
first paragraph into two separate ones? The first could
explain why your mother lived on the island, and the sec-
ond could show what life on the island was like.


Paragraph 2

--Fascinating story! Does your mother remember the names
of some of the other criminals imprisoned on Alcatraz
while she lived there?


Paragraph 3

--Remember that your subject is your mother's childhood
memories of Alcatraz. Should the fate of Royal Cline's
murderer take over the story?
```

Paragraph 4

--Try to expand this paragraph a little. Since "The Rock" is almost like a character, why not say a few closing words about it?
--We enjoyed the story very much. Good work.

6 REVISE YOUR DRAFT. If you agree with the suggestions your group gave you, conduct a follow-up interview if needed, and write another draft of your paper, making the desired changes. If you are not sure you agree with the group's feedback or if you want more specific help, discuss your work with your instructor or a tutor.

Once you have revised, your instructor may ask you to reconvene your small group and read all the new drafts. Did each writer make the needed changes? Should any other changes be made?

Once you have made the desired changes in the content of your paper, do any refining that is needed. For additional help with specific grammatical or punctuation problems, see the appropriate section in the Handbook.

Sample Revised Drafts

Following are revised final drafts of the rough draft by John Watson (page 81) and of Bonnie Lowe's interview transcript (page 78). Note how each of these student writers has revised and refined the rough original.

```
               LIFE ON "THE ROCK"
                   (final draft)
                   by John Watson
```

1   Alcatraz Federal Penitentiary sounds like a foreboding place, but for three years, from 1935 to 1938, my mother lived on "The Rock"; she was "incarcerated" there at the tender age of four, when she came to live with her uncle, Royal Cline, a prison guard. While all guards' families were required to live on Alcatraz Island, no one could forget that "The Rock" imprisoned the country's most dangerous criminals.

2   When I asked my mother to tell me about the years she lived there, she recalled that "the water boat from San Francisco was the only way on or off the island. It brought water and food twice a day. It also took prisoners to and from the island. The guards were everywhere; there were walkways on the

walls where guards were stationed. Some guards walked the grounds, and others were stationed in the different shops where prisoners worked."

At the time my mother lived on Alcatraz, some of the biggest criminals of the Depression Era were imprisoned there: "Machine Gun" Kelly, "Creepy" Karlis, and Al Capone called "The Rock" home. In fact, Mom has a jewelry box made by Al Capone. She told me the interesting story: "I took Uncle Royal's lunch to him every day, and sometimes I would see Capone being exercised in the yard alone, although I didn't know who he was at the time. I would wave at him through the fence, and he would wave back. Uncle Royal ran the furniture shop where Capone worked, and he asked Uncle Royal who the little girl was that he saw every day. When my uncle said I was his niece, Capone asked him to give a jewelry box he'd finished to 'the little girl.'" My mother still has the jewelry box. It has become a small family treasure.

Not all of her memories of Alcatraz are happy, though. In May 1938, my mother's uncle was killed by an inmate attempting to escape from "The Rock." Royal Cline was the first prison officer ever killed at Alcatraz. The murderer, my mother remembers, was put in solitary confinement, where, she later learned, he remained for ten years. Only after a later prison riot brought about prison reform was Royal Cline's killer released from solitary. The years of confinement, however, had driven the murderer insane.

Shortly after Royal Cline's death, his family and my mother left Alcatraz Island. The penitentiary itself has long since been abandoned; no one lives on the tiny island stuck out in San Francisco Bay. My mother remembers, though, and while the memory of her uncle's death saddens her, she looks back with fondness at the days she spent on "The Rock."

NEW RAMAH PRIMITIVE BAPTIST CHURCH,
YESTERDAY AND TODAY (final draft)
by Bonnie Lowe

Nestled quietly within a grove of oak trees, six miles north of Haynesville, Louisiana, stands a small country church.

It looks so peaceful and reassuring, as if it were inviting the entire world to come inside. Walking up the front steps and through the front door, you can sense the love and devotion that must have gone into its construction. If only these walls could talk, they would tell countless stories of sermons, hymns, prayers, and tears--stories about the five generations of family members who have belonged to this, the New Ramah Primitive Baptist Church. Sitting down and running your hands over the pews, silky smooth from years of wear, opens a doorway into the past.

It is now 1860, and members reverently enter the church. Quietly walking to their seats, they give only an occasional nod to a friend. Once the congregation has filled the ten or so rows of wooden pews, the service begins. The elder who leads the singing walks to the pulpit and briefly sings an octave scale. Each member listens for the right note and prepares to sing. No musical instruments are allowed in the church. It is God's love flowing through hearts and souls that creates the congregation's hymns. According to Primitive Baptist doctrine, it would be a sin to drown the music out with a piano or organ.

Once the singing is over, the pastor walks slowly to the pulpit and bows his head in prayer. Thanking God for allowing him to be there, he asks for wisdom as he uses the Lord's words. For the next few minutes there are announcements of births, deaths, weddings, and illnesses.

After the announcements the pastor reaches into his pocket to take out a handkerchief; laying it on the pulpit, he opens the Bible. Slowly he looks over his congregation, pauses, and then, taking a deep breath, starts his sermon. His words flow quickly and continually, in a single tone of voice, almost as though his hour-long sermon flowed from his initial breath. His only gesture is to wipe his mouth at frequent intervals, a gesture required because of the speed with which he speaks. During his sermon the pastor mentions his unworthiness to repeat God's words and occasionally asks forgiveness for any offense he might cause as he preaches. When the sermon is over, he signals his conclusion to the elders.

The head elder will either lead a closing prayer or make final announcements. The announcements are usually about church upkeep, but sometimes they are about a member's nonpayment of debt. Primitive Baptists believe that church members should pay all debts they incur. If a merchant feels a debt is being ignored, he will speak to the church elders about it. The elders will then go to the member and speak with him about the debt. In most cases it is just unusual circumstances that prevent prompt payment. The elders arrange for extended payments in order to resolve the issue.

But every once in a while, there is a member who has no intention of paying a bill. If after the elders talk to the debtor and he still refuses to pay, they call him up in front of the whole congregation at the next church meeting. In the presence of everyone, the member is again asked to take care of the debt. If he still refuses, the congregation withdraws his membership and forces him to pay his debt using any means they have to use. If he does not have enough money to pay the whole debt, the church makes up the difference. Because of this practice, members of the Primitive Baptist church always have credit, wherever they go.

On this particular day there are no announcements, only a prayer to close the service. Once the service is over, the congregation is slow to leave. For many of them this is the only time to see friends and relatives, and they listen closely, trying to catch up on all of the latest news. As the pastor walks through the crowd, someone quietly hands him fifty cents, another a dollar. The Primitive Baptists do not pay a salary to the pastor. They believe he should be a humble man of modest means in order to spread the word of God without being corrupted by worldly desires. The members pay him only what they feel will take care of his necessities. There are many times he leaves without even enough money for his weekly expenses, but this time there is more than enough to pay for his immediate needs. Graciously accepting a ride to town, he and his driver join the parade of wagons creaking noisily down the dirt road.

Over the years few changes have been made to the New Ramah Primitive Baptist Church. The original meetings were held once a month due to poor lighting and the great distances people had to come. But in the early 1940s the building was completely taken apart board by board. It was rebuilt with the original lumber and only a few new pieces. During this construction plumbing and electricity were installed. With the installation of electricity and the easy use of the automobile, the services were changed to the first and third Sundays of the month. An old frame house was donated to the church, and it is now used to hold Sunday dinners for the congregation. The elders no longer have the ability to control any member's debt, so instant credit is no longer the norm.

These are about the only changes that have taken place. In nearly every other way the church and its practices are just as they were over a century ago.

PERSONAL SUMMARY

1. Review the goals at the beginning of this chapter, and check off each one that you have successfully accomplished.

2. Summarize the main lessons you have learned by working through this chapter.

_____

_____

_____

3. List the subjects covered in this chapter that you still need more work on.

_____

_____

_____

ADDITIONAL WRITING

1. For a number of years, students at Louisiana State University in Shreveport have been collecting family and cultural stories, including the two you just read, and compiling them in a series of booklets we have titled *Ancestral Voices*.

   We invite you to join us in the project. To do so, simply follow the instructions for the writing assignment and set up an editorial board of students, who will help your instructor do the final revising. Each writer can be responsible for typing his or her work, or you can use a pool of volunteer typists.

   Ask your instructor for additional instructions for putting your booklet together. When preparing copies for distribution, remember to give interviewees a personal copy.

   If you will send us one of your booklets, we will be happy to send you the latest edition of ours. What follows is a part of the introduction to our first collection, along with our mailing address.

   > *Ancestral Voices* is a collection of stories that we have gathered from relatives and others or experienced ourselves as children. We have found out that collecting together parts of our heritage to share with you, our reader, has been a challenging, rewarding, and enriching experience. The knowledge we have gained and the personal growth we have experienced have been enough reward in themselves for all the hard work we devoted to make the project a success. . . .
   >
   > To complete the introduction, we would like to recall some of Mark Twain's advice to would-be writers. Twain insisted, "To be a writer, one must observe three rules: (1) write; (2) write; (3) write." We have followed his advice as we have rewritten our pieces a number of times before we were satisfied with the final version. Twain also urged amateur writers to "write without pay until somebody offers pay; if nobody offers within three years, sawing wood is what you were intended for." Of course, we already believe that our book is a success; nevertheless, no matter what others think about our work,

we share Mark Twain's view when he said, "I have been complimented many times and they [my admirers] always embarrass me; I always feel they have not said enough."

Ancestral Voices
English Department
Louisiana State University
Shreveport, Louisiana 71115

2. Look back at the piece you wrote for this chapter's assignment. In a few hundred words, explain how the subject you wrote about still has significance for you or someone else today.

ADDITIONAL READING

Rodriguez, Richard. *Hunger of Memory: The Education of Richard Rodriguez.* Boston: Godine, 1982. Tells of the author's cultural struggles and frustrations as a young Chicano, who ultimately became a successful writer.

Terkel, Studs. *Working.* New York: Pantheon Books, 1974. In interviews with the author, people from all walks of life talk about their work.

Wigginton, Eliot. The *Foxfire* series, vols. 1–8. Garden City, N.Y.: Anchor/Doubleday, 1972–1984. In interviews with high school students, people from rural Appalachia describe folkways and customs of days gone by.

Part Two

WRITING FOR PUBLIC REASONS

Public Writing from Personal Opinion

> *In this chapter, you will:*
> ✔ Improve your critical thinking ability
> ✔ Use evidence to support your opinions
> ✔ Write a formal essay

In the chapters in Part One, you wrote for a variety of personal reasons, expressing different aspects of yourself and your past. The writing you have done and the knowledge and ability you have gained provide a good foundation on which to build.

In Part Two we turn to more formal types of writing in which you will aim to have an effect on a public audience. This shift toward public writing takes us more into the world of opinions and ideas, so important in academic and professional settings.

As before, you will continue to ask questions in order to direct your thinking and your writing, but the questions will challenge you to listen more carefully, think more critically, and explore ideas in more depth. Also, you will continue to use concrete details, examples, and facts, not so much for their own sake but rather as evidence to support your opinions and ideas in order to make a point.

Again, you will draw on conflict and multiple points of view to stimulate creative thought. As you consider conflicting, or opposing, ideas and viewpoints, you may challenge your own prejudices or discover a new and better way of looking at a problem and then present it to others in a clear, balanced way.

READINGS

An aspect of modern life that has created considerable conflict and controversy, generating opinions in nearly everyone, is the change in men's and women's roles and the social effects of these changes. To get an idea of how much we've changed, contrast modern-day attitudes toward male-female relationships with those expressed in this excerpt from my grandmother's "sex" manual (mentioned in Chapter Three), *Creative and Sexual Science, or Manhood, Womanhood and Their Mutual Inter-relations* (1906).

The law governing man's treatment of woman is that all things should be treated in accord with their own natures. As in handling cannon-balls we may pitch and pound, because they are hard, but in handling watches we must treat them delicate; so men may bang men about as they would rough boxes—yet as those who use the sword must expect some time to perish by the sword, so those who will bang must expect to be banged, and serve them right—but since woman is exquisitely sensitive and delicately organized, every genuine man should and will treat her kindly, and in a delicate, considerate, refined, polite manner; avoiding whatever can give her pain, and doing what contributes to her pleasure.

[As for women,] gratitude is due from all receivers to all givers, as much as wages for work. All should pay somehow for all they get. Woman's natural dependence on man, consequent on maternity, demands that she "return thanks" for whatever she receives from him. And here payment is deserved.

While many modern readers would disapprove of most of the values expressed here, many others would want at least some of them preserved, thus showing how controversial some gender-related issues still are. Even within the sexes themselves there is heated disagreement; women disagree with women, and men disagree with men.

Still controversial is the present-day feminist, or women's liberation, movement, now several decades old. Two of the early responses, one defending and one opposing the modern movement, are excerpted here. The first selection is by Gloria Steinem, a leading supporter of feminism, who has been a highly active member of the women's movement for almost thirty years and who was one of the cofounders of *Ms.* magazine. In the work you are about to read, she explains how the movement has affected our language and our lives.

The second selection is from a book written by Phyllis Schlafly, a well-known opponent of feminism and a defender of traditional attitudes toward gender-related issues. Schlafly worked hard during the 1970s and 1980s to help defeat the Equal Rights Amendment to the United States Constitution, which would have guaranteed equal rights under law to persons of both sexes. In the passage you will read, she explains her opposition to the women's liberation movement especially as it has affected our language.

In both selections the authors present their opinions, or points of view, in an effort to persuade readers to share them. Imagine, as you read, that the two women are engaged in a debate that you are listening to. Like a judge hearing the opposing viewpoints of two witnesses, listen carefully to what both sides have to say in order to get a more complete and balanced picture from which you can draw your own conclusions.

You will be asked to read both selections twice—the first time mainly to understand the writers' opinions, the second time to evaluate what they say, weighing the evidence they provide so that you can arrive at your own point of view. Because these selections are the most challenging ones you have yet been presented, you may want to read them more than twice.

Preparing to Read

Before you read the first selection, written by Steinem, think about your own attitudes toward the changes brought on by women's liberation and how they have affected you, either directly or indirectly.

If you are male, ask yourself whether you believe you've suffered reverse discrimination of some kind, or perhaps whether your spouse's or your mother's working has affected you somehow. If you are female, ask yourself which aspects of the women's movement you support and which ones you're opposed to.

If, at the moment, you have no strong opinions or interest in the topics being discussed, ask yourself why. Can you imagine how gender-related issues may affect you in the future?

As you read, keep the following points in mind.

1. Try to avoid two extremes, either closing your mind to a point of view that may differ from your own or accepting the opinions of the writer without question.

2. Do your best to hear all the author has to say so that you can accurately summarize her point of view without any distortion.
3. Don't automatically accept everything Steinem says, either because you consider her an authority or because her opinions are similar to your own; the important point is to think for yourself.
4. Recognize that Steinem's essay was one of the early responses to a movement now several decades old. Do you think her opinions are widely accepted today? Or do they sound like ones that are still being challenged? Or do they seem irrelevant?

From
"Words and Change"
by Gloria Steinem

transformations:
changes

1   New words and phrases are one . . . measure of change. They capture transformations of perception, and sometimes of reality itself.

2   We have terms like *sexual harassment* and *battered women*. A few years ago, they were just called *life*.

3   Now, we are becoming the [people] we wanted to marry. Once women were trained to marry a doctor, not be one. . . .

4   Now, we've made the revolutionary discovery that children have two parents. A decade ago even the kindly Dr. Spock held mothers solely responsible for children.

5   In 1972, a NASA official's view of women's function in space was "sexual diversion" on "long-duration flights such as Mars." Now, women are simply *astronauts*. . . .

6   Until recently, an older woman on campus was an oddity. Now, so many women have returned for a college education once denied them that the median age of the female undergraduate is twenty-seven years old, and colleges are becoming community resources with a new definition of "student." . . .

7   Until the 1970's women had to choose between *Miss* or *Mrs.*, thus identifying themselves by marital status in a way men did not. Now, more than a third of American women support *Ms.* as an alternative, an exact parallel of *Mr.*, and so do government publications, business, and most of the media. . . .

Much of this newness is simple accuracy—for instance, changing *congress-men* to *congresspeople*, or MEN WORKING to PEOPLE WORKING—and even those changes can spell major differences in power. . . .

The nature of *work* has been a major area of new understanding, beginning with the word itself. Before feminism, work was largely defined as what men did or would do. Thus, a *working woman* was someone who labored outside the home for money, masculine-style. Though still alarmingly common, the term is being protested, especially by homemakers who work harder than any other class of worker, and are still called people who "don't work." Feminists have always tried to speak of work *inside the home* or *outside the home*, of *salaried* or *unsalaried workers*. Attributing a financial value to work in the home would go a long way toward making marriage an equal partnership, as the Equal Rights Amendment would also do, and toward ending the semantic slavery inherent in the phrase *women who don't work*.

semantic: related to the meanings of words

It would also begin to untangle the *double-role problem* identified in the sixties—that is, the double burden of millions of women who work both inside and outside the home—by defining human maintenance and home care as a job in itself, a job that men can and should do as well as women. . . .

Power is also being redefined. Women often explain with care that we mean power to control our lives but not to dominate others. . . .

Of course, an importance of words is their power to exclude. *Man, mankind,* and the *family of man* have made women feel left out, usually with good reason. *People, humanity,* and *humankind* are more inclusive. So are rewrites like "Peace on Earth, Good Will to People." Feminists also tried to educate by asking men to imagine receiving a *Spinster of Arts* or *Mistress of Science* degree [as opposed to a *Bachelor of Arts* or *Master of Science* degree] and then working hard for a *sistership* [as opposed to a *fellowship*]. Wouldn't they feel a little left out? . . .

Battered women is a phrase that uncovered major, long-hidden violence. It helps us to face the fact that, statistically speaking, the most dangerous place for a woman is in her own home, not in the streets. *Sexual harassment* on the job also exposed a form of intimidation that about a third of all women workers suffer. Talking about it openly inspired women to come forward and legal remedies to be created. By identifying *pornography* (literally, "writing about female slavery") as the preaching of woman hatred, and thus quite different from *erotica*, with its connotation of love and mutuality, there was also the beginning of an understanding that pornography is a major way in which violence and dominance are taught and legitimized; that it is as socially harmful as Nazi literature is to Jews or Klan literature is to blacks.

Even *female sexual slavery* (once known by the nineteenth-century racist term *white slavery*, because for the most part it was the only form of slavery to which whites were also subjected) has been redefined and exposed by this wave of feminism. We know now it flourishes in many of our cities where prostitution and pornography are big business and a fact of international life. . . .

The feminist revolution has been a contagious and progressive recurrence in history for thousands of years. The last wave won for many women of the world a *legal identity* as human beings, not the possessions of others. Now we seek to complete that step for all women, and to gain *legal equality*, too. But there will be many more waves of feminism before male-supremacist cultures give way.

In this wave, words and consciousness have forged ahead, so reality can follow. Measuring the distance between the new and the old evokes the unique part of history that lives in each of us.

Thinking about Your Reading

1. One goal of Steinem's essay is to compare old and new terms and their meanings for the purpose of measuring social changes resulting from the feminist movement. What social change is she measuring when she says, "Once women were trained to marry a doctor, not be one" (3)?

2. Steinem uses the term *semantic slavery* (9) to describe how words or labels can lock people into stereotypes. In your opinion, do words and labels have the power to enslave, limit, or exclude people? Why or why not?

3. Note that another important goal of the passage is to define terms to help measure the social changes the movement has promoted. Of all the terms Steinem defines or discusses, which one do you consider most important? Summarize, or put in your own words, the points that Steinem makes about this term. In your opinion, why is it most important?

4. What do you think Steinem means by the phrase *double-role problem* (10), which she uses to describe the dilemma of some women?

5. Why do you think the author uses the phrases *Spinster of Arts* and *Mistress of Science* (12), especially since there really are no such expressions?

6. In one paragraph, summarize the main points Steinem makes in her essay.

7. Imagine what the perfect world according to Steinem would be like, based on your reading and understanding of her essay, and describe that world, especially as it relates to male-female relationships and roles.

Preparing to Read

If we consider Gloria Steinem a feminist, we might look at Phyllis Schlafly as a traditionalist. **Before you read** her selection, think again about how some of the feminist issues already discussed affect you. For example, how do you feel about the use of expressions such as *mankind* and *Goodwill to Men* to include all people? If, at the moment, you have no strong opinions or interest in gender-related issues, think about how they may affect you in the future.

Also anticipate ways in which you think Schlafly's views will differ from Steinem's.

As you read, remember these points:

1. Keep an open mind, neither shutting out a point of view that may differ from your own nor accepting the opinions of the writer without question.
2. Do your best to hear all the author has to say so that you can accurately summarize her point of view without any distortion.
3. Don't automatically agree with everything Schlafly says, either because you consider her an authority or because her opinions are similar to your own; the important point is to think for yourself.
4. Recognize that Schlafly's essay was one of the early responses to a movement now several decades old. Do you consider her opinions to be either out of date or irrelevant? Or do they sound like ideas that are popular today?

From
The Power of the Positive Woman
by Phyllis Schlafly

precipitates: sets up

neuterize: make sexless

expunged: removed

By its very nature . . . the women's liberation movement precipitates a series of conflict situations—in the legislatures, in the courts, in the schools, in industry—with man targeted as the enemy. Confrontation replaces cooperation as the watchword of all relationships. Women and men become adversaries instead of partners.

Neuterizing Society. A basic objective and tactic of the women's liberationists is to neuterize all laws, textbooks, and language in newspapers, radio, and television. Their friends in state legislatures are ordering computer printouts of all laws that use such "sexist" words as *man, woman, husband,* and *wife.* They are to be expunged and replaced with neuter equivalents. Some state legislators

acquiesced: given in

have acquiesced rather than face charges of "sexism." Others have rejected this effort and labeled it the silliness that it is.

The feminists look upon textbooks as a major weapon in their campaign to eliminate what they call our "sex-stereotyped society" and to restructure it into one that is sex-neutral from cradle to grave. Under liberationist demands, a publisher issued a booklet called "Guidelines for Creating Positive Sexual and Racial Images in Educational Materials." Its purpose is to instruct authors in the use of sex-neutral language, concepts, and illustrations. . . .

amity: friendship

Henceforth, you may not say *mankind*, it should be *humanity*. You may not say *brotherhood*, it should be *amity*. *Manpower* must be replaced by *human energy*; *forefathers* should give way to *precursors*. *Chairman* and *salesman* are out; and "in" words are *chairperson* and *salesperson*.

You are forbidden to say "man the sailboat." The acceptable substitute is not given; presumably it is "person the sailboat." You must not say "the conscientious housekeeper dusts her furniture at least once a week." You must say "*the* furniture" [instead of *her* furniture] because otherwise you would imply that the housekeeper is a woman—and that would be intolerable. You may not say "the cat washed herself"; it must be "the cat washed itself," because it would be sexist to imply that the cat is female. . . .

Women must be shown participating actively "in exciting worthwhile pursuits," which, by apparent definition, do not include being a homemaker. The guidelines warn that books will not be tolerated that indicate that "homemaking is the true vocation for a woman." . . .

Baby-care doctor Benjamin Spock was one of those whom the feminists targeted as obnoxious because of the alleged "sexism" in his bestselling baby books. His principal offense was that, in advising mothers how to care for their babies, he repeatedly used the pronoun *he* instead of *she*. Obviously, it would be a semantic hurdle of significant magnitude to write a baby book and say "he or she" every time the author refers to the baby. Until women's liberationists became so vocal, normal mothers understood that *he* is used in the generic sense to mean babies of both sexes.

The feminists continued their campaign against Dr. Spock's "sexism" until they finally convinced him that modern liberated society should treat males and females exactly the same. In his latest book he eliminated "sexist" language. The only trouble was, Dr. Spock bought the whole bag of "liberation." He walked out on his faithful wife Jane, to whom he had been married for forty-eight years, and took up with a younger woman. Dr. Spock was truly "liberated" from traditional restraints.

It is no gain for women, for children, for families, or for America to propel us into a unisex society. Our strength is in our diversity, not in our sameness....

Understanding Differences. Another silliness of the women's liberationists is their frenetic desire to force all women to accept the title *Ms.* in place of *Miss* or *Mrs.* If Gloria Steinem and Betty Friedan want to call themselves *Ms.* in order to conceal their marital status, their wishes should be respected.

But that doesn't satisfy the women's liberationists. They want all women to be compelled to use *Ms.* whether they like it or not. The women's liberation movement has been waging a persistent campaign to browbeat the media into using *Ms.* as the standard title for all women. The women's liberationists have already succeeded in getting the Department of Health, Education and Welfare to forbid schools and colleges from identifying women students as a *Miss* or *Mrs.*

All polls show that the majority of women do not care to be called *Ms.* A Roper poll indicated that 81 percent of the women questioned said they prefer *Miss* or *Mrs.* to *Ms.* Most married women feel they worked hard for the *r* in their names, and they don't care to be gratuitously deprived of it. Most single women don't care to have their name changed to an unfamiliar title that at best conveys overtones of feminist ideology and is polemical in meaning, and at worst connotes misery instead of joy....

Amaury de Riencourt, in his book *Sex and Power in History*, shows that a successful society depends on a delicate balancing of different male and female factors, and that the women's liberation movement, which promotes unisexual values and androgyny, contains within it "a social and cultural death wish and the end of the civilization that endorses it...."

An effort to eliminate the differences by social engineering or legislative or constitutional tinkering cannot succeed, which is fortunate, but social relationships and spiritual values can be ruptured in the attempt. Thus the role reversal being forced upon high school students, under which guidance counselors urge reluctant girls to take "shop" and boys to take "home economics," further confuse a generation already unsure about its identity. They are as wrong as efforts to make a left-handed child right-handed.

frenetic: frantic

gratuitously: unjustifiably
ideology: beliefs
polemical: argumentative
connotes: implies

androgyny: combination of the qualities of both sexes

Thinking about Your Reading

1. Schlafly compares Dr. Spock's use of the traditional pronoun *he* in his earlier bestselling baby books with his use of the phrase *he or she* in his latest

book (7). Find two reasons why Schlafly believes that *he* should be used instead of the phrase *he or she*, and copy them here.

_____

_____

_____

_____

2. Why do you think the author puts quotation marks around "sexist," "sexism," and "sex-stereotyped society" (2, 3)?

_____

_____

_____

_____

3. What label does she use to describe feminist attempts to eliminate sexual references from legislation (2) and to promote the use of *Ms.* in place of *Miss* or *Mrs.* (10)?

_____

4. What is Schlafly's opinion of the feminists' objective to eliminate "sex-stereotyping" and to "neuterize" all laws, textbooks, and language in newspapers, radio, and television?

_____

_____

Chapter Four / Public Writing from Personal Opinion

5. From Schlafly's point of view, what are the potential effects of feminist attempts to eliminate the differences in the sexes?

6. In a single paragraph, summarize the main points Schlafly makes in her essay.

7. Imagine what the perfect world according to Schlafly would be like, based on your reading of the passage from her book, and describe that world, especially as it relates to male-female relationships and roles.

_____

_____

_____

_____

_____

◆◆◆

WRITING ASSIGNMENT

Writing and Critical Thinking

When examining opposing views toward an issue, you will find yourself agreeing with some ideas and disagreeing with others as you develop your own point of view. In the process of making these judgments, you are engaging in the mental activity known as *critical thinking*. You are attempting to make sense of some issue by evaluating a set of ideas and facts—and then perhaps going on to present some ideas and facts of your own, which may in turn need to be evaluated and refined.

The power that drives this critical-thinking process comes in part from your ability to distinguish between opinions that are well supported with evidence and ones that are merely prejudices with little or no support. Not only does the ability to make such distinctions help you evaluate the opinions of others, but it also helps you create, evaluate, and present your point of view.

For what purposes might you express well-supported opinions? Sometimes simply to explain an issue, sometimes to argue a point, sometimes to deal with an emotional topic more objectively in order to persuade your audience to adopt your point of view and take some course of action. These are just some of the possibilities.

By noting how other writers present their opinions and either support them or fail to support them with adequate evidence, you can improve your critical thinking and your writing.

Using Evidence

An *opinion* is a judgment, belief, or attitude; *evidence* is made up of details that support an opinion and can be checked out and verified as true or probable. In other words, an opinion is an *abstract idea* that tends to be more general, whereas evidence is *concrete support* that tends to be more specific.

> OPINION (abstract, general): I believe that a man can contribute just as much to the home as a woman can.

> EVIDENCE (concrete, specific): My husband buys the groceries, cooks the meals, and pays the bills; I take care of the floors and the yard; and we share the other responsibilities of homemaking, depending on who prefers to do what job and who has more free time on any given day.

Both kinds of material—opinions and evidence—are vital to good writing.

TYPES OF EVIDENCE. Various types of evidence can be used to support opinions. Some basic types are *facts*, *testimony of an authority*, *statistics*, *examples*, and *illustrations*. As you read, you may note other types.

Here are some examples of basic types of evidence.

1. *Opinion supported with facts*. In the opinion of Herb Goldberg, a psychotherapist and professor of psychology at California State University in Los Angeles, lower salaries do not mean that women are discriminated against in the workplace. He believes that women typically make less money than men because, on the average, they (1) invest less in on-the-job training, (2) have less work experience, and (3) tend to be less mobile, among other things. (From Bruno Leone and M. Teresa O'Neill, *Male/Female Roles: Opposing Viewpoints*. St. Paul, Minn.: Greenhaven Press, 1983, p. 90.)

2. *Opinion supported with testimony of an authority.* Susan Byrne, editor of *Psychology Today*, believes that one of the problems with American families may be that "we feel it's more important to follow our own personal stars than to preserve the family." In response to her assertion, Dr. Urie Bronfenbrenner, Professor of Psychology at Cornell University and author of several volumes on human development, replies: "That's right. Move the old folks to Florida so they can live their life and we can live ours. It's all very understandable. This whole way of life is fine if you're young, sexy, and full of verve. But if you happen to be a child, or sick, or lonely, or old—and all of us are at some time—you need somebody else. If that somebody else is doing his own thing, he's not there." (From Bruno Leone and M. Teresa O'Neill, *Male/Female Roles: Opposing Viewpoints.* St. Paul, Minn.: Greenhaven Press, 1983, p. 130.)
3. *Opinion supported with statistics.* According to Claudia Wallis, author of "Onward, Women!" (*Time*, December 4, 1989), changes brought on by the women's movement are good and are regarded favorably by most other women. To support her opinion, she cites a recent *Time/CNN* survey that indicated that 77 percent of 1,000 women questioned think that the movement has improved life for women.
4. *Opinion supported with examples.* Medical research reflects male bias. A health article in the March 5, 1990, issue of *Time* magazine, reported that there is a predominance of male-only medical research studies. For example, in one study of 22,071 subjects, all of whom were male, researchers found that small doses of aspirin can reduce the risk of heart attack. The article goes on to say that drugs that are found to be effective in men may be effective in women as well, but the information gap becomes important if the sexes respond differently to a given treatment. For many drugs and treatments, doctors cannot be sure how women will respond because of the predominance of male-only studies. The National Institutes of Health reportedly spends just 13 percent of its budget studying women's health.
5. *Opinion supported with illustrations.* Men are the victims of reverse discrimination. At Corporation A, a male and a female candidate are interviewed for the same job. The man is slightly more qualified than the woman, but to satisfy affirmative action guidelines, the woman is hired instead of the man. He then goes to Corporation B, where he and another female candidate are interviewed. The two are judged

equally qualified; so once more, because of affirmative action guidelines, the woman is hired. Finally, the man goes to Corporation C, where he is interviewed again, along with a female candidate. This time she is judged to be more qualified than he; so she is hired. Three qualified women have gotten a good job, but the qualified man is still looking.

For Further Thought

The opinions that follow appeared in the "Letters" section of the December 25, 1989, issue of *Time* magazine in response to an article in the "Living" section of *Time*, December 4, 1989, titled "Onward, Women!" Because your answers may differ from those of others, it's a good idea to discuss responses in class.

Underline each writer's main opinion. In the space provided, identify the type of evidence used as support—facts, testimony of an authority, statistics, examples, illustrations, combination of these, or another type.

EXAMPLE

Whether you refer to it as feminism or the women's movement, this bloodless political revolution has changed America forever. If it had not been for us strident, hairy-legged activists, you gals in your 20s earning $80,000 a year selling blue-chip stocks, happy in the knowledge [that] your dayworker and dog walker can handle the home front, would still be separating wash in front of a TV game show.

Shylah Boyd
New York City

TYPE(S) OF EVIDENCE: illustration

1. Pondering the supposedly lazy male who fails to do his share of chores around the home, I thought about the "housework" my three brothers do. They constantly make general repairs, remodel rooms, mow lawns, chauffeur children, etc. They rarely have an idle moment.

Kristine Benishek
Worcester, Mass.

TYPE(S) OF EVIDENCE:

2. As a 20-year-old Vassar undergraduate, I think my generation's hesitancy to align itself wholeheartedly with the feminist movement is due to the lack of consistent role models. Ours range from Cher [flamboyant singer and actor] to Michelle Pfeiffer [actor] to Pat Schroeder [representative in U.S. Congress] to Faye Wattleton [Planned Parenthood director]. This variety is enough to bewilder any woman.

Wendy Wasserman
Larchmont, N.Y.

TYPE(S) OF EVIDENCE: _____

3. When you described me [author of *Why Men Are the Way They Are*, quoted in the *Time* article] as a feminist, you missed the all-important distinction I make between being an equal-rights-only feminist and an equal-rights-and-responsibilities feminist. I talk about women's obligation to register for the draft as much as I do about women's equal rights in the armed forces. I care as much about men working in more hazardous jobs as I do about women having to take lower-paying jobs. In brief, I oppose an Equal Rights Only Amendment and I support an Equal Rights and Responsibilities Amendment.

Warren Farrell
Encinitas, Calif.

TYPE(S) OF EVIDENCE: _____

4. I am tired of hearing about the wage gap. Women are born to nurture children. Men have more of themselves tied up in their work. They are more assertive on the job and more likely to forgo a pleasant working environment for higher pay. Women often opt for a package that produces less money. What's wrong with that? Men can't have it all. Neither can women.

James A. Kern
Miami, Fla.

TYPE(S) OF EVIDENCE: _____

Evaluating Evidence

Not only are writers expected to support their opinions with evidence, but that evidence must also be appropriate for the given situation. If it is inappropriate or missing, the opinion may be considered *prejudiced* or *biased*. To evaluate the appropriateness of evidence, here are some questions to ask:

Appropriate		*Prejudiced or Biased*
Is it sufficient	or	insufficient or missing?
Is it relevant	or	irrelevant?
Is it representative	or	unrepresentative?
Is it verifiable	or	not verifiable?
Is it reliable	or	unreliable?
Is it free of exaggeration, ridicule, or sarcasm	or	exaggerated, ridiculing, or sarcastic?
Is it clear	or	confusing?
Is it up to date	or	out of date?

For Further Thought

Answer the following questions. Because your answers may differ from those of others, it's a good idea to discuss responses in class.

1. Do you think the examples listed under "Types of Evidence" on pages 107–109 illustrate appropriate characteristics of evidence? Explain any problems you note.

_____

_____

_____

_____

2. Review characteristics of prejudiced or biased evidence listed above. Then identify the problems with the characteristics of the evidence shown in items *a*

through *e*. If you don't see a problem with a particular item, put "none" in the blank.

To be sure you can distinguish opinions from evidence, you may want to underline the main opinion expressed in each item. The first one has been completed as an example.

EXAMPLE
Women are less motivated to work hard than men are. The two women I work with are the laziest people I've ever known.

Problem(s): insufficient, probably exaggerated, maybe sarcastic

a. Men can't be trusted.

   Problem(s): _____

   _____

b. Women are naturally more mentally creative than men; after all, they are the only ones who can bear children.

   Problem(s): _____

   _____

c. The guy I used to date doesn't care about women's feelings; he quit seeing me just because I called him "pie face."

   Problem(s): _____

   _____

d. "Men may bang men about as they would rough boxes, . . . but since woman is exquisitely sensitive and delicately organized, every genuine man should and will treat her kindly, and in a delicate, considerate, refined, polite manner; avoiding whatever can give her pain and doing what contributes to her pleasure" (taken from *Creative and Sexual Science, or Manhood, Womanhood and Their Mutual Inter-relations*, published in 1906).

Problem(s): _____

_____

e. Men are sometimes favored in the work environment. For example, as more men have become elementary-school teachers, salaries have increased at a much faster rate than they did when the majority of teachers were women.

Problem(s): _____

_____

For Further Thought

Your critical thinking ability is enhanced as you look at a subject from different perspectives. In Chapter Two you examined an event from two points of view—yours as a child and yours as an adult—in order to develop some new insight. While reading the Steinem and Schlafly essays in this chapter, you are examining an issue from two external perspectives in order to develop your own point of view.

The questions below are designed to help you further refine your views through a critical, comparative examination of the Steinem and Schlafly essays. Read them once more from start to finish before attempting to answer the questions. Once you've answered them, discuss your responses in class.

1. Find two or three examples of opinions in both essays that are well supported with evidence. Copy each set of opinions and evidence in the blanks below, and label the type of evidence you find. Ask your instructor for help if you think the evidence is some type other than the basic ones listed earlier (facts, testimony of an authority, statistics, examples, or illustrations).

Steinem

a. _____

b. _____

c. _____

Schlafly

a. _____

b. _____

c. _____

2. Remember that in order for one's opinion to be convincing to others, it must be supported with appropriate evidence. If there is a problem with the evidence, we consider the opinion to be prejudiced or biased. Find one or more opinions expressed by either Steinem or Schlafly that you don't think are well supported.

Copy the ill-supported opinions here, and explain in each case whether you consider the evidence to be missing altogether or whether it is insufficient, irrelevant, unrepresentative, unverifiable, unreliable, exaggerated, ridiculing, or sarcastic.

3. In your opinion, which selection shows less prejudice or bias, and why?

4. A key to understanding different points of view is to understand how terms are interpreted and used by those holding a particular opinion. How would Steinem define the title of *Ms.*? _____

How would Schlafly define it? _____

Could differing definitions explain one's support of its use and the other's rejection? Explain. _____

5. Both authors offer statistical evidence to support their opposing attitudes toward the use of *Ms.* Steinem says that "now more than a third of American women support *Ms.* as an alternative" (7), whereas Schlafly says that a poll "indicated that 81 percent of the women questioned said they prefer *Miss* or

Mrs. to *Ms.*" (10). Even if the two writers are referring to the same poll, are their comments necessarily contradictory? Explain.

_____

_____

_____

_____

If the same poll were taken today, do you think the results would be similar?

_____ Provide evidence to support your belief. _____

_____

_____

_____

6. Compare Steinem's and Schlafly's attitudes toward the use of the word *mankind* and similar words.

_____

_____

_____

_____

Why does Steinem object to the use of such terms? Why does Schlafly not object?

_____

_____

What is your opinion? Support it.

7. Compare Steinem's and Schlafly's attitudes toward homemaking as a profession.

Which opinion is closer to your own?

Why?

8. Notice that Steinem's initial negative attitude toward Spock and his work becomes positive whereas Schlafly's attitude shifts from positive to negative. Why do you think they each change their opinions?

9. Overall, are you more in agreement with Steinem's opinions or Schlafly's? Why? _____

Write It Out: An Opinion Essay

Select a significant topic associated with some gender-related issue, and write an essay on your chosen subject by using the method that follows.

You may want to address a problem or issue raised by the Steinem and Schlafly passages, combining the knowledge you've gained from reading, observation, and personal experience as evidence to support your opinions. As you work, think about your purpose for writing and the audience you are writing for.

Suggested Essay Topics

- The changing roles of women or men and how these changes have affected marriage, children, the workplace, the military, the church, or some other institution
- Balancing career and family responsibilities (from either the husband's or the wife's point of view)
- Effects (positive or negative) of divorce
- Parents without partners
- Outlawing abortion (for or against)
- Positive or negative effects of the women's movement on male-female relationships
- Equal rights versus equal rights and responsibilities
- The rights of homosexuals
- A topic of your choice on any aspect of family relationships, same-sex relationships, opposite-sex relationships, male roles, or female roles.

Before beginning to write, record the subject you want to write about, the audience you want to write for, and your purpose for writing. Later as you work, you may find the need to modify your subject, purpose, or audience.

EXAMPLE

The sample student essay by Tammy Stevens appears on page 128.

SUBJECT: **Continuing unfair treatment of women on and off the job**

PURPOSE AND AUDIENCE: **To write an opposing-opinion essay in response to a newspaper editorial for the purpose of informing the readership of a young woman's point of view that differs from that expressed in the editorial**

SUBJECT _____

PURPOSE AND AUDIENCE _____

The method outlined here is offered as a guide for writing an essay rather than a rigid set of rules. Feel free to adapt the guide to suit your own needs, but don't skip any parts or subparts of the writing process as described in Chapter Two.

1 **FREEWRITE.** To explore your subject, answer the following six questions by writing freely whatever comes to your mind as a response. Try to answer all six questions in as much detail as possible because each one is designed to challenge your thinking further. *Don't worry if you repeat yourself.* (If you have trouble answering any of the questions, you may need to ask your instructor for help, or you may want to learn more about your subject through reading, talking, or observing before you write.)

You can freewrite on the computer, in your journal, or on note cards. You may want to answer some of the questions during one writing period and the rest at another, or you may prefer to do all of your freewriting during one block of time.

1. *What do you know about your subject?* Example (written by student Tammy Stevens): What do I know about *unfair treatment of women on and off the job?*

   > I know that working women are being told that the old problems have been solved—they haven't. Women, especially younger women, don't make as much as men. We have tougher times getting higher-paying jobs, and even women with higher-paying jobs don't get promotions like men do. We still do most of the housework and take care of the kids. Employers still discriminate against women— Marcy had to give up her job when she got pregnant. The old saying's true—a woman has to work twice as hard as a man to get half the credit. It's still a man's world.

2. *What do you understand or not understand about your subject?* Understanding requires a level of critical thinking that knowing doesn't necessarily require. You might know that you are getting paid less but not understand why until you find evidence that explains the reasons.
3. *What is a typical situation involving your subject?* Tammy might describe a scene at work or home, for example.
4. *What are different features or aspects of your subject?* Look at your subject part by part. For the sample subject, unfair treatment of women on and off the job, Tammy might write about these separate aspects: problems as workers, problems as wives, problems as mothers.

5. *When you put all these features or aspects of your subject together, what do you have?* Look at your subject as a whole. Tammy might begin her answer with a sentence like "Women face problems at work as well as at home."

6. *What is your opinion of your subject?* Tammy's opinion might include a statement such as this: "Many women are treated unfairly as workers, wives, and mothers."

2 DISCUSS YOUR FREEWRITING. Review your freewriting in small groups in class. Explain your purpose and the audience you plan to write your essay for. Ask your group for help with any of the questions you had trouble with. Take some time in class to write down what you learned from your small group.

3 USE THE STAIRCASE METHOD OF FREEWRITING. In your earlier freewriting, you took as much time as you wanted or needed in order to record all the ideas you could come up with that related to different aspects of your topic. Then you discussed your work with others. The purpose of this initial freewriting and the follow-up discussion was to include as many ideas as possible.

Now you will bring greater depth and focus to your ideas by freewriting once more, this time concentrating your energy into a compressed period.

a. At one sitting, respond to the statements you see below each stairstep in the figure on page 123 without looking back at your earlier freewriting. Allow yourself three to five minutes on each stairstep. Again you can write in your journal or on note cards; if a computer is available, you may use that.

b. Write nonstop, *repeating yourself if necessary* in order to keep going and moving quickly from step to step.

c. Don't worry about "correctness" in any way.

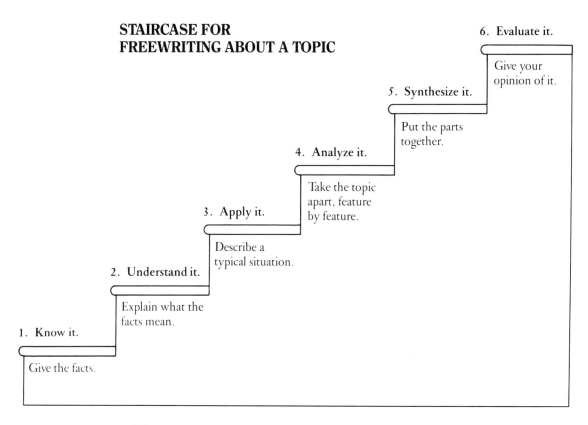

STAIRCASE FOR FREEWRITING ABOUT A TOPIC

1. Know it. — Give the facts.
2. Understand it. — Explain what the facts mean.
3. Apply it. — Describe a typical situation.
4. Analyze it. — Take the topic apart, feature by feature.
5. Synthesize it. — Put the parts together.
6. Evaluate it. — Give your opinion of it.

4 **QUESTION YOUR FREEWRITING.** Reread both sets of your free-written material (Steps 1 and 3). On a sheet of paper in your journal or on a note card, make up a list of questions—as many as you can think of—that are related to the material. The questions may or may not be answered in your freewriting, and there may be some overlap in your questions.

Here are some of the questions Tammy prepared:

1. Are women still treated unfairly on and off the job?
2. Who treats working women unfairly?
3. When do women encounter setbacks because of their roles as wives and mothers?
4. How does the workplace discriminate against women?
5. Why are women stuck with nearly the same status they had before the women's movement began?

If you find it difficult to make up questions, rely on the journalist's question words *who*, *what*, *when*, *where*, *how*, and *why* to get you started.

5 **FIND THE MAIN POINT AND KEY SUBPOINTS.** Review all of your freewritten material and the related questions you asked; then, from that material, try to come up with a single main question, the one that you consider the most interesting, the most significant, or the best developed in the material.

Tammy's main question: *Are women still treated unfairly on and off the job?*

Write that question at the top of a clean sheet of paper. Turn the question into a statement of your main opinion on your subject, adding to it, taking away from it, or changing it in any way that you need to. This opinion statement may later become the main point of your essay.

Tammy's main opinion (main point): *Women are still treated unfairly on and off the job.*

Try to find two to four subpoints related to the main point that are developed or touched on in your freewritten material; you might find these subpoints on different pages. Turn each subpoint into a complete statement, or *topic sentence* (for a review of topic sentences see pages 28–29). If you are unable to find at least two subpoints, try to think of some now, and write them down as statements.

❑ Subpoint 1: *Women often have most of the responsibility for raising children.*
❑ Subpoint 2: *Women are still discriminated against in the workplace.*
❑ Subpoint 3: *Sometimes women are not treated equally as marriage partners.*

6 **DIAGRAM YOUR POINTS.** Decide what order you want to put your points in, and put them in a diagram as shown in the following figure.

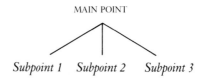

MAIN POINT

Subpoint 1   Subpoint 2   Subpoint 3

Tammy's diagram is shown at the top of page 125.

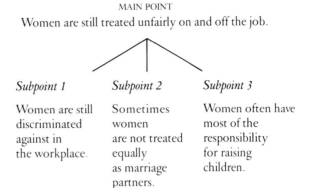

MAIN POINT
Women are still treated unfairly on and off the job.

Subpoint 1 *Subpoint 2* *Subpoint 3*

Women are still discriminated against in the workplace.
Sometimes women are not treated equally as marriage partners.
Women often have most of the responsibility for raising children.

7 FIND THE LEAD (INTRODUCTION) AND THE END (CONCLUSION). Read back through your freewritten material. Find the sentence or group of sentences related to your main point that someone else would find most attention-getting, interesting, or thought-provoking. Circle and label this material as the *lead*. Tammy chose as her lead "We've come a long way, baby—or have we?"

Find the part that is related to the main thought you want to leave with your reader. Circle and label material as the *end*. Tammy chose as her end, "We may have come a long way, but don't call us baby, and don't tell us how far we can go."

8 GET FEEDBACK. Discuss your main point and subpoints in class either in small groups or with the whole class if time allows. Use the following checklist.

1. Are the main points and subpoints opinions rather than facts?
2. Can the opinions be appropriately supported with evidence?
3. What is your purpose for writing?
4. Who is your audience?
5. Is the lead statement interesting or attention-getting?
6. Does the end contain the main point you want to leave with your audience?

9 CREATE A BARE-BONES OUTLINE. Using your diagram, lead, end, and group feedback, create a bare-bones outline as shown at the top of page 126, and modify it as necessary.

❏ *Introductory paragraph*
  lead + statement of main point
❏ *Body paragraph 1*
  subpoint statement 1 (topic sentence)
❏ *Body paragraph 2*
  subpoint statement 2 (topic sentence)
❏ Further body paragraphs as needed
❏ *Concluding paragraph*
  end

As you write, feel free to change, add, or delete any part in any way that you need to.

10 FIND YOUR EVIDENCE. Look through all of your freewriting to find evidence to support your opinions (main point and subpoints).

In addition to your freewriting helping you discover what you know and what you understand, it can also help you discover what you don't know and what you don't understand. If you don't find enough evidence in your freewriting, talk to others, think about your personal experience, read about your subject, and record any related observations you have, either in your journal or on note cards.

11 WRITE A ROUGH DRAFT. Add your evidence to your bare-bones outline, and write a rough draft.

12 SHARE YOUR DRAFT. As you did in Chapter Three, bring your rough draft to class. In small groups, review each person's draft, checking especially for the completeness and effectiveness of the evidence offered.

13 REVISE YOUR ROUGH DRAFT. Use your group feedback and the checklist that follows to evaluate your rough draft. Then rework and refine your draft in order to prepare a final draft.

Self-Check Evaluation

The checklist that follows should help you evaluate your work in order to produce a successful final draft.

1. Have I followed all instructions I was given? _____
2. Did I have an effective lead that makes readers want to keep reading? _____
3. Is my main opinion or point either clearly stated in the introduction or at least clearly implied? _____
4. Is my main point a significant opinion that I can support adequately with appropriate evidence? _____
5. Are the separate parts of the body related to the main point and to each other? _____
6. Have I used sufficient supporting evidence (facts, testimony of an authority, statistics, examples, illustrations) to prove my main point and all subpoints? _____
7. Is my evidence relevant? Representative? Verifiable? Free of exaggeration, ridicule, and sarcasm? Clear? Up to date? _____
8. Have I taken into account reasonable objections to my point of view? _____
9. Is my conclusion a natural and logical outgrowth of what I said in the introduction and body? _____
10. Have I kept the same point of view throughout? _____
11. Do all of my body paragraphs fit in with the overall plan suggested in my introduction? _____
12. Do all of the body paragraphs have topic sentences that are clearly related to my main point? _____
13. Does each body paragraph treat only one topic? _____
14. Have I developed each body paragraph with six to eight sentences of related facts? _____
15. Have I arranged the paragraphs in the most logical and effective order? _____

Sample Student Essay

The following is not intended as a model but rather as a sample to show how one student responded to the assignment. Look back at Tammy's statement of her audience and purpose on page 120 and decide whether you think she accomplished what she originally planned to do. Are her opinions supported with appropriate evidence? How do you think she might have revised her essay to make it more effective?

IT'S STILL TOUGH TO BE A WOMAN
(final draft)
by Tammy Stevens

Even though the cigarette advertisements tell us "You've come a long way, baby," it's still hard to be a woman today, especially a working woman. "Women's lib" may have gotten a lot of press, but it still hasn't liberated some of us. In spite of what some people think, many of the old problems haven't been solved. Working women of my generation face many of the same frustrations that our working mothers faced. Many women are still treated unfairly in the workplace and in their roles as wife and mother.

While more women are working than ever before, we don't command the respect in the workplace that men do. Women still make less money than men for doing the same jobs. A woman makes something like 59 cents for every dollar a man makes. While women are working more, many of the jobs are still in areas traditionally occupied by women. Women with these jobs find that the average salary is low. Even if a woman breaks out and becomes a doctor or a lawyer, it is likely that she won't advance as far or as fast as the men around her. In the past, companies have justified men's quicker advancements and higher salaries "because the man supports his family." Even if this were a valid justification, however, it is no longer true. Two-income families are the rule instead of the exception. Also many women are single parents and the sole support of their households.

Even if a woman has a career of her own, relationships at home generally haven't changed much. Things like housecleaning are still looked on by many as female chores--in spite of the fact that more men are claiming to help with those chores. Even in families where all of the housework is supposed to be split 50-50, many of my friends tell me that the wives still do three-fourths of the work. My husband and I are a good example. He has a full-time job; I work part-time and go to school part-time. On Saturday, our "cleanup day," I scrub the counters, do the bathrooms, and vacuum. He takes out the trash, putters around in the yard a bit, and then plops down in front of the

TV to watch the fooball game--before I'm halfway through with "my" jobs!

While I can't speak from personal experience, taking care of children seems to be another family responsibility assigned to women most of the time. My friends with children tell me that many women who work outside the home are still expected to take care of the kids by themselves. One complaint I hear a lot is that whenever their children get sick, it is nearly always the mothers, instead of the fathers, who have to take time off from work. In other words, women are expected to risk setbacks in their careers while men are not. At least women with children are usually well acquainted with career setbacks--most of the women I know lost points with their employers when they became pregnant. One friend even had to give up her job.

I've talked about only the most obvious problems of unfair treatment that women find in their work and family relationships--other women, and probably some men, know that there are some more subtle problems. Like it or not, it's still a man's world. We may have come a long way, but don't call us baby, and don't tell us how far we can go.

PERSONAL SUMMARY

1. Review the goals at the beginning of this chapter, and check off each one that you have successfully accomplished.

2. Summarize the main lessons you have learned by working through this chapter.

_____

_____

_____

_____

3. List the subjects covered in this chapter that you still need more work on.

_____

_____

_____

_____

_____

_____

ADDITIONAL WRITING

1. Using personal experience or an extended illustration, write an essay in the form of a story (as you did in Chapter Two). Your purpose here is to support an opinion on a gender-related topic of your choice through personal experience. (For an example, see page 258 in the Handbook.)
2. Find a news report, an article, or an editorial concerning an issue on which you have an opinion, and write a letter to the editor about it. Be sure to support your opinion with appropriate evidence in order to convince other readers to see the subject from your point of view.

ADDITIONAL READING

Schlafly, Phyllis. *The Power of the Positive Woman*. New York: Random House, 1977. A supporter of traditional values, Schlafly discusses the differences between feminists and what she calls "positive women."

Steinem, Gloria. *Outrageous Acts and Everyday Rebellions*. New York: Holt, Rinehart and Winston, 1983. In a series of essays written over an extended period, Steinem explains the value of the women's liberation movement as she sees it.

Opposing Viewpoints Series. St. Paul, Minn., and San Diego, Calif.: Greenhaven Press. In addition to volumes on male/female roles and sexual values, other books in the series present opposing views on a variety of controversial and timely issues, such as the health crisis, ecology, and chemical dependency.

Chapter Five
Public Writing from Sources

> *In this chapter, you will:*
> ✔ Improve your comprehension of what you read
> ✔ Use sources in your writing
> ✔ Get further practice in revising your essays

Take a moment to reflect on all the work you have done in your writing course so far. Looking back to the beginning of the term helps you realize how far you've come in a short amount of time. If you have continued to study and practice, you are prepared for even greater challenges. You can look with pride on your accomplishments and know that with continuing effort, you will continue to make gains.

With each bit of success you experience, the more motivated you will be to put forth your best effort. Especially important is the time—and quality of time—you give to your reading. Not only will reading give you material to respond to, interact with, and write about, but because reading and writing use interrelated thinking skills, the better you read, the better you will write.

READING

Of all the selections in this text, the one you are about to read will probably challenge you most. Written by the renowned Jewish psychiatrist Viktor Frankl, this passage from *Man's Search for Meaning* documents one of the most hideous crimes against humanity committed in world history: the massive persecution and extermination of Jews in a Nazi* labor and extermination camp in Auschwitz, Poland.

Preparing to Read

Before you read, call to mind other abuses or crimes against humans you are aware of. These might range from the deliberate and systematic abuse of an entire people, such as apartheid in South Africa, to the random acts of violence and abuse, such as drug-related murders or violent sexual crimes against children, that plague our inner cities, our suburbs, and even rural America. Later you will be asked to select some abuse or crime against humans as a subject to write about; the reading you are about to engage in will serve as a springboard for that writing.

As you read, keep the following points in mind:

1. Notice from whose viewpoint this true story is told. Through whose eyes do we see the action?
2. Visualize the pictures drawn with words; listen to the sounds; activate all your senses in order to become more deeply involved in your reading.
3. Take special note of passages that show the courage of human beings in the most horrible of circumstances.
4. Jot down questions that come to mind, either something you don't understand or something you wonder about. Make an educated guess at what your final answers will be, and then verify or modify your hunches as you continue to read.
5. Try to figure out the meaning of unfamiliar words from the way they are used in the passage and from what you already know. Circle all those you aren't sure of.

---

*The National Socialist (Nazi) party rose to power in Germany in 1933 under the leadership of Adolf Hitler and mounted a campaign of systematic persecution and killing of Jews and members of other ethnic and political groups that Hitler considered a threat to his dictatorship. The Nazis' annihilation of more than six million Jews is known as the Holocaust.

From
Man's Search for Meaning
Viktor Frankl

Fifteen hundred persons had been traveling by train for several days and nights: there were eighty people in each coach. All had to lie on top of their luggage, the few remnants of their personal possessions. The carriages were so full that only the top parts of the windows were free to let in the grey of dawn. Everyone expected the train to head for some munitions factory, in which we would be employed as forced labor. . . .

Suddenly a cry broke from the ranks of the anxious passengers, "There is a sign, Auschwitz!" Everyone's heart missed a beat at that moment. Auschwitz—the very name stood for all that was horrible: gas chambers, crematoriums, massacres. Slowly, almost hesitatingly, the train moved on as if it wanted to spare its passengers the dreadful realization as long as possible: Auschwitz!

With the progressive dawn, the outlines of an immense camp became visible: long stretches of several rows of barbed wire fences; watch towers; search lights; and long columns of ragged human figures, grey in the greyness of dawn, trekking along the straight desolate roads, to what destination we did not know. There were isolated shouts and whistles of command. We did not know their meaning. My imagination led me to see gallows with people dangling on them. I was horrified, but this was just as well, because step by step we had to become accustomed to a terrible and immense horror. Eventually we moved into the station. . . .

Fifteen hundred captives were cooped up in a shed built to accommodate probably two hundred at the most. We were cold and hungry and there was not enough room for everyone to squat on the bare ground, let alone to lie down. One five-ounce piece of bread was our only food in four days. . . .

Nearly everyone in our transport lived under the illusion that he would be reprieved, that everything would yet be well. We did not realize the meaning behind the scene that was to follow presently. We were told to leave our luggage in the train and to fall into two lines—women on one side, men on the other—in order to file past a senior **SS** officer. . . . He was a tall man who looked slim and fit in his spotless uniform. What a contrast to us, who were untidy and grimy after our long journey! He had assumed an attitude of careless ease, supporting his right elbow with his left hand. His right hand was lifted, and with the forefinger of

SS: the Nazis' special police

that hand he pointed very leisurely to the right or to the left. None of us had the slightest idea of the sinister meaning behind that little movement of a man's finger, pointing now to the right and now to the left, but far more frequently to the left.

It was my turn. Somebody whispered to me that to be sent to the right side would mean work, the way to the left being for the sick and those incapable of work, who would be sent to a special camp. I just waited for things to take their course, the first of many such times to come. . . .

The SS man looked me over, appeared to hesitate, then put both his hands on my shoulders. I tried very hard to look smart, and he turned my shoulders very slowly until I faced right, and I moved over to that side.

The significance of the finger game was explained to us in the evening. It was the first selection, the first verdict made on our existence or non-existence. For the great majority of our transport, it meant death. Their sentence was carried out within the next few hours. Those who were sent left were marched from the station straight to the crematorium. This building, as I was told by someone who worked there, had the word "bath" written over its doors in several European languages. On entering, each prisoner was handed a piece of soap, and then—but mercifully I do not need to describe the events which followed.* Many accounts have been written about this horror.

We who were saved, the minority of our transport, found out the truth in the evening. I inquired from prisoners who had been there for some time where my colleague and friend P—— had been sent.

"Was he sent to the left side?"

"Yes," I replied.

"Then you can see him there," I was told.

"Where?" A hand pointed to the chimney a few hundred yards off, which was sending a column of flame up into the grey sky of Poland. It dissolved into a sinister cloud of smoke.

"That's where your friend is, floating up to Heaven," was the answer. But I still did not understand until the truth was explained to me in plain words.

But I am telling things out of their turn. From a psychological point of view, we had a long, long way in front of us from the break of that dawn at the station until our first night's rest at the camp.

Escorted by SS guards with loaded guns, we were made to run from the station, past electrically charged barbed wire, through the camp, to the cleans-

---

*The doors were sealed, and poison gas was piped through the shower heads.

ing station; for those of us who had passed the first selection, this was a real bath....

We waited in a shed which seemed to be the anteroom to the disinfecting chamber. SS men appeared and spread out blankets into which we had to throw all our possessions, all our watches and jewelry. There were still naive prisoners among us who asked, to the amusement of the more seasoned ones who were there as helpers, if they could not keep a wedding ring, a medal, or a good-luck piece. No one could yet grasp the fact that everything would be taken away. I tried to take one of the old prisoners into my confidence. Approaching him furtively, I pointed to the roll of paper in the inner pocket of my coat and said, "Look, this is the manuscript of a scientific book. I know what you will say; that I should be grateful to escape with my life, that that should be all I can expect of fate. But I cannot help myself. I must keep this manuscript at all costs; it contains my life's work. Do you understand that?"

Yes, he was beginning to understand. A grin spread slowly over his face, first piteous, then more amused, mocking, insulting, until he bellowed [a vulgar curse] at me in answer to my question.... At that moment I saw the plain truth and did what marked the culminating point of the first phase of my psychological reaction: I struck out my whole former life.

Suddenly there was a stir among my fellow travelers, who had been standing about with pale, frightened faces, helplessly debating. Again we heard the hoarsely shouted commands. We were driven with blows into the immediate anteroom of the bath. There we assembled around an SS man who waited until we had all arrived. Then he said, "I will give you two minutes, and I shall time you by my watch. In these two minutes you will get fully undressed and drop everything on the floor where you are standing. You will take nothing with you except your shoes, your belt or suspenders, and possibly a truss. I am starting to count—now!"

With unthinkable haste, people tore off their clothes. As the time grew shorter, they became increasingly nervous and pulled clumsily at their underwear, belts and shoelaces. Then we heard the first sounds of whipping, leather straps beating down on naked bodies.

Next we were herded into another room to be shaved: not only our heads were shorn, but not a hair was left on our entire bodies. Then on to the showers, where we lined up again. We hardly recognized each other; but with great relief some people noted that real water dripped from the sprays.

While we were waiting for the shower, our nakedness was brought home to us: we really had nothing now except our bare bodies—even minus hair; all we possessed, literally, was our naked existence. What else remained for us as a material link with our former lives? For me there were my glasses and my belt; the latter I had to exchange later on for a piece of bread. . . .

Thus the illusions some of us still held were destroyed one by one. . . .

I had been convinced that there were certain things I just could not do: I could not sleep without this or I could not live with that or the other. The first night in Auschwitz we slept in beds which were constructed in tiers. On each tier (measuring about six-and-a-half to eight feet) slept nine men, directly on the boards. Two blankets were shared by each nine men. We could, of course, lie only on our sides, crowded and huddled against each other, which had some advantages because of the bitter cold. Though it was forbidden to take shoes up to the bunks, some people did use them secretly as pillows in spite of the fact that they were caked with mud. Otherwise one's head had to rest on the crook of an almost dislocated arm. And yet sleep came and brought oblivion and relief from pain for a few hours. . . .

In spite of all the enforced physical and mental primitiveness of the life in a concentration camp, it was possible for spiritual life to deepen. Sensitive people who were used to a rich intellectual life may have suffered much pain (they were often of a delicate constitution), but the damage to their inner selves was less. They were able to retreat from their terrible surroundings to a life of inner riches and spiritual freedom. Only in this way can one explain the apparent paradox that some prisoners of a less hardy make-up often seemed to survive camp life better than did those of a robust nature. In order to make myself clear, I am forced to fall back on personal experience. Let me tell what happened on those early mornings when we had to march to our work site.

There were shouted commands: "Detachment, forward march! Left-2-3-4! Left-2-3-4! Left-2-3-4! Left-2-3-4! First man about, left and left and left and left! Caps off!" These words sound in my ears even now. At the order "Caps off!" we passed the gate of the camp, and searchlights were trained upon us. Whoever did not march smartly got a kick. And worse off was the man who, because of the cold, had pulled his cap back over his ears before permission was given.

We stumbled on in the darkness, over big stones and through large puddles, along the one road leading from the camp. The accompanying guards kept shouting at us and driving us with the butts of their rifles. Anyone with very sore feet supported himself on his neighbor's arm. Hardly a word was spoken; the icy wind did not encourage talk. Hiding his mouth behind his upturned collar, the man marching next to me whispered suddenly: "If our wives could see us now!

I do hope they are better off in their camps and don't know what is happening to us."

That brought thoughts of my own wife to mind. And as we stumbled on for miles, slipping on icy spots, supporting each other time and again, dragging one another up and onward, nothing was said, but we both knew: each of us was thinking of his wife. Occasionally I looked at the sky, where the stars were fading and the pink light of the morning was beginning to spread behind a dark bank of clouds. But my mind clung to my wife's image, imagining it with an uncanny acuteness. I heard her answering me, saw her smile, her frank and encouraging look. Real or not, her look was then more luminous than the sun which was beginning to rise. 28

A thought transfixed me: for the first time in my life I saw the truth as it is set into song by so many poets, proclaimed as the final wisdom by so many thinkers. The truth—that love is the ultimate and the highest goal to which man can aspire. Then I grasped the meaning of the greatest secret that human poetry and human thought and belief have to impart: the salvation of man is through love and in love. I understand how a man who has nothing left in this world still may know bliss, be it only for a brief moment, in the contemplation of his beloved. In a position of utter desolation, when man cannot express himself in positive action, when his only achievement may consist in enduring his sufferings in the right way—an honorable way—in such a position man can, through loving contemplation of the image he carries of his beloved, achieve fulfillment.... 29

In front of me a man stumbled and those following him fell on top of him. The guard rushed over and used his whip on them all. Thus my thoughts were interrupted for a few minutes. But soon my soul found its way back from the prisoner's existence to another world, and I resumed talk with my loved one: I asked her questions, and she answered; she questioned me in return, and I answered. 30

"Stop!" We had arrived at our work site. Everybody rushed into the dark hut in the hope of getting a fairly decent tool. Each prisoner got a spade or a pickaxe. 31

"Can't you hurry up, you pigs?" Soon we had resumed the previous day's positions in the ditch. The frozen ground cracked under the point of the pickaxes, and sparks flew. The men were silent, their brains numb. 32

My mind still clung to the image of my wife. A thought crossed my mind: I didn't even know if she were still alive. I knew only one thing—which I have learned well by now: Love goes very far beyond the physical person of the 33 beloved. It finds its deepest meaning in his spiritual being, his inner self. Whether or not he is actually present, whether or not he is still alive at all, ceases somehow to be of importance. . . .

This intensification of inner life helped the prisoner find a refuge from the emptiness, desolation and spiritual poverty of his existence, by letting him escape into the past. When given free rein, his imagination played with past events, often not important ones, but minor happenings and trifling things. His nostalgic memory glorified them and they assumed a strange character. Their world and their existence seemed very distant and the spirit reached out for them longingly: in my mind I took bus rides, unlocked the front door of my apartment, answered my telephone, switched on the electric lights. Our thoughts often centered on such details, and these memories could move one to tears.

As the inner life of the prisoner tended to become more intense, he also experienced the beauty of art and nature as never before. Under their influence he sometimes even forgot his own frightful circumstances. If someone had seen our faces on the journey from Auschwitz to a Bavarian camp as we beheld the mountains of Salzburg with their summits glowing in the sunset, through the little barred windows of the prison carriage, he would never have believed that those were the faces of men who had given up all hope of life and liberty. Despite that factor—or maybe because of it—we were carried away by nature's beauty, which we had missed for so long. . . .

One evening, when we were already resting on the floor of our hut, dead tired, soup bowls in hand, a fellow prisoner rushed in and asked us to run out to the assembly grounds and see the wonderful sunset. Standing outside we saw sinister clouds glowing in the west and the whole sky alive with clouds of ever-changing shapes and colors, from steel blue to blood red. The desolate grey mud huts provided a sharp contrast, while the puddles on the muddy ground reflected the glowing sky. Then after minutes of moving silence, one prisoner said to another, "How beautiful the world *could* be!" . . .

When the transport of sick patients for the "rest camp" was organized, my name (that is, my number) was put on the list, since a few doctors were needed. But no one was convinced that the destination was really a rest camp. A few weeks previously the same transport had been prepared. Then, too, everyone had thought that it was destined for the gas ovens. When it was announced that anyone who volunteered for the dreaded night shift would be taken off the transport list, eighty-two prisoners volunteered immediately. A quarter of an hour later the transport was canceled, but the eighty-two stayed on the list for the night shift. For the majority of them, this meant death within the next fortnight.

fortnight: two weeks

ruse: trick

Now the transport for the rest camp was arranged for the second time. Again no one knew whether this was a ruse to obtain the last bit of work from the sick—if only for fourteen days—or whether it would go to the gas ovens or to a genuine rest camp. The chief doctor, who had taken a liking to me, told me furtively one evening at a quarter to ten, "I have made it known in the orderly room that you can still have your name crossed off the list; you may do so up till ten o'clock."

I told him that this was not my way; that I had learned to let fate take its course. "I might as well stay with my friends," I said. There was a look of pity in his eyes, as if he knew. . . . He shook my hand silently, as though it were a farewell, not for life, but from life. Slowly I walked back to my hut. There I found a good friend waiting for me.

"You really want to go with them?" he asked sadly.

"Yes, I am going."

Tears came to his eyes and I tried to comfort him. Then there was something else to do—to make my will:

"Listen, Otto, if I don't get back home to my wife, and if you should see her again, then tell her that I talked of her daily, hourly. You remember. Secondly, I have loved her more than anyone. Thirdly, the short time I have been married to her outweighs everything, even all we have gone through here."

Otto, where are you now? Are you alive? What has happened to you since our last hour together? Did you find your wife again? And do you remember how I made you learn my will by heart—word for word—in spite of your childlike tears?

The next morning I departed with the transport. This time it was not a ruse. We were not heading for the gas chambers, and we actually did go to a rest camp. Those who had pitied me remained in a camp where famine was to rage even more fiercely than in our new camp. They tried to save themselves, but they only sealed their own fates. Months later, after liberation, I met a friend from the old camp. He related to me how he, as camp policeman, had searched for a piece of human flesh that was missing from a pile of corpses. He confiscated it from a pot in which he found it cooking. Cannibalism had broken out. I had left just in time.

Thinking about Your Reading

Before answering the questions, you may want to spend some time reflecting on the profound impact of the Holocaust—six million or more people annihilated for no reason other than the fact that they were born Jews. Our response to the Holocaust, whether in the form of questions or comments, cannot do justice to a tragedy so atrocious our minds can hardly comprehend it. But we honor the dead as we struggle to express our response to this crime against humanity, and we serve future generations as we work for a better, more humane world by examining other abuses and crimes against humans. It has been said that those who fail to learn from history are destined to repeat it.

1. Describe the emotions you felt as you read Frankl's story. What parts did you find most moving?

_____

_____

_____

_____

_____

_____

_____

2. Does the passage leave you with a generally hopeless, pessimistic attitude or a hopeful, optimistic attitude toward human nature? Explain your reaction.

_____

_____

3. Based on your knowledge of human nature, what character traits do you think Frankl reveals in himself as he describes the following?

a. His reflections on his wife

_____
_____

b. The will he makes for his wife

_____
_____

c. His refusal to have his name taken off the list of prisoners to be sent to the "rest camp"

_____
_____

4. Imagine for a moment that you owned nothing material. What kind of inheritance could you leave someone, and who would you leave that inheritance to? _____

_____
_____
_____
_____

5. What similarities do you note between the horrors of Auschwitz and another abuse or crime against humans it brings to mind?

_____

_____

_____

_____

6. Divide into teams of classmates. Working together, try to figure out the meaning of the words and phrases listed here from the context in which they are used in the Frankl passage (the paragraph number is given) and from what you already know. If you are unsure of the meaning, find the most appropriate definition in your dictionary. Each team might take one column of words to define and then share the results with the other teams.

I	*II*	*III*	*IV*
1 munitions (1)	8 sinister (5)	16 oblivion (24)	23 contemplation (29)
2 crematorium (2)	9 naive (17)	17 paradox (25)	24 intensification (34)
3 gas chamber (2)	10 seasoned (17)	18 robust (25)	25 refuge (34)
4 desolate (3)	11 furtively (17)	19 luminous (28)	26 nostalgic (34)
5 gallows (3)	12 bellowed (18)	20 transfixed (29)	27 destination (37)
6 transport (5)	13 culminating (18)	21 proclaimed (29)	28 confiscated (45)
7 reprieved (5)	14 truss (19)	22 aspire (29)	
	15 tiers (24)		

7. The following poem was written by Rose Van Thyn, a survivor of Auschwitz. After reading the poem, write a letter to Mrs. Van Thyn expressing your personal response to the Holocaust.* Or if you know someone else who has survived the Holocaust, you may prefer to address your letter to that person.

*Mrs. Van Thyn lives in my hometown. If you would like for her to receive your letter, please send it to Rose Van Thyn, c/o Patricia Teel Bates, Louisiana State University, Shreveport, LA 71115.

Close the curtains, neighbors of Buchenwald† and Dachau;†
The train is passing by,
Loaded with all kinds of people.
Young and old, they don't know where they are going.
They have never been told.
Close the curtains, neighbors of Bergen-Belsen;†
The train is passing by,
Loaded with children.
Yesterday they were still playing in the street, unaware.
Benjamin was playing marbles;
Sara got new shoes and a ribbon for her hair.
They will not survive.
Today is the last day of their lives.

Close the curtains, neighbors of Auschwitz;
Close the windows too
So you will neither see nor smell
The smoke in the darkened sky.
The train is passing by,
Loaded with families.
They are being sent.
To this desolate place where their lives will end.
They will be forever gone,
But their memory lives on.

WRITING ASSIGNMENT

If you compare yourself to the billions of human beings who have inhabited this planet, you are one of the most privileged and one of the best educated. With privilege and education comes opportunity—the opportunity to share your knowledge and understanding with others for the betterment of those who live about you. One way to do so is through your writing. In the writing you are about to undertake, you will educate yourself and write for the purpose of educating others.

†A Nazi concentration camp.

Write It Out: An Essay Using Sources

In much of your writing up to now, you've relied mainly on your experience, observations, and opinions as a primary resource, using ideas and details from others to supplement your own. Now the emphasis will shift, with outside sources assuming a more prominent role.

Using outside sources and following the guide presented here, write an essay that examines a serious abuse or crime against humans. As indicated earlier, your subject might be a deliberate and systematic abuse against an entire people, such as apartheid in South Africa, or it might be a type of random offense, such as sexual crimes against children. The subject you choose might be a well-recognized and widespread problem such as alcohol-related homicide or it might be a less well-known, seldom-discussed, but nonetheless serious crime like date rape. Or it could be any social problem you consider to have potentially serious consequences.

The general purposes of the essay are to educate your readers and to propose a solution that addresses the abuse or crime you choose to write about. Your general audience might be the individuals who are most likely to learn and benefit from your proposed solution. (Shortly, you will select a specific audience.)

1 SELECT A TOPIC. To begin your work, consider a list of potential topics to write about.

EXAMPLES
anti-Semitism (hostility toward Jews)
mistreatment of native Americans
racism
capital punishment
paroling murderers
sale (or use) of illegal drugs
child abuse
pornography
date rape
teen suicide
mistreatment or neglect of people with AIDS

Add other possible topics to the list by brainstorming alone or with others. Then, circle the topic that interests you most.

Even after you've chosen your topic, you will probably need to restrict it further by selecting a specific problem or angle to write about. For example, if you are considering the topic of pornography, you might restrict yourself to the problem of child pornography.

2 EXPLORE SOURCES. To be sure that you will be able to write successfully about your topic using outside sources, you will want to check to see how much reliable up-to-date information is available. Sources you may have found helpful in previous writing projects include testimony of authorities, reliable eyewitness accounts, news reports, television documentaries, and even movies.

Perhaps you know someone—or maybe there is someone on your college campus—with special knowledge about your topic. If so, consider interviewing that person as one of the sources for your paper. You can make use of the interviewing techniques you practiced in Chapter Three.

You may also find useful information in books or magazines that you have at home. Or you can locate other printed materials by using your library's card catalog or computer search service, the *Reader's Guide to Periodical Literature*, the *Social Sciences Index*, the *New York Times Index*, or the vertical file. Public or private nonprofit agencies can also provide good sources of published information, such as videotapes, pamphlets, and brochures. The *Editorial Research Reports* is another valuable source.

If you need help with any of these materials or sources, ask your instructor or another resource person. Your librarian, in particular, will be glad to point out a number of possible sources.

> **Ask Yourself**

1. What writing topic do I plan to investigate?

   _____

2. What specific problem or angle interests me?

   _____

3. What are some possible sources of information on this topic?

   _____

   _____

   _____

3 SUMMARIZE THE PROBLEM. Consider the topic or problem you have chosen, and identify the abuse or crime against humans involved. In a few sentences, summarize *what* the problem is and *why* it is a serious human problem. Also identify the specific purpose you hope to accomplish by examining the problem. Who might be the specific audience for your paper? (Remember that the general purposes of the assignment are to educate the reader and to propose a solution that addresses the problem; the general audience may be the people most likely to learn and benefit from the proposed solution.)

Here is the *summary statement of the problem* written by a student working on the topic of teen suicide.

- *Topic Problem*

  Suicide is the second greatest killer of teenagers in the United States today. Not only do these fatalities bring an abrupt and tragic end to the victims' lives, but they also bring grief and guilt to the lives of family members and friends, who may spend the rest of their lives agonizing over what they might have done to save the troubled youth.

❑ *Audience*
Family members and friends who are in contact with the troubled teen might be able to save a life if they were aware of the warning signals that commonly precede teen suicide. They also need to know how to deal with their own grief and guilt if a teenager close to them commits suicide.

❑ *Purpose*
The purpose of my essay is to inform readers of the facts surrounding teen suicide so that they might help prevent this devastating tragedy or deal with their grief and guilt if it does occur.

Ask Yourself

1. How would I summarize the topic or problem of my essay?

_____

_____

_____

_____

_____

2. What is my specific purpose?

_____

_____

_____

3. Who will be the specific audience for my paper (in addition to my instructor and classmates)? Who might learn and benefit from my proposed solution?

_____

_____

4 COLLECT YOUR INFORMATION (SUMMARIZE, PARAPHRASE, AND QUOTE). One of the most important steps in writing an essay based on sources is actually collecting your information. To use your time most effectively, decide what subtopics you should take notes on. Some important subtopics to consider are (1) the human tragedy or harmful effects of the problem you are writing about, (2) principal causes of the problem, (3) possible solutions that address the causes, and (4) facts, statistics, examples, illustrations, and other details that will help accomplish your purposes.

Go back to the useful sources you identified earlier during your exploratory search and take notes. If you are interviewing someone, you might tape-record the interview and then translate your material into writing. It's especially helpful to put your notes on cards so that they can be more easily arranged and rearranged. Each time you change sources or subtopics, use a different card. Also, be sure to label each card with the subtopic and the source. Once you have collected your information, you can put related cards together.

You should put material in your own words as you work, rather than waste time copying, word for word, from your sources and ending up with masses of material you won't use. Sometimes you will want to condense information from a source into two or three sentences or just a few words that capture the main points. This is referred to as *summarizing*, and it means that you are eliminating minor points that the speaker or author makes and retaining the most important ones.

At other times you will want to include the main points as well as specific supporting details. In this case your wording will be about the same length as that of the source but will be written *in your own language*. This is known as *paraphrasing*.

Occasionally you will use *direct quotations*, the exact words of your source. (For help in punctuating direct quotations, see page 256 in the Handbook.) It's a good idea to use direct quotations only when you need the precise wording to make your point; otherwise, they lose their impact, causing your essay to look more like a "cut-and-paste" job than like your own work.

To make your writing more convincing and to give credit where credit is due, be sure to choose up-to-date, reliable sources; identify each source by name; and give a brief description like the one shown in the sample summary, paraphrase, and direct quotation that follow. You can identify your sources either within the essay itself or at the bottom of the page on which the source material is used (see the sample essay at the end of this chapter). As you become a more advanced writer, you will learn other techniques for identifying, or documenting, your sources.

Failure to give credit, whether you are summarizing, paraphrasing, or directly quoting your sources, is known as *plagiarism*, a serious offense that carries significant penalties.

The excerpt that follows is from *They Always Call Us Ladies*, the autobiography of Jean Harris. A prominent educator who was convicted of killing a doctor with whom she had had a fifteen-year relationship, Mrs. Harris has recorded observations and opinions related to her experience as an inmate at the Bedford Hills Correctional Facility in New York.

❑ *The Original Material*
Infants and children of inmates make up the darkest part of the story of crime, yet they are the only source we can count on for light in the future. It is a well-established fact that what happens to us in infancy sets the scene for the rest of our lives, sets it, quite possibly, indelibly. To be accurate, I should go back to the fetal stage, not start with birth. For many humans, infancy itself is too late. The drugs and liquor and cigarettes and candy bars some mothers have indulged themselves and their unborn babies in, the milk and fruit and grains they didn't feed them, can be the beginning of a very troubled life. If mothers' drugs were administered with dirty needles, birth itself can be little more than a death sentence. Yet it is true in America today, and in many other countries where we have withheld drastically needed funds, that while we insist upon the birth of a fetus, we do tragically too little to see that the fetus is healthy, and that someone in its world is waiting

and able to take good care of it, or even give it a place to live. So many of these small people die in the preamble of their lives.

- ❏ *Identification of the Source and Summary of the Material*
  In her prison autobiography *They Always Call Us Ladies*, Jean Harris deplores the tragic circumstances often surrounding the prenatal existence and birth of some children. Before they are born, many are already doomed, having been exposed to harmful substances and denied their right to proper nourishment and care.

- ❏ *Identification of the Source and Paraphrase of the First Sentence*
  Jean Harris, a prisoner and author of *They Always Call Us Ladies*, notes that children born to inmates constitute the most tragic aspect of crime, but she also sees children as our only hope for a better world.

- ❏ *Identification of the Source and Use of Exact Words (Direct Quotation)*
  Jean Harris, a prisoner and author of *They Always Call Us Ladies*, is critical of the fact "that while we insist upon the birth of a fetus, we do tragically too little to see that the fetus is healthy, and that someone in its world is waiting and able to take good care of it, or even give it a place to live."

For Further Thought

Copy a block of material from one of your sources. Then summarize, paraphrase, and quote some of it. Be sure in each case to name and briefly describe your source:

1. Original: _____

_____

_____

_____

_____

2. Summary of the passage: _____

_____

_____

_____

_____

3. Paraphrase: _____

_____

_____

_____

_____

4. Quotation: _____

_____

_____

_____

_____

5 DEVELOP YOUR THESIS, OR MAIN POINT. After reading through the notes you've collected, prepare the main point you want to make in your essay. Sometimes called a thesis statement, it is actually only a "working thesis" because you will no doubt change and improve it as you work with your subject. (Of course, you might even change the topic itself. Until the final draft is complete, you may change your mind about any aspect of your work.)

One way to create a working thesis is to reread your summary statement of the problem (page 147) and ask yourself what is the most important question your essay can answer. The answer to the question—or the question itself—can be your thesis. It may be an opinion statement comparable to the one you prepared in Chapter Four, or you may simply present a factual statement, saving your opinions for the conclusion of your paper, where you offer your solutions. Examples of topics, questions, and thesis statements follow:

- *Topic:* Nuclear Waste
- *Question:* In light of their destructive potential, should we allow nuclear plants to continue to operate or permit new plants to be built?
- *Thesis:* We should not allow nuclear plants to continue to operate. . . .

- *Topic:* Apathy about AIDS
- *Question:* What can be done to halt the spread of AIDS?
- *Thesis:* The government must make a major investment in research and education if we are to halt the spread of AIDS.

The significance of your paper will depend in part on the significance of your thesis, so you will need to get feedback on how promising it appears to be before going too much further into the project.

To refine your thesis in response to your feedback, do a bit more brainstorming. Working quickly, make a list of all the key points and subpoints that come to mind as you think about your topic. When you run out of ideas, try recalling points and subpoints that you learned from your sources, or reread your notes. Continue to add points and subpoints to your list.

Ask Yourself

1. What are my topic, question, and thesis statement? (Write them out.)

_____

_____

Chapter Five / Public Writing from Sources

2. What points and subpoints shall I use? (After getting feedback, use brainstorming to help you make a list of points and subpoints.)

3. What is my refined thesis?

6 **ORGANIZE YOUR MATERIAL.** Three useful ways of organizing your source material are the *bare-bones outline* and *tree diagram*, illustrated in Chapter Four, and the *mental map*, which will be described in this chapter.

Perhaps the best feature of the outline is its familiarity and its usefulness in showing how a piece of writing is organized.

Here is a possible bare-bones outline, or *organizational plan*, for the notes you have collected. Remember that this is just one of many possibilities.

Sample Bare-bones Outline

I. Introduction
   A. Lead
   B. Thesis
II. Body
   A. Causes of the problem
   B. Effects of the problem
III. Conclusion
   A. Solution 1
   B. Solution 2

The *tree diagram* can be an effective organizer because it allows you to add new points easily and enables you to see at a glance if any of the branches of the diagram are overemphasized or underemphasized.

Let's say you were about to develop a tree diagram on the topic of alcohol-related homicides. Assume that before preparing the diagram, (1) you have restricted your topic to treat only the homicides resulting from drunk driving, (2) you've already collected a good bit of information, and (3) you've prepared a working thesis. The sample on page 155 shows how one student writing on this topic organized her subtopics.

After preparing the diagram, the student decided that her material would be better organized if she began her paper with a single dramatic illustration and rounded out her introduction with statistics providing background on the problem of homicides resulting from drunk driving. She chose to weave her other examples and illustrations into the body of her paper to show society's general apathy regarding drunk driving and to demonstrate the failures of the legal system. This organizational plan led logically to her

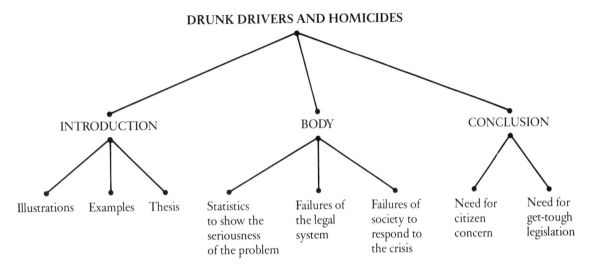

SAMPLE TREE DIAGRAM

conclusion, which stressed the need for individual citizen concern and get-tough legislation.

The mental map is an effective way to show relationships in material resulting from brainstorming. The term *mental map* refers to the fact that it allows for material to be organized into what we might think of as a chart or map of the writer's thoughts and the pattern they form. You can create your personalized combination of graphic symbols, like circles, boxes, and lines, to show pathways or relationships. There is no right or wrong form, so experiment with your own.

In my system, I place a circle in the center of the map to represent the main point, put boxes around the circle to represent subpoints, add triangles beyond the boxes to represent details that support the subpoints, and draw lines connecting the symbols along a pathway and radiating outward like spokes of a wheel.

Note the example of a mental map on page 156 to see how it can be made. The student who prepared it also wrote on the topic of homicides and drunk driving. (His final draft appears at the end of this chapter.)

Organize your essay using the bare-bones outline, the tree diagram, the mental map, or some other plan of your choice. Remember that it is subject to change as you write and learn more about your topic.

SAMPLE MENTAL MAP

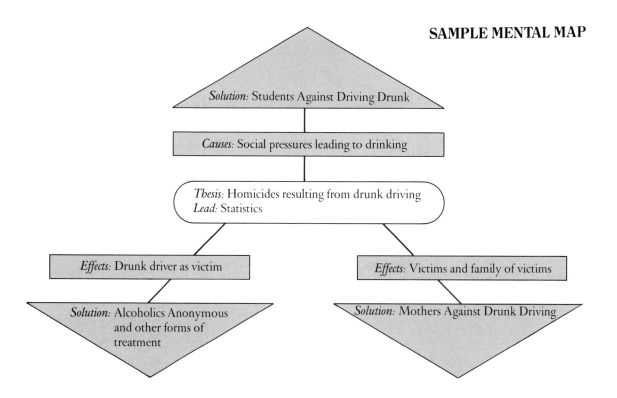

7 DRAFT YOUR ESSAY. The first draft of the paper you produce will be in the form of notes from your sources that you have organized according to your plan. Be sure that you have plenty of facts, examples, illustrations, statistics, and other details to develop your thesis fully and to support your subpoints. This development makes your paper more believable and helps to convince your readers to accept the solutions you propose.

As you review your source material, look for good points or subpoints not on your plan, and add them where you think they fit.

Once you've drafted and organized your notes, you are ready to put them into essay form, keeping in mind the general purposes of the introduction, body, and conclusion for a project such as the one you are working on. These purposes are summarized below.

Purposes of the Introduction

❑ To encourage the reader to bring prior knowledge to the reading

- ❏ To attract and hold the reader's attention
- ❏ To provide background information and set the stage for the thesis, or main point
- ❏ To state the thesis, or main point
- ❏ To help accomplish the purpose for writing

Purposes of the Body
- ❏ To develop and support the thesis
- ❏ To help accomplish the purpose for writing

Purposes of the Conclusion
- ❏ To bring the subject to a close
- ❏ To make a final impression
- ❏ To help accomplish the purpose for writing

For this particular assignment, which examines a serious abuse or crime against humans in order to educate the reader and propose a solution, the first draft of your essay might follow the rough plan presented next. Notice that it is a modified and expanded version of the organizational plan shown on page 154. (Feel free to use any approach that seems appropriate for your purposes; this is just one of many possibilities.)

SAMPLE ESSAY PLAN

Plan for the Introduction
- ❏ Attention-getting statement of the problem
- ❏ Statement of the effect of the problem as it affects the reader
- ❏ Statement of the main point (thesis) of the essay, which identifies key causes of the problem

Plan for the Body
- ❏ First body paragraph—topic sentence identifies one subpoint of the problem and develops it through the use of facts, examples, illustrations, and other supporting details.

- ❏ Second body paragraph—topic sentence identifies a second subpoint and develops it through the use of facts, examples, illustrations, and other supporting details.
- ❏ Further body paragraphs as needed.

Plan for the Conclusion
- ❏ Statement of solutions that counteract the negative effects of the problem and take into account each of the causes discussed in the essay

8 EVALUATE YOUR DRAFT. The checklist that follows should help you evaluate your essay in order to produce a successful final draft.

1. Have I followed all instructions I was given? _____

2. Have I chosen an interesting, significant topic? _____

3. Is the solution I propose significant and realistic? _____

4. Is my topic focused enough to be covered in depth in my essay? _____

5. Do I have an effective introduction that is helpful and interesting to readers? _____

6. Is my main point, or thesis, either clearly stated in the introduction or at least clearly implied? _____

7. Is my title interesting and closely related to my main idea? _____

8. Does the introduction suggest a purpose for the essay? _____

9. Does each paragraph fit in with the overall purpose suggested by the introduction? _____

10. Does each paragraph have a topic sentence or a clearly stated topic that is closely related to the thesis? _____

11. Does each paragraph treat only one topic? _____

12. Is each paragraph well developed with sentences containing vivid concrete details? _____

13. Are the paragraphs arranged in the most logical and effective order? _____

14. Have I used enough supporting evidence (facts, figures, examples, illustrations, and other details) to prove my main point and all subpoints? _____

    Is the supporting material appropriate? _____

15. Have I named and briefly described all my sources? _____

16. Is my conclusion a natural and logical outgrowth of what I said in the introduction and body? _____

17. Does my conclusion contribute to my purpose? _____

18. Have I kept my audience in mind throughout? _____

9 REWORK YOUR DRAFT TO MAKE YOUR POINT CONVINCING. After evaluating your essay with the help of the checklist and with helpful feedback from readers, you may see the need for a number of changes, including a more attention-getting introduction than the one you developed earlier in the writing process.

Read back through the introduction you had intended to use, and see if it contains anything striking or dramatic. One of the ways to stimulate your reader's interest is to provide background for the thesis in the form of a "minidrama," complete with characters, action, and setting, that will draw the reader into the scene. A student who wrote on the topic of arson for profit prepared the following introduction in response to the suggestion that he create a minidrama.

> The taxi glided slowly through the crowded East Side traffic before easing into the cold gray slush piled against the curb. The cab rolled to a stop. The driver, following his passenger's lead, glanced out of the side window at the charred debris of the burned-out tenement building. Recognizing the scene from the pictures in last month's newspapers, he recalled the details surrounding the fire. The fire had started at 3:00 A.M. in the basement and quickly raced upward, engulfing the dry, rotten wood of the structure in a matter of minutes. As the six-story torch lit up the city's skyline, the firemen arrived, but the flammable liquid that had been poured into the building's heating ducts had given the fire too much of a head start. By dawn, it had been brought under control, but not before it had claimed the building and eleven victims. Nine of the victims had been children, too young and innocent to understand the greed responsible for their death.

If one of the purposes of your essay is to persuade the reader to do or believe something, keep in mind three strategies that speakers and writers since the ancient Greeks have used to persuade their audiences:

- ❑ *Strategy 1: Emotional Appeal*
  A good example of an emotional appeal is the sample introduction to the paper on arson for profit just presented. Be careful to make your emotional material believable; otherwise, it takes away from your purpose instead of helping to accomplish it. As a general rule, the more biased an audience, the more readily it is influenced either favorably or unfavorably by an emotional appeal.

- ❑ *Strategy 2: Logical Appeal*
  Using logical arguments is an important way to win over your audience to your way of thinking. Requirements of good logic include

accuracy and completeness of details along with well-supported opinions.

In the following example, note that the writer uses faulty logic; the statements are a series of opinions that cannot possibly be proved or adequately supported. Also notice the contradiction in the sentence that uses the expressions *in most cases* and *invariably* in reference to the author's belief that women can't keep a secret. Common sense tells us that no character trait is invariably true about the members of a particular sex (or any other group). Finally, notice that there is no proof for any of the statements.

EXAMPLE OF FAULTY LOGIC

Generally, a woman can confide in a male friend and not have to worry about "being discussed in the locker room." Men just seem to have the ability to keep secrets, whereas women are just the opposite. In most cases, after they have sworn themselves to secrecy, women will invariably repeat the secret, sometimes ruining another person's reputation in the process. This is not intentionally done in a cruel, malicious way: it is simply not the nature of women to keep secrets.

❏ *Strategy 3: Credibility*

There are a number of ways to enhance your credibility—that is, to persuade your readers to trust or believe in what you say. One of the most effective is to use reliable, up-to-date sources and to identify and describe those sources accurately. Compare the two paragraphs that follow. The first offers an unsupported opinion that comes across as self-serving; the second contains more factual statements taken from authoritative sources. Notice the increased credibility of the second example.

EXAMPLE 1 (LACKS CREDIBILITY)

One reason I am in favor of capital punishment is related to the expense involved in keeping criminals imprisoned. I do not want my tax money used to keep criminals alive. Less expense is involved in hanging or electrocuting a person than providing room and board even for a few years, much less for the rest of the criminal's lifetime.

EXAMPLE 2 (HAS CREDIBILITY)

    I agree with C. L. Black, author of *Capital Punishment: The Inevitability of Caprice and Mistake*, that capital punishment should be abandoned for at least two reasons: some people will be killed because of mistakes made in the process of administering "justice," and some will be arbitrarily selected to receive the death penalty because of "discretion" given to juries and judges. The death penalty should be abandoned for these two reasons if no others.

10 REFINE YOUR DRAFT. The process of refining your writing involves checking such features as spelling, punctuation, capitalization, subject-verb agreement, and other areas of grammar and usage explained in the Handbook.

Sample Student Essay

Here is the final draft written by a student in response to this chapter's assignment. His topic is traffic fatalities due to drunk driving. As you read, think about what the writer might have done to make his essay more effective.

```
           DRINKING, DRIVING, DYING
                 by Bill Rice
```

    Every 27 minutes in America a drunk driver kills another person, according to the National Highway Traffic Safety Administration. It is estimated that up to 90% of all auto fatalities and injuries are related to drinking and driving. In the past ten years alone an estimated 250,000 people, about five times the number of Americans killed in the Vietnam War, have been killed in alcohol-related crashes. Alcohol-related crashes are the number one killer of people between the ages of 16 and 24. On an average weekend night, one out of every ten cars you pass on the road is driven by a drunk driver. Linda Weltner, writing in the June 6, 1986, Boston *Globe*, expresses the tragedy in graphic terms: "Every 27 minutes somebody drinks, somebody drives, somebody dies" in an alcohol-related automobile crash.

It has become an American tradition to get intoxicated at every get-together. For some people, drinking brings a false sense of power, as if they were indestructible or invincible. Others just need that little extra boost of courage so they have the confidence to deal with the pressures of life or someone of the opposite sex. Speakers at Alcoholics Anonymous meetings report an endless number of excuses that people use to justify drinking and getting high on alcohol. However, drinking is one thing; driving after drinking is another. Though nobody in his or her right mind would drive with the intent to kill someone, alcohol clouds people's judgment. Far too many are mistakenly convinced that their driving will not be affected by just a few drinks.

Who are the victims of this tragedy? Not only the ones who are killed and become further statistics. There are living victims too. Think about those who are condemned to go through life feeling the pain, the sorrow, and the hurt caused by the death of their loved ones slaughtered on the highway. Consider, for example, the child who will never again feel the warm and tender touch of a loving mother. No one can take the pain away; only time can help ease the hurt and lonely feelings.

Or consider the family of Tommy Sexton, whose story was featured on ABC's 20/20. On a summer day, Tommy Sexton and two friends were returning from a fishing trip when drunk driver David Watkins smashed into their car and killed Tommy instantly. A month later, parents Tom and Dot Sexton sat in a southern Maryland courtroom and watched as defendants in criminal cases were called before the judge. The first man was accused of car theft, and the judge sentenced him to two years in jail. Then came the case of David Watkins. The judge placed him on two years' probation and fined him $200. The Sextons were stunned, and rightly so.

The drunk driver who becomes an instant murderer becomes a real victim too. He must bear the burden of guilt and shame, knowing he killed someone and devastated the lives of family members and loved ones left behind. He will relive the moment of that fatal crash many times over. He will hear screeching tires and screams of pain and see mental pictures of mutilated bodies strewn about the highway. He will have to live with himself knowing he created it all because of his negligence.

Take Larry Mahoney, for example, whose tragic story was reported on the national news and retold in the May 30, 1988, issue of U.S. News and World Report. A 34-year-old father who, according to a friend "wouldn't hurt anybody for the world," drove down the wrong side of a Kentucky road and slammed his pickup truck into a school bus, killing 24 children and 3 adults. Mahoney has been sentenced to 16 years in prison. He was a previous offender.

Every 27 minutes, somebody drinks, somebody drives, and somebody dies. What can we do to stop this senseless slaughter on our nation's highways? What the Sextons and others have done is to become active members of MADD (Mothers Against Drunk Driving) and lobby for stiffer legislation to get drunk drivers off the highways. MADD has also lobbied successfully to get the legal drinking age raised to 21. Another activist organization is SADD (Students Against Driving Drunk). SADD is prevention- and youth-oriented and opposes underage drinking, drug abuse of all kinds, and deaths due to drinking and driving.

If you have a problem with alcohol, David Ellis, author of Becoming a Master Student, says the first step is to admit that you have a problem. To get help, you can contact an organization such as Alcoholics Anonymous, listed in your phone book, or see a trained health professional. Finally, I would add, if you're going to drink, don't drive. Your next 27 minutes could be your last.

PERSONAL SUMMARY

1. Review the chapter goals at the beginning of this chapter, and check off each one you have successfully accomplished.

2. Summarize the main lessons you have learned by working through this chapter.

3. List the subjects covered in this chapter that you still need more work on.

4. At the beginning of the semester, you wrote a note to yourself that you sealed in an envelope to be opened later in the semester. In your note, you described what you hoped to accomplish this semester and explained the changes you would have to make in your study and work habits in order to reach your goals.

Now open the envelope and read your note. Put a check by the goals you have already reached and the changes in your work and study habits you have made in order to achieve those goals.

In an essay one to two pages long, outline the additional changes you need to make in order to reach the goals you have not yet achieved, and identify what you need to learn more about in order to reach your goals. Using the index of this text, locate the information you need and then, as the conclusion of your essay, summarize that information.

ADDITIONAL WRITING

Follow all instructions for "Write It Out" beginning on page 144, but write on some environmental issue that you consider to be a crime against nature.

ADDITIONAL READING

Frankl, Viktor. *Man's Search for Meaning*. New York: Beacon Press, 1962. Frankl tells not only of the horrors he endured as an inmate in a Nazi concentration camp but also of the spiritual and psychological insights he gained and later used in healing others' emotional ills.

Opposing Viewpoints Series. St. Paul, Minn., and San Diego, Calif.: Greenhaven Press. A number of volumes in this series treat such topics as the arms race, war and human nature, crime and criminality, and America's prisons.

Chapter Six
Writing for the Workplace

> *In this chapter you will:*
> ✔ Practice the conventions of professional writing
> ✔ Use writing to prepare for a career
> ✔ Observe the importance of writing imaginatively even in everyday writing tasks

Why are you going to college? No doubt you have your unique reasons and goals, but if you are like many other students, you probably hope to gain skills that will lead to a promising career. Obviously, some professions require more writing than others. But whether your chosen field demands a significant level of ability or not, chances are good that the more verbally skilled you are, the more quickly you will advance in your profession.

According to a nationwide sample of business executives, the ability to write is one of the most useful skills in the professional world.* Almost half of those who were surveyed rated writing skills either 9 or 10 on a scale of 1 (unimportant) to 10 (important) in helping them to be more productive, and over half of the executives ranked these skills either 9 or 10 in helping them to advance professionally.

---

*For a copy of the survey summary, write Communispond at 485 Lexington Avenue, New York, NY 10017. One respondent noted that generally as an individual advances within a company, the less important one's technical background becomes and the more important communication skills and the ability to work with people become. In key positions, these abilities are critical and are often the deciding factors in the selection of a particular candidate for a promotion.

Ask Yourself

1. What career field do I hope to enter when I complete my college work? What kinds of writing do I expect to do in my chosen career field (letters, memos, summaries, reports, proposals, analyses, evaluations, critiques, reviews)?

_____

_____

_____

_____

2. If I were to take a job today that required me to write frequently, what would my greatest strengths and my greatest weaknesses be? _____

_____

_____

_____

_____

3. In what ways can writing be an asset to me on the job?

_____

_____

_____

_____

4. What writing skills do I want to improve over the next four years so that I will be a competent writer in my chosen profession? _____

_____

_____

For Further Thought

Interview two or three people already working successfully in your field of interest. List the kinds of writing they do.

_____

_____

_____

Approximately how much time do they spend writing each week? _____

READING

You have probably already improved your writing skills in a variety of ways as you've done the writing assignments of earlier chapters, and no doubt you will continue to make significant gains during your coming years in school. The following article offers some strategies for helping you make those gains. It is especially helpful for you to read at this point because it builds on the skills you have developed in earlier chapters and anticipates other skills you will develop by the end of the term. In other words, it serves as both review and preview.

Preparing to Read

Before you read the article, review the questions asked in the preceding section and the answers you gave. **As you read**, ask yourself these questions:

1. How can I become more imaginative as a writer?
2. What role does reader interest play in imaginative professional writing?
3. What are good resources for developing one's imagination?

From
"Imagination Helps Communication"
by the Royal Bank of Canada

1. A basic skill in every profession and in most businesses is the ability to organize and express ideas in writing and in speaking.

2. No matter how clever an engineer may be technically, an executive managerially, and a researcher creatively, they do not show their worth unless they communicate their ideas to others in an influential way. . . .

3. What are the writer's tools? A wide range of language, for variety and interest; active verbs, to keep the action moving; similes, which create word pictures; metaphors and anecdotes or stories to make meanings clear; and rhythm, which contributes to smooth, easy reading.

4. To these tools, the writer adds imagination, always being careful to bring it within the scope of facts. Art in writing must not be used as an escape from reality. . . .

5. Imagination in writing finds expression through the use of accurate and illuminating equivalents for thoughts. You may show your imagination by dealing with something unfamiliar; by calling to attention a commonplace fact that is generally overlooked; by bringing into view familiar things in new relationship; or by drawing together relevant thoughts in a bouquet tied with your own ribbon.

6. An imaginative writer can look out upon the sprawling incoherence of a factory or a city or a nation or a problem and give it intelligible statement. . . .

A letter in which something significant is attempted—a sale, a correction, a

incoherence: lacking clarity or intelligibility

changing of opinion, the making of a friend—cannot be written in a neutral and bloodless state of mind. In letter writing, imagination must supply personal contact. When you . . . write a letter you are entering into a personal relationship with the readers. They are no longer statistics in a mass market. You and your readers are human beings talking things over. . . .

No matter what your professional writing is about, the reader will want to know: "How does this affect me?"

It is a literary vice not to seek out the readers' interest. You may tell them what you want in **impeccable** language and forceful manner, but you fall short of success unless you pay attention to what they want or can be made to desire. Your ideas must enter, influence, and stick in the mind of the recipient.

As a writer, you may protest that some of the failure in communication may be blamed on the receiver, but it is your responsibility as sender to determine in advance, to the best of your ability, all potential causes of failure and to tune your transmission for the best reception. . . .

You need to study your audience and then write what you want them to understand in the form that is most likely to appeal to them. . . .

If you do not wish your letters to be read yawningly, write them wide awake. When a good idea strikes you . . . , ride that idea on the dead run; don't wait to ponder, criticize and correct. You can be critical after your imaginative spell subsides.

The search for the exact word should never so **usurp** the writer's attention that the larger movements of thought . . . are made to falter and so lose their fire. The first draft of a piece of writing should be done at white heat. The smoothing and polishing may follow later.

To be dynamic and forceful, we don't need to give the impression of breathlessness. Strong words lose their force if used often. Don't say "the roof is falling in" when you mean that a crack in the ceiling needs patching. If you habitually term a dull party "a disaster," what have you left that is vivid enough to cover your feelings about an earthquake?

From the moment that writers lose their reverence for words as accurate expressions of their thoughts, they become second-rate. Even experienced writers testify to their constant search for the right word . . . .

There is no better way to learn the feeling of words than through reading poetry. The use of synonyms so necessary in poetry gives us a grasp of language and readiness in its use. Exercise your imagination by looking up wide choices of words meaning the same thing, in varying shades of strength and attractiveness. . . .

---

impeccable: flawless

usurp: take over

Our writing creates pictures in the reader's mind. We use metaphors to sharpen and extend the reader's understanding of our ideas by representing . . . images drawn from the world of experiences. . . . Metaphors are not confined to poetic writing; they occur in science and business writing: the flow of electricity, the stream of consciousness, the thinking machine, getting at the root of the problem, falling into error, indulging in mental gymnastics. . . .

If the imagination is to yield any product useful to the writer, it must have received material from the external world. Images do not spring out of a desert.

Writers will train their minds to roam, to seek food, to experience events. They will read widely, observing words at work in a multitude of combinations. . . .

The books in an executive's office should not consist solely of directories, almanacs, and the like. In literature are recorded all the thoughts, feelings, passion, and dreams that have passed through the human mind and these can play their part in the efficiency of the professional writer today. Even on the battlefield, Napoleon had in his tent more than three hundred volumes ranging through science, art, history, poetry, travels, romance, and philosophy.

To do all that has been suggested takes time. It requires preparation, practice, and participation: preparation through reading and study, practice through revising and rewriting, and participation through putting something of yourself into your writing.

Thinking about Your Reading

1. In your own words, explain what it means to write imaginatively in the workplace.

_____

_____

_____

_____

Chapter Six / Writing for the Workplace

2. How do you interpret this statement: "Art in [professional] writing"—that is, imagination in professional writing—"must not be used as an escape from reality" (4)?

_____

_____

_____

_____

3. Look back at the model of a writing process on page 22. What main parts and subparts is the following passage referring to?

_____

> "When a good idea strikes you . . . , ride that idea on the dead run; don't wait to ponder, criticize and correct. You can be critical after your imaginative spell subsides.
>
> "The search for the exact word should never so usurp the writer's attention that the larger movements of thought . . . are made to falter and so lose their fire. The first draft of a piece of writing should be done at white heat. The smoothing and polishing may follow later" (12, 13).

Do you agree or disagree with the author? _____ Why or why not?

_____

_____

_____

_____

4. Explain how the following statement applies to your experience as you have learned more about writing: "To do all that has been suggested takes time. It requires preparation, practice, and participation" (21).

_____

_____

5. Review the reading passage "Imagination Helps Communication," and prepare a checklist of helpful ideas for improving your writing.

_____

_____

_____

_____

_____

WRITING ASSIGNMENT

The Conventions of Professional Writing

Effective professional writing is an art that requires imagination and a craft that calls for the use of certain tools, or writing *conventions*. You might think of these conventions as customs or traditions. Just as families have holiday customs—such as a traditional Thanksgiving meal of turkey, dressing, and pumpkin pie—so do professional and business organizations follow certain customs, or conventions, in their writing practices.

Take, for example, the conventions used in professional correspondence, such as business letters. When you write a letter in *block format* (the most widely used convention for business letters), you send a message to your reader that you have formal, efficient business in mind. Because the block format is associated *conventionally* with business, the person who receives your letter will know not to expect an informal, chatty rundown of recent events in your life.

The following business letter is written in modified block format. At the top of the letter are the sender's address (at the right-hand side unless

```
                                        Louisiana State University
                                        Department of English
                                        One University Place
                                        Shreveport, Louisiana 71115
                                        November 26, 1990

Philip Yam
The Woodcutter's Workshop
21 Maple Street
Camden, Maine 04843

Dear Mr. Yam:

At a recent artisans' fair, I saw a demonstration of your
newest creation: a canvas hammock with an optional frame
attachment. According to your sales representative, the
frame is designed to convert the hammock into a collaps-
ible outdoor rocking chair. Is it possible to order frames
larger than those used in the demonstration?

If you have a brochure or catalog that describes this or
any of your other products, please mail me the informa-
tion.

                                        Sincerely yours,

                                        Patricia T. Bates

                                        Patricia T. Bates
```

letterhead paper—printed with the company's return address—is used) and the date. Just below, to the left, is the "inside address"—the address of the receiver. Directly below the inside address is a greeting (such as "Dear Dr. Jensen" or "Dear Personnel Manager," followed by a colon [:]). The paragraphs making up the body of the letter come next. Beneath the final paragraph is a "complimentary closing" (such as "Sincerely yours," followed by a comma) and the sender's signature. Beneath the written signature, the sender's name is typed. If any item is enclosed with the letter, a line such as "Encl: Résumé" should be placed beneath the signature line, aligned with the left-hand margin.

Notice, in the body of the letter, one major diffference between paragraphs as they appear in block-format business letters and as they appear in the essays you write for your composition class: in block format, the first line of a paragraph is not indented.

In addition to the traditional format shown here, other conventions of professional writing are correct standard grammar, spelling, and punctuation; clear wording; concise sentences and paragraphs; and a courteous tone. You might remember these conventions as the *four C*'s: correctness, clarity, conciseness, and courtesy.

Correctness in professional writing is generally understood to mean the use of standard English, standard punctuation, and accurate spelling, all of which are explained in the Handbook. Correctness also means using accurate facts and details. The importance of correctness is illustrated by the fact that a misspelled word can cost an applicant a job and a misquoted price can cost a company a customer.

Clarity is critical in professional communication. If writing is not clear, readers cannot make sense of it. Here are some rather simple guidelines to follow in order to write more clearly:

1. Say what you mean—no more, no less.
2. Use details your reader will understand and relate to.
3. Ask someone who will give you honest feedback to tell you whether your writing is clear or unclear.

Conciseness means stating your point quickly and directly, without distracting details or unnecessary words. In professional correspondence, brevity is a virtue. Business letters are rarely more than one and a half pages long. (Most are considerably shorter.) And unlike the paragraphs in academic essays, paragraphs in professional correspondence rarely contain more than three or four sentences, if that many.

Other forms of professional writing such as reports and proposals vary widely in length, but the principle of conciseness still applies. For example, an "executive summary" may appear at the beginning of a business document to give readers a concise account of the full content.

But conciseness does not mean simply a bare-bones recital of facts. In order to write concisely, prepare a first draft saying all you want to say. Then revise your draft by getting to the point immediately, combining ideas where you can, and eliminating unimportant or vague words and phrases. Be careful, though, not to eliminate needed content. As I tell my technical-writing students, "Blow it up; then boil it down."

Courtesy in professional writing, especially in business letters, requires the writer to adopt the readers' point of view, keeping the readers' concerns in mind while writing. This is sometimes referred to as a "you" attitude, in contrast to an "I" attitude. Writing from the readers' perspective means writing to satisfy their needs, not just the writer's; using sincere ordinary language that readers will understand instead of technical jargon; and adopting an appropriately personal tone, neither overly familiar and informal nor stiff and overly formal.

To test your writing for courtesy, put yourself in the readers' place and ask, "How would I feel if I were receiving this? Would I feel that my needs and interests had been overlooked? Would I be confused or bored? Would I be offended or put off?" If you have succeeded in maintaining a "you" attitude, chances are good that your writing will capture your readers' imagination, convincing them of the truth of what you are saying—that you are the best candidate for the job, your product is the best, or whatever.

If an emphasis on the conventions of correctness, conciseness, clarity, and courtesy suggests that there is little room in the workplace for imagination, keep in mind that today's complex problems require more imaginative solutions than ever. But in the workplace (as in any writing situation, really), a writer must use imagination within the limits of reader expectations in order to be successful. These expectations, or conventions, help the reader understand and accept a piece of writing. If the writer fails to follow the expected conventions, the reader is less likely to accept the message.

What is more, the writer who follows the conventions has an advantage before even writing the first word, since no time is wasted puzzling over how to begin, where to put certain information, or what to include. At least some of the writing problem is solved before the writer starts to work.

Write It Out: A Job Application Letter and Résumé

First, find a newspaper ad for a job that you would like to have and that you feel qualified to hold (preferably a job that will help prepare you for the career you hope to have someday or perhaps an advanced position where you now work). (If you cannot find such an ad, design your own—but try to be realistic.) Then write a letter of application, to be accompanied by a résumé, which outlines your qualifications for the job. A method for planning, drafting, and revising your letter and résumé is outlined here.

You may want to use your journal for Steps 1 through 4, which will guide you in developing a body of material to draw on as you draft your letter and résumé. Ask your instructor to check your ad before you proceed with Step 1.

1 SET CAREER GOALS. In one or more paragraphs, state your short-range and long-range career goals. Mention goals that are both ambitious and achievable.

> EXAMPLE
> While in college I want to get a part-time job as a peer counselor so I can get some experience and help pay my way through school. After college, I plan to work in some mental health–related field for a couple of years to make enough money to go to grad school. I want to get a doctorate in clinical psychology and specialize in the treatment of drug abuse.

2 ASSESS YOUR STRENGTHS. Make a list of all the jobs (paid or unpaid, part-time or full-time) you have held over the past three to five years, the location, and the period of time you held them.

> EXAMPLE
> Substance abuse counselor trainee assigned to work with adolescents, part-time on weekends, from April 1990 to the present, at the Chemical Dependency Center, a drug treatment facility.

Resident caretaker on weekends from January 1989 to April 1990 at Serenity House, a halfway house for recovering alcoholics.

For each job, list at least three skills or traits that you believe contributed to your success.

EXAMPLE

insight, knowledge, training, experience, cooperativeness, punctuality

Of the skills or traits you have listed, choose two or three that you consider to be your greatest assets. Write a brief paragraph on each, beginning with an identification of the skill or trait. Then follow up by explaining how, when, and where you developed and demonstrated it.

EXAMPLE

experience: I've had a lot of part-time experience working with substance abusers. I've worked weekends as a counselor trainee in a chemical dependency treatment center and as a resident caretaker at a halfway house for recovering alcoholics. At CDC I helped lead an adolescent group of users and was supervised by Dr. Dick Williams. At Serenity House, I took incoming phone calls, planned rec activities, and helped with new residents.

3 WRITE A "NUTSHELL" BIOGRAPHY. In one or more paragraphs, highlight experiences other than those at work that should help you on the job. Be sure to include all activities that have taught you or trained you in some significant way. Don't forget to mention hobbies, groups you've done volunteer work for, school experience, and other relevant activities.

EXAMPLE

I'm majoring in psychology, and I've learned a lot about addiction and mental illness. I have a 3.75 average in the four psychology courses I've taken, and I've attended a good many seminars on chemical dependency. Besides classroom knowledge, I've learned a lot from my volunteer work. I helped put together an annual drug awareness week and a drug abuse hotline. Both are now in their second year on campus.

4. PREPARE TO DRAFT. To clarify your goals before drafting your letter, complete the following exercise in the spaces provided or in your journal.

1. Describe your point of view and your qualifications to write this letter.

   EXAMPLE
   I'm a 25-year-old man who works part-time and goes to college part-time. I want a job that requires skills in counseling drug abusers and pays better than the one I have now. I've researched the requirements of the job and my qualifications; so I'm well prepared to write the letter.

   _____

   _____

   _____

   _____

2. Describe your reader's needs and expectations or point of view. Learn as much as you can about your reader, and record your findings.

   EXAMPLE
   The reader is the director of a campus counseling center and probably has a Ph.D. in clinical psychology and special training in the treatment of drug abuse in adolescents. I don't yet know the director's name but will try to find out before I write the final draft of my letter.

   _____

   _____

   _____

   _____

3. Summarize the main points you want to make.

   EXAMPLE
   I am knowledgeable, experienced, and motivated; my background supports my claims.

   _____

   _____

5 **DRAFT YOUR LETTER.** In Steps 1 through 4, you created a body of material you can now draw on in order to draft your letter. A sample plan follows to help you organize your points. Feel free to modify or adapt the plan to suit your needs. Remember that the purpose of a letter of application and a résumé is to get an interview. (The purpose of the interview is to get the job.) Your letter will highlight the most important features of your résumé.

As you write, remember that writing is an art that requires some imagination, as well as a craft that calls for certain conventions. In this case you will need to be especially attentive to the conventions of correctness, conciseness, clarity, and courtesy. Your imagination can come into play as you put yourself in your reader's place and imagine how you can appeal to the reader's interest. Write with the "you" attitude in mind from beginning to end.

Sample Plan for a Job Application Letter

In the **introduction**, identify the position you are applying for, state how you learned about the job, and explain how the position fits in with your career goals. In a one-sentence summary, cite the chief strengths you would bring to the job.

In the **body**, expand on the strengths identified in the one-sentence summary, giving the highlights from your education, work experience, and other activities as evidence to show that you have the qualifications that you claim. It isn't necessary to provide complete details of your education and employment since they will be outlined in your résumé. The body can consist of one or more paragraphs.

In the **conclusion**, make a summary statement regarding the good match between the job requirements and your skills or traits. Politely request further contact or an interview.

The rough draft that follows was written by student Scott Brown.

Job Application Letter (rough draft)

3130 Sherwood Forest Boulevard
Baton Rouge, LA 70807
January 30, 19--

Campus Counseling Center
Louisiana State University
Baton Rouge, LA 70803

Dear Director,

I want to apply for the position of peer drug-abuse counselor. My long-range career goal is to earn a Ph.D. in clinical psychology and specialize in the treatment of drug addiction.

As a sophomore psychology major at LSU, I have learned a good deal already about addictive disease. I have a 3.75 average in the four psychology courses I have taken thus far: introductory psychology, adolescent psychology, psychology of addiction, and clinical psychology. I have attended numerous seminars dealing with the various aspects of chemical dependency.

I have also had considerable volunteer and part-time experience working with substance abusers.

My résumé, which I have enclosed, will give you additional details about my background. I would appreciate the opportunity for an interview.

Sincerely,

Scott Brown

Scott Brown

Encl.: Résumé

Job Application Letter (final draft)

3130 Sherwood Forest Boulevard
Baton Rouge, LA 70807
January 30, 19--

Dr. Suzanna Jensen, Director
Campus Counseling Center
Louisiana State University
Baton Rouge, LA 70803

Dear Dr. Jensen:

I want to apply for the position of peer drug abuse counselor that you advertised in the November 11 issue of the Daily Reveille. Because of my knowledge, experience, and motivation, I believe I can make a significant contribution to your program. My long-range career goal is to earn a Ph.D. in clinical psychology and specialize in the treatment of drug addiction.

As a sophomore psychology major at LSU, I have learned a good deal already about addictive disease. I have a 3.75 average in the four psychology courses I have taken thus far, and I have attended numerous seminars dealing with the various aspects of chemical dependency.

I have also had considerable volunteer and part-time experience working with substance abusers. As you probably know, I helped to establish our annual drug awareness week and a drug abuse hotline, both of which are now in their second year on campus. I have worked weekends as a counselor trainee in a chemical dependency treatment center and as a resident caretaker at a halfway house for recovering alcoholics.

My résumé, which I have enclosed, will give you additional details about my background. If my qualifications suit your need for a knowledgeable, experienced, and motivated peer drug-abuse counselor, I would appreciate the opportunity for an interview. I can be reached from 1 p.m. to 5 p.m. Monday through Friday at (504) 797-5835. In the evenings I can be reached at (504) 555-8395.

Sincerely,

Scott Brown

Scott Brown

Encl.: Résumé

6 **GET FEEDBACK ON YOUR DRAFT.** After you have drafted your application letter, ask someone else to read it over and comment on it from the perspective of a potential employer.

Scott Brown got the following suggestions from his instructor. What other changes would you have suggested to him?

_____

_____

_____

Sample Feedback

1. Remember to find out the director's name, and address your letter to him or her. Use a colon in place of the comma since this is a business rather than personal letter.
2. In your introduction, convey the "you" attitude by mentioning the specific characteristics you will bring to your work. You might also indicate where or how you heard about the job.
3. There is no need to name your psychology courses here since you will identify them in your résumé.
4. It's good to practice the principle of conciseness, but don't omit the highlights of your experience.
5. Don't forget to convey the "you" attitude in your conclusion. Be sure to indicate when and how you can be contacted.

7 **REVISE YOUR DRAFT.** Evaluate, rework, and refine your letter, using the following questions as a guide:

1. Have I overstated or understated my case? _____

2. Have I appealed to my reader's interest? _____

3. Did I keep my letter on a single page? _____

4. Have I created vivid word pictures that help my reader see my ability? _____

5. Have I presented myself as a knowledgeable, educated, imaginative worker? _____

6. Have I profited from available resources, put something of myself in my writing, and revised and rewritten as needed? _____

7. Overall, have I followed the conventions of professional writing? _____

For Further Thought

Notice the changes Scott Brown made in revising his job application letter. How does he show imagination?

_____

_____

Which conventions of professional writing has he followed? (Before answering this question, you may need to review pages 174–178.)

_____

_____

8 **WRITE YOUR RÉSUMÉ.** Now complete the second half of this assignment by preparing a résumé which outlines your qualifications for the job you are applying for. Use details from the material you wrote earlier and follow the format of the example or another format you might prefer. Your instructor or a career counselor may have other suggestions regarding an effective format. Once you have finished your résumé, reread your letter of application to see if you need to make any further changes so that the letter and résumé complement each other.

Sample Résumé

SCOTT BROWN

Temporary Address:	Permanent Address:
3130 Sherwood Forest Boulevard	249 Kings Highway
Baton Rouge, LA 70807	Shreveport, LA 71104
(504) 555-8395	(318) 555-9384

Immediate Objective

To obtain a position as a peer drug-abuse counselor at the LSU campus counseling center.

Career Objective

To obtain a position as a clinical psychologist and to specialize in the treatment of drug addiction.

Educational Background

Sophomore psychology major
Louisiana State University
Bachelor of Arts expected May 1992
Grade point average in psychology 3.75 (4.0 scale)

Psychology coursework includes 12 hours: introductory psychology, adolescent psychology, addiction pathology, introductory clinical psychology. Other coursework includes 15 hours of continuing-education seminars on chemical dependency.

Related Activities

Established annual drug awareness week on the LSU campus. Instituted a drug abuse hotline on the LSU campus.

Experience

<u>1990-present</u>. Counselor trainee at Chemical Dependency Center. Assisted in leading an adolescent group of drug abusers under the supervision of a psychiatrist.

<u>1989-1990</u>. Resident caretaker at Serenity House, a halfway house for recovering alcoholics. Was responsible for answering phone and planning recreational activities. Assisted with admitting new residents and oriented new residents to house rules.

References

On file in the Career Center at Louisiana State University. Available upon request.

The sample résumé on page 186 was prepared by student Scott Brown. What changes would you have suggested to him?

_____

_____

PERSONAL SUMMARY

1. Review the chapter goals at the beginning of this chapter, and check off each one you have successfully accomplished.

2. Summarize the main lessons you have learned by working through this chapter.

_____

_____

_____

_____

_____

_____

3. Do the following exercise if your instructor has not already asked you to do so: At the beginning of the semester, you wrote a note to yourself that you

sealed in an envelope to be opened later in the semester. In your note, you described what you hoped to accomplish this semester and explained the changes you would have to make in your study and work habits in order to reach your goals.

Now open the envelope and read your note. Put a check by the goals you have already reached and the changes in your work and study habits you have made in order to achieve those goals.

In an essay one to two pages long, outline the additional changes you need to make in order to reach the goals you have not yet achieved, and identify what you need to learn more about in order to reach your goals. Using the index of this text, locate the information you need and then, as the conclusion of your essay, summarize that information. (If your instructor gives you a final examination, this exercise will be a good review.)

ADDITIONAL WRITING

Begin to compile a writing portfolio by selecting one or two of the best papers you have written this semester, along with your letter of application and your résumé, and revise each piece with your instructor's or a lab tutor's help. Refer to the revising checklists in Chapters Four, Five, and Six, as appropriate. After completing your revisions, put them in a binder.

Over the next four years of college, you may want to continue to add to your writing portfolio, eliminating the weakest papers and keeping the strongest ones.

ADDITIONAL READING

Bolles, Richard N. *What Color Is Your Parachute?* Berkeley: Ten Speed Press, 1985. A job hunter's manual that stresses the importance of researching one's skills and attributes, as well as characteristics of prospective employers, in order to succeed in the job market.

Munschauer, John L. *Jobs for English Majors and Other Smart People*. Princeton: Peterson's Guides, 1986. Explores job-hunting strategies for those with liberal education backgrounds who are seeking careers in traditional and nontraditional markets.

Part Three

HANDBOOK

When you think about the study of English, what comes to mind first? Perhaps the study of grammar. It seems that people generally feel one of two ways about studying grammar. They either hate it or love it. Whichever group you find yourself in at this point, you may share the belief with many other students that there is no real rhyme or reason for the so-called rules, or principles, of English grammar.

One of the purposes of this Handbook is to show you that these principles fit into some general patterns. By understanding these patterns, you will begin to see how a knowledge of grammar can help you achieve your purposes as you write.

Finally, let me add one more note of encouragement. Believe it or not, you are a grammar expert already. With some thought, you can create any number of grammatical sentences that you have never seen or heard before. You can accomplish this extraordinary mental feat because you know the rules of English grammar. That is, you know the main rules for putting English words together to make sense, even though you may not be able to explain those rules to someone else.

To prove this to yourself, put a checkmark next to the groups of words that you think are grammatically correct.

1. Grammar English hard explain to is.
2. English grammar is hard to explain.
3. English grammar is not hard to use.
4. Use English hard not to grammar is.

You also generally know whether groups of words are complete sentences or not. Again prove this to yourself by checking off the groups of words that seem to you to be complete.

1. Abraham Lincoln, the sixteenth president of the United States.
2. George Washington, our first president, died in 1799.
3. Why do we celebrate July 4?
4. The land of the free, the home of the brave.

If you checked 2 and 3 in each list, you have shown how much you know. With a little more understanding of how and why these rules work as they do, you will be prepared to write more effectively as you progress through college and into the professional world.

SENTENCE STRUCTURE

Think for a minute about the difference between a grocery list and a business letter. How do the structures of the two differ? Among other things, the first is merely a list of words, whereas the second uses words to make up sentences and probably paragraphs as well. We can no doubt agree that the business letter is a form of "writing," whereas the shopping list is not. Further, we can probably agree that the letter would be more meaningful to a variety of readers than the list would.

Sentences are the basic grammatical units of language that allow us to put words together in *meaningful* ways. Therefore, an understanding of how words fit together to make sentences is basic to an understanding of grammar.

Subjects and Predicates

A complete sentence has at least two grammatical parts. Consider an earlier example.

English grammar is hard to explain.

The two parts are the subject and the predicate. The *subject* is the topic of the sentence, or what that sentence is about; the *predicate* tells something about that topic, or makes a comment about it. These two parts, when put together, can express a complete thought and can be shown in a branching diagram.

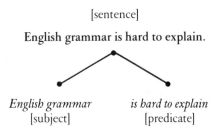

English grammar is what the sentence is about. *Is hard to explain* tells something about English grammar.

Consider a second sentence, written in the form of a question (see top of next page).

Sentence Structure

[sentence]
Will the Rolling Stones be in Chicago next week?

the Rolling Stones   Will be in Chicago next week
[subject]   [predicate]

The Rolling Stones is what the sentence is about. *Will be in Chicago next week* asks for information about the Rolling Stones. Later we will see how these main sentence parts, especially the predicate, can be subdivided into other branching patterns.

Identifying Subjects and Predicates

Break the following sentences down into their main parts by writing out the subjects and predicates in the appropriate spaces.

1. Tomeka Raphael hopes to join Moa Afrika.

   _____   _____
   [subject]   [predicate]

2. Does Annie Yew enjoy strenuous running?

   _____   _____
   [subject]   [predicate]

3. Quinton Hawks plays the piano.

   _____   _____
   [subject]   [predicate]

4. Does Braden Kelly want to be a doctor?

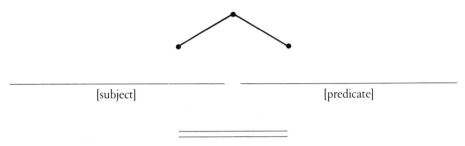

[subject] [predicate]

Sentence Fragments

The clarity of your writing depends partly on your ability to write complete sentences. If either the subject or the predicate is missing, or if your thought is incomplete, your readers may misunderstand you, because you've written a **sentence fragment**—part of a sentence—rather than a complete sentence.

When talking, we can often communicate successfully with sentence fragments, in part because our listeners are with us. If they get confused because part of a sentence is missing, we can generally clear up that confusion. However, when people read what we have written, they are not normally with us; so we have no opportunity to clarify incomplete thoughts or even know if our writing has confused our readers.

Consider the two-part sentence pattern once more. Which part, subject or predicate, is missing in the following group of words?

The land of the free

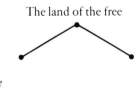

The land of the free

To test your writing in order to determine whether or not it consists of complete sentences, apply the following tests.

❑ *Is the subject missing?*

Then left the package on the steps. (*Who* left the package?)

Correct by adding a subject: Then *he* left a package on the steps.

Sentence Structure

❏ *Is part or all of the predicate missing?*

A girl leaving the building. (*Leaving* can't be a complete predicate without a helper like *was* or *is*. To learn more about the use of helping verbs with verbs ending in *-ing*, see pages 221–222.)

Correct by adding a helping verb: A girl *was* leaving the building.

❏ *Are both the subject and the predicate missing?*

Late at night in the fall on the beach. (*Who* did *what?*)

Correct by adding a subject and predicate: *He walked* late at night in the fall on the beach.

❏ *Is a complete thought expressed?*

After I left the room. (*What* happened after I left the room?)

Correct by completing the thought: After I left the room, *the phone rang*.

Correcting Sentence Fragments

Correct each fragment by adding either a subject or a predicate or both a subject and predicate, or correct it by completing the thought.

1. Bloomed everywhere.

   _____

   _____

2. Spring coming quickly this year.

   _____

   _____

3. In the park.

   _____

   _____

4. When Oscar moved to Austin.

_____

_____

When the fragment and the sentence next to it make a complete thought, put them together.

FRAGMENT: *Leaving the building.* She seemed to be in a hurry.
CORRECTION: Leaving the building, she seemed to be in a hurry.

FRAGMENT: He knocked. *And then left the package on the steps.*
CORRECTION: He knocked and then left the package on the steps.

Joining Fragments and Sentences

Correct each fragment by joining it to the sentence next to it.

1. Having lived in Texas all his life. Oscar would never choose to live anywhere else.

_____

_____

2. Oscar Rodriguez lived in San Antonio. And then moved to Austin.

_____

_____

Check Yourself

Correct the following fragments by revising them in any of the ways you have learned.

Sentence Structure

1. Sparked a fire.

2. Firefighters extinguishing the blaze.

3. In Greenwich Village.

4. When the fire chief arrived.

5. Who was wearing a helmet and a yellow plastic overcoat.

6. Seeing bright lights and hearing a loud siren. The crowd trapped in the burning restaurant knew that help was on the way.

7. Irving Benoit was the head waiter. Who led the diners through the kitchen to the back exit.

_____

_____

Editing Practice

Underline the sentence fragments in the student-written paragraphs that follow. Then rewrite the paragraphs on a separate sheet of paper, correcting the fragments in the ways you consider to be most effective or appropriate. You may add extra words if you think they are needed. Be sure to make appropriate changes in punctuation and capitalization, and spell all words correctly. (For help with punctuation, capitalization, and spelling, see pages 249–277.)

When my mother was a child. Her family would take leisurely Sunday afternoon rides in the country. One of their favorite places Pawnee Bill's Trading Post in Pawnee, Oklahoma. Mother can vividly remember the bare wood building with a wagon wheel or two lying around outside the Trading Post. Inside there was the usual assortment of goods. Including tourists' trinkets, hand-sewn moccasins, corn-cob pipes, and postcards. The main attraction, though, was Pawnee Bill. Who had once been an Indian scout.

Pawnee Bill must have been about eighty years old when my mother first met him. A small man in stature, he was only about five feet five inches tall. Had shoulder-length hair and a snow-white beard. He wore the traditional Indian scout attire. Consisting of a fringed buckskin shirt and pants with leather boots and a big hat. Other than selling an arrowhead or two, sitting around spinning yarns was about all Pawnee Bill did in those days. My mother can still remember him talking of Buffalo Bill Cody—known as Wild Bill—who was a friend of his. It is ironic that Pawnee Bill survived battles with the Indians but was killed some years later in an automobile accident. I think my mother is lucky to have seen a frontiersman from out of the past.

For Further Practice

Select a piece of writing you did earlier in the semester, and proofread it to be sure that it has no fragments. If you find any errors, review the material in this section and correct the errors.

Run-ons and Comma Splices

Put in a nutshell, the grammatical problem of sentence fragments is: What are the essential parts of a sentence? Or asked another way, when is a group of words a sentence fragment instead of a complete sentence?

Now let's look at a related problem: How do we know where one sentence stops and another sentence begins? Or asked another way, when is a group of words more than one sentence, which needs to be broken into two or more sentences in order to be grammatically correct? The two problems, or errors, we consider here are the *run-on* and the *comma splice*.

The *run-on* is simply two sentences incorrectly run together as one, with no punctuation between the two—that is, two complete sentences placed side by side without punctuation in between. The *comma splice* is two sentences run together with only a comma in between.

To understand these two types of errors, let's reconsider how words are normally put together in an extended piece of writing—say, a letter. We've already noted that words are used to make up sentences, and sentences, in turn, are put together to form paragraphs. Take, for example, the following paragraph written by a teacher who is hoping to get his first novel published.

> I have enclosed my novel on computer diskettes. I sent it to an agent in New York last week. He called me today to say that he likes it and wants more copies so that he can start submitting it to potential publishers. That's a step farther than I've gotten before. Cross your fingers. If

trying to read the novel on your computer is a pain, let me know and I'll send you a printed copy.

How many sentences does this paragraph contain? If we were to put each *sentence* (a group of related words, containing a subject and predicate and expressing a complete thought) into a series of branching diagrams, they would form a pattern something like that shown in the accompanying diagram. If the page were wide enough, we could expand the diagram until all six of the sentences were represented and connected as a paragraph in this way.

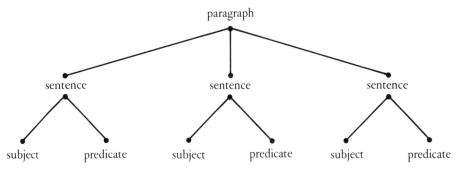

With this visual representation and our definition of a sentence in mind, let's go back and answer the problem question: How do we know when to stop one sentence and start another? The answer is simple: when each subject and predicate group that makes complete sense stops and another such group starts.

Now let's take a closer look at why run-on errors make writing hard to read. Again, a run-on sentence error is two sentences run together as one with no punctuation between the two. Our sample paragraph contains no run-on errors, but suppose the first two sentences had been written this way:

I have enclosed my novel on computer diskettes I sent it to an agent in New York last week.

The subject of the first complete thought is *I*. The predicate is *have enclosed my novel on computer diskettes*. The subject of the second complete thought is *I*. The predicate is *sent it to an agent in New York last week*.

When the two complete thoughts are run together with no punctuation between them, they are more difficult to read and comprehend.

Sentence Structure

The simplest way to correct a run-on error is to use an end mark such as a period after each complete thought. Of course, you will capitalize the first word after the period.

RUN-ON: **The deliveryman knocked on the door he left the packages on the steps.**

CORRECTION: **The deliveryman knocked on the door. He left the packages on the steps.**

Correcting the Run-on with a Period

By using a period and by capitalizing appropriately, separate each of the following groups of words into two complete sentences.

1. Winter in Detroit can be depressing with its dreary days spring brings needed relief.

_____

_____

2. Winter sports are fun ice skating is my favorite.

_____

_____

When the two parts of a run-on are short and closely related, as in the deliveryman example, the two parts may be separated by a semicolon (;). You may also want to add another transitional word or phrase that shows the logical relationship between the two thoughts. Called *logical connectives*, these are words and phrases like *however, nevertheless, therefore, then, in addition*, and *in fact*. (For more information on coordinating ideas, see the section beginning on page 208.)

RUN-ON: **The deliveryman knocked on the door he left the packages on the steps.**

CORRECTION: **The deliveryman knocked on the door; then he left the packages on the steps.**

Correcting the Run-on with a Semicolon

Use a semicolon to separate the following groups of words into complete, correctly punctuated sentences.

1. In the spring the ice and snow eventually melt then the sun warms the earth.

_____

_____

2. Summer is my favorite time of the year I like autumn too.

_____

_____

The comma can be used to separate two sentences if a comma and a coordinating conjunction (such as *and*, *but*, *or*, *nor*, or *for*) are used.

RUN-ON: **The deliveryman knocked on the door he left the packages on the steps.**

CORRECTION: **The deliveryman knocked on the door, and then he left the packages on the steps.**

Note: Do not use the comma by itself to separate two complete sentences. A comma alone will not correct the run-on problem. It will simply create another error, the comma splice, to be discussed in more detail shortly.

Sentence Structure

Correcting the Run-on with a Comma and a Coordinating Conjunction

Use a comma and a coordinating conjunction (*and, but, or, nor, for*) to correct these run-on errors.

1. After being rescued, the small boy ate several cookies he drank two glasses of milk.

   _____

   _____

2. Noveen loves to read she doesn't like the classics that her instructor recommends.

   _____

   _____

You can also fix a run-on sentence by adding a subordinator (such as *while, after, since, because, who,* or *which*). (For more information on subordinating ideas, see the section beginning on page 209.)

> RUN-ON: **The deliveryman knocked on the door he left the packages on the steps.**
> CORRECTION: **After the deliveryman knocked on the door, he left the packages on the steps.**

Correcting the Run-on with a Subordinator

Use a subordinator (such as *while, after, because, when, since, who,* or *which*) to correct these run-on errors. Be careful not to create a fragment.

1. She lived with my family she worked at the train station nearby.

   _____

   _____

2. The student makes good grades she studies.

   _____

   _____

The *comma splice* is a sentence error similar to the run-on. In this case, two sentences are run together with only a comma to separate them.

> COMMA SPLICE: **The mother and daughter resemble each other, they have similar hairstyles.**

The subject of the first complete thought is *the mother and daughter*. The predicate is *resemble each other*. The subject of the second complete thought is *they*. The predicate is *have similar hairstyles*. Finally, notice that only a comma separates the two complete thoughts.

As with the run-on error, one way to correct a comma splice error is to use an end mark such as a period after each complete thought. Of course, you will capitalize the first word after the period.

> COMMA SPLICE: **The mother and daughter resemble each other, they have similar hairstyles.**
> CORRECTION: **The mother and daughter resemble each other. They have similar hairstyles.**

Correcting the Comma Splice with a Period

Substitute the period for the comma to correct these comma splices.

Sentence Structure

1. Daniel Martinez makes great pralines, for many years he has enjoyed making candy.

2. Al Vekovius will be the guest speaker, he is entertaining and smart.

When the two parts of a comma splice are short and the thoughts are closely related, as in the mother-and-daughter example, the two parts may be separated by a semicolon (;). You may also want to add a logical connective to show the relationship between the two thoughts.

Of course, when using a semicolon, you won't capitalize the first word that follows it.

COMMA SPLICE: The mother and daughter resemble each other, they have similar hairstyles.
CORRECTION: The mother and daughter resemble each other; in addition, they have similar hairstyles.

Correcting the Comma Splice with a Semicolon and a Logical Connective

Use a semicolon or a semicolon and a logical connective like *therefore, however, in addition,* or *then* to correct the following comma splice errors.

1. The tailor sews for many customers, he makes all the clothes his children wear.

_____

_____

2. Main Street is a short street, it is the most important street in the village.

_____

_____

The comma can be used to separate two sentences as long as a coordinating conjunction (such as *and, but, or, for,* or *nor*) is used.

> COMMA SPLICE: **The mother and daughter resemble each other, they have similar hairstyles.**
> CORRECTION: **The mother and daughter resemble each other, and they have similar hairstyles.**

Correcting the Comma Splice with a Comma and a Coordinating Conjunction

Use a comma and a coordinating conjunction (such as *and, but, or, for,* or *nor*) to correct these comma splices.

1. We came to the party with high hopes, we didn't stay long.

_____

_____

2. The potato chips were mostly stale, the guests were mostly jerks.

___

You can also fix a comma splice by adding a subordinator (such as *while, after, since, because, who,* or *which*).

COMMA SPLICE: **The mother and daughter resemble each other, they have similar hairstyles.**

CORRECTIONS: **The mother and daughter who resemble each other have similar hairstyles.**
The mother and daughter resemble each other because they have similar hairstyles.

Correcting the Comma Splice with a Subordinator

Use a subordinator (such as *while, when, if, because, who,* or *which*) to correct these comma splices.

1. Branwell eats cereal for breakfast, he eats a big lunch.

___

2. Sheranda finished the test early, she was well prepared.

___

COORDINATION AND SUBORDINATION

Coordination

When two main ideas appear in a sentence, the best way to showcase both of them equally is to tie them together by coordinating them in a compound sentence. You may coordinate the two ideas with a **coordinating conjunction**, a **logical connective** and a **semicolon**, or just a **semicolon**.

Coordinating Conjunctions and Their Meanings

And means addition (a similar idea, what you would expect to follow).

Julio studied his notes, *and* he made an A.

But and *yet*, when they indicate contrast (the reverse of what you would expect to follow).

Julio studied his notes, *but* he made an F.
Julio studied his notes, *yet* he made an F.

For when it indicates cause (gives a reason).

Julio made an A, *for* he had studied his notes.

Or means choice (another possibility).

Julio must study his notes, *or* he will make an F.

Nor means additional negative (neither one is possible).

Julio didn't study his notes, *nor* did he pass the test.

So when it means "therefore" (one event causes another event to happen).

Julio studied his notes, *so* he should pass the test.

Logical Connectives and Their Meanings

Logical connectives show logical relationships between ideas. In order to use them effectively, it is helpful to learn what they each mean.

Certain logical connectives mean "in addition to": *also, besides, moreover, furthermore, afterward, then.*

Julio always studies for a test; *moreover,* **he always makes an A.**

Certain logical connectives indicate contrast: *however, nevertheless, still.*

Julio always intends to study for his tests; *however,* **he rarely does.**

About the only logical connective indicating an alternative is *otherwise.*

Julio must study for his tests; *otherwise,* **he will make an F.**

Several words indicate cause or result: *accordingly, consequently, hence, therefore, thus.*

Julio studied for his test; *consequently,* **he made an A.**

Note that a semicolon is used before a logical connective that joins two main clauses, because the logical connective is not grammatically strong enough to join the clauses with just a comma. A comma normally follows the logical connective.

The Semicolon

Match and join two short, closely related main clauses with just a semicolon.

Julio studies; he makes A's.

Subordination

When two main ideas appear in the same sentence, but one is of secondary or minor importance compared to the other, the way to show which idea is most important is to *subordinate* the less important idea in a dependent clause with a subordinate conjunction.

Subordinate Conjunctions and Their Meanings

Some subordinate conjunctions give reasons or tell why: *as, since, because, in order that, so that, as long as.*

Because Julio studied for his test, he made an *A.*

Some subordinate conjunctions tell time, or when: *after, as soon as, before, since, when, whenever, while, until, as, once.*

When Julio studies for a test, he makes an *A.*
Julio makes *A*'s *when* he studies.

Some subordinate conjunctions tell place (where) or manner (how): *wherever, where, how, as if, as though.*

Julio looks *as if* he is studying.

Some subordinate conjunctions tell condition: *although, if, though, unless, provided, once.*

If Julio studies, he will be satisfied with the results.

Notice punctuation. The introductory subordinate clause is usually followed by a comma. A comma usually does not precede the subordinate clause coming at the end of a sentence.

The relative pronouns that introduce subordinate clauses are *who, whom, whose, which,* and *that.* They are called *relative* because they relate or join a subordinate clause to a main clause.

Julio, *who* studies hard, always makes good grades.

Notice the punctuation. Use a comma before and after subordinate clauses that cut into the middle of sentences if they give additional information about a word already limited, or restricted, as the word *Julio* is in the sample sentence. If the subordinate clause restricts the word modified in the main clause, no commas are used.

All students *who* study hard deserve good grades.

The word *who* may introduce restrictive or nonrestrictive clauses. *Which* usually introduces nonrestrictive clauses. *That* always introduces restrictive clauses.

Coordinating and Subordinating

Combine the following pairs of clauses into a single sentence by adding a coordinating conjunction, a logical connective, or a subordinate conjunction. You may want to reverse the order of the pairs. (In many cases, there is more than one possible solution. Try experimenting with different answers, and note how different coordinators and subordinators give the final sentence different meanings, or produce a sentence that makes little sense. Remember to use capitalization and punctuation correctly.)

1. He was a left-handed quarterback.
   His skill amazed the coach.

   _____

   _____

2. Elvis was loved by millions.
   He couldn't handle the pressure of such fame.

   _____

   _____

3. Buy a deluxe tofu-and-bean-sprout all-natural health salad.
   You will receive a free stick of beef jerky.

   _____

   _____

4. I was strolling through the park.
   I saw three squirrels playing keep-away with a walnut.

   _____

   _____

5. I jumped from the airplane.
   I realized I had forgotten my parachute.

   _____

   _____

6. I was concerned with making sure I had all my camera equipment.
   I just forgot all about that darn parachute.

   _____

   _____

Check Yourself

Correct the following run-on sentences and comma splices by revising them in any of the ways you have learned.

1. The Superdome is located in New Orleans athletic events are held there.

   _____

   _____

Coordination and Subordination 213

2. The New Orleans Saints football team plays its home games in the Superdome the team attracts large crowds.

3. New Orleans has many top restaurants Antoine's is one of the most famous.

4. While attending Mardi Gras festivities college students camped out near the Mississippi River they saw ships from all over the world.

5. They visited the French Market they ate doughnuts called *beignets*.

6. Starving artists need money they draw portraits of the tourists.

7. Visitors can buy fried alligator on a stick and turtle soup, for dessert they can try pralines or cherries jubilee.

_____

_____

8. St. Louis Cathedral in Jackson Square is still a popular attraction, many of its historical treasures were destroyed in a recent fire.

_____

_____

9. My brother hates large crowds, he refuses to visit the city on New Year's Eve.

_____

_____

10. He watches celebrations, they are shown on TV.

_____

_____

Editing Practice

Underline the run-on and comma splice errors in the student-written paragraph that follows. Then rewrite the paragraph on a separate sheet of paper, correcting the run-ons and the comma splices in the ways you consider to be most effective or appropriate. Be sure to make the needed changes in punctuation and capitalization, and spell all words correctly.

Coordination and Subordination

1. Home remedies are an important part of our American culture, the remedies used in the early 1900s were often prepared from items found around the home. There were home remedies for every problem from the common cold to a bee sting. Garlic was frequently used for instance, if someone had a cold, it was sometimes rubbed on a person's chest. Garlic was also used to keep high blood pressure down to a reasonable level. For an earache or a toothache, rags were heated and then placed on the patient's ear or cheek. Whiskey was frequently given to babies suffering with colic, sometimes whiskey was placed in hot tea to treat a sore throat. Bee stings were relieved with a wad of chewing tobacco placed on the sting. Home remedies are an interesting part of our American heritage in some ways they may have even influenced modern medicine.

Repeat all the directions for the previous exercise in order to correct any run-ons, comma splices, or fragments you find in the student-written paragraph that follows.

2. In just a little over a year I have developed an ability. Which I am immensely proud of. I have taught myself to play a musical instrument from an instruction booklet, my obsession with this new form of self-expression has found me practicing endlessly. Locking myself in my room for countless hours at a time. Deep into the night plunking away attempting to read music. I look back at my humble beginnings I recall my fingers bleeding. My brain straining to remember where to put my fingers. At times I felt ridiculously feeble-minded, I refused to give up. Perhaps the reason that I have achieved a certain amount of success. But practice became excruciatingly boring at times. Not the actual playing, just the attempt to learn how. It took me months to simply search and peck out my first tunes, I slowly memorized them by sheer repetition. After I had memorized my first tune, I played it over and over until my hands ached and my fingertips cried, "No more!" But I sounded so good to myself creating music that if I had heard the song a thousand times, I would still have enjoyed it.

For Further Practice

Select a piece of writing you did earlier in the semester, and proofread it to be sure that you have no fragments, run-ons, or comma splices. If you find any errors, try to identify the problem by looking back at the material in this section. Then correct your errors.

VERB FORMS

We have established that the sentence has two basic parts, the *subject* and the *predicate* (or complete predicate):

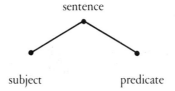

The Rolling Stones will be in Chicago next week.

[The Rolling Stones]   [will be in Chicago next week.]

In some sentences the complete predicate consists of one or two words: He *runs*, I *will sing*. But often the predicate consists of multiple parts: the verb (or simple predicate) and its *modifiers* (words that complete or add meaning to the verb).

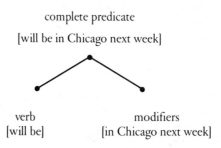

Similarly, the verb can often be broken into two parts: the helping verb and the main verb.

Verb Forms

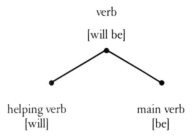

As the heart of a sentence, the verb provides vital information about the subject, or topic, being written about. The verb is also a key indicator of the particular dialect a writer or speaker is using. Since academic and professional settings normally require the effective use of the dialect known as standard English, it is especially useful to master standard verb forms. Altogether there are five standard verb forms, each of which serves a different function. Different forms are used to show present, past, and future time. Also, different forms are used depending on whether the subject is singular (*boy*) or plural (*boys*).

The five standard verb forms are the base form, the *s* form, the *ed* form, the *en* form, and the *ing* form.

Base Form

The base form of a verb, as its name suggests, is the simplest form.

walk   learn   go   eat   think   do

When used alone without a helping verb, the base form expresses the present time. When used with the helping verb *will*, it expresses future time. The base form is used with the personal pronouns *I, you, we,* and *they*; with plural nouns, such as *boys*; and with plural combinations, such as *he and I*.

Present Time

I walk.
You walk.
We walk.
They walk.
The boys walk.
He and I walk.

Future Time

I will walk.
You will walk.
We will walk.
They will walk.
The boys will walk.
He and I will walk.

Recognizing Base Forms

Fill in each blank with the base form of the verb in parenthesis.

1. (to visit)   I _____ my sister each week.

2. (to take)   I will _____ a trip with her soon.

S Form

As its name indicates, the *s* form ends in *s*.

walks   learns   goes   eats   thinks   does

The *s* form expresses present time. It is used with the pronouns *he*, *she*, and *it* and with singular nouns.

He walks.
She walks.
It walks.
The boy walks.

Using the S Form

Fill in each blank with the *s* form of the verb shown in parenthesis.

1. (to call)   My brother _____ home once a month.

2. (to talk)   He _____ to my parents for at least an hour.

Ed Form

As its name suggests, the *ed* form of verbs generally ends in *ed*.

walked   learned

The *ed* form indicates past time when there is no helping verb (such as *has* or *have*). It is used with all pronouns and nouns, whether singular or plural.

> I walked.
> She walked.
> The boy walked.
> The boys walked.

Exceptions: Some verbs, such as *ate, went, thought*, and *did*, are referred to as irregular because their past form does not end in *ed*. These forms are used with all pronouns and nouns to show past time when there is no helping verb. And for this reason, they are still known as *ed* forms, even though they do not actually end in *ed*. (For more information on irregular verbs, see page 223.)

> I ate.
> She ate.
> The boy ate.
> The boys ate.

Using *Ed* Forms

Fill in each blank with the *ed* form of the verb shown in parenthesis.

1. (to stroll)   Yesterday the elderly couple _____ through Central Park.

2. (to take)   Last week they _____ a carriage ride there.

En Form

The *en* form may or may not end in *en*, according to whether it is regular or irregular. The name of the form comes from the way some irregular verbs, such as *take*, create one of their forms (*taken*).

> walked   learned   eaten   gone   thought   done

The *en* form is always used with a helping verb. The tense or time of the verb depends on the tense or the time of the helping verb. *Has*, for example, is used to help express action completed at the present time when the subject is *he*, *she*, *it*, or a singular noun:

> He has walked.   He has eaten
> She has walked.   She has eaten.
> It has walked.   It has eaten.
> The boy has walked.   The boy has eaten.

The past form of a helping verb is used with the *en* form to help express action completed at a definite time in the past and is used with all pronouns and nouns. Here are some examples.

> By Saturday she had walked ten miles.
> By Saturday we had walked ten miles.
> By Saturday the boys had walked ten miles.

> By dinnertime she had eaten the whole cake.
> By dinnertime we had eaten the whole cake.
> By dinnertime the boys had eaten the whole cake.

To help express action completed at a definite time in the future, the helper *will* or *shall*, along with a present helping verb, such as *have*, is used with all nouns and pronouns. Consider these examples.

> By Saturday she will have walked ten miles.
> By Saturday you will have walked ten miles.
> By Saturday the boys will have walked ten miles.

Note: For all regular verbs, the *ed* form and the *en* form are identical: I *walked*. I *have walked*. For some irregular verbs, the *ed* form and the *en* form are identical: I *thought*. I *have thought*.

Using *En* Forms

Fill in each blank with the *en* form of the verb shown in parenthesis.

1. (to give)   The crowd has _____ the pitcher a standing ovation.

2. (to write) The owner of the baseball team has _____ a letter of congratulations to the manager.

3. (to see)   Have you _____ the St. Louis Cardinals play ball this season?

4. (to watch) I have _____ the relief pitcher warm up.

Ing Form

The *ing* form always ends in *ing*.

walking   earning   going   eating   thinking   doing

To be a complete verb, the *ing* form of a verb must be accompanied by some form of the helping verb *be*. (*Am*, *is*, and *are* indicate present time; *was* and *were* indicate past time.)

Present Time

With the pronoun *I*, *am* is used. With the pronouns *he*, *she*, and *it* and all singular nouns, *is* is used. With the pronouns *you*, *we*, and *they*, all plural nouns, and all plural combinations, *are* is used.

EXAMPLES:
I am walking.   You are walking.
He is walking.   They are walking.
The boy is walking.   The boys are walking.
We are walking.   He and I are walking.

Past Time

With the pronouns *I*, *he*, *she*, and *it* and all singular nouns, *was* is used. With the pronouns *you*, *we*, and *they*, plural nouns, and plural combinations, *were* is used.

EXAMPLES:

I was walking.   You were walking.
He was walking.   They were walking.
The boy was walking.   The boys were walking.
We were walking.   He and I were walking.

Using the *Ing* Form

Fill in each blank with the *ing* form of the verb shown in parenthesis.

1. (to work)   When you are _____ in your garden, wear a hat and a long-sleeved shirt.

2. (to study)   Paul is _____ for his finals, which start on Monday.

3. (to lick)   The children were _____ their ice cream cones because the ice cream was melting quickly.

4. (to sleep)   I was _____ when the phone rang.

Regular and Irregular Verbs

We have already used these terms, but let's define and clarify them further.

Regular verbs are classified by the way they create their basic forms. If they add *ed* or *d* to the base to create the *ed* form and the *en* form, they are called regular verbs. The same word is used for the *ed* form and the *en* form. As mentioned earlier, the label "*ed* form" is taken from this regular formation of verb parts.

Walked (*ed* form)
Has walked (*en* form)

Most of the verbs in our language are regular, so once you learn how to use these forms, you will be able to handle most verbs without any difficulty. Here are some examples:

Regular Verbs

Base	S Form	Ed Form	En Form	Ing Form
ask	asks	asked	asked	asking
dance	dances	danced	danced	dancing
help	helps	helped	helped	helping
march	marches	marched	marched	marching
move	moves	moved	moved	moving
use	uses	used*	used	using

Recognizing Regular Verb Forms

Indicate whether the verbs in italics are in the *ed* form or the *en* form. Remember that the *ed* form does not use a helper, but the *en* form does.

1. We noticed that Jeffrey *marched* to the tune of a different drummer. _____

2. He *has* always *marched* in his own special way. _____

3. Althea *has danced* since she was five years old. _____

4. Once she *danced* with a national ballet company. _____

Irregular verbs are classified by the irregular way in which they create the *ed* and *en* forms. They do not follow a pattern. Two or more forms for a verb may be identical; take, for example, the *ed* form *set* and the *en* form *set* for the base form *set*. Or a vowel may change, as with the *ed* form *came* and the *en* form *come* for the base form *come*. Or vowels may change and letters may be added, as with the *ed* form *took* and the *en* form *taken* for the base form *take*.

As mentioned earlier, the label of the *en* form comes from the way such words as *take* create one of their forms (*taken*).

*Note the multiple meanings of this word:
  I *used* five sheets of paper.
  I *used* to take an afternoon nap.

The irregular verbs in our language are the ones that present the most difficulty in standard English. If you can master the verbs in the following list, you will be on your way to mastering the standard English verb system, an accomplishment that may help you academically as well as professionally.

Irregular Verbs

Base	*S* Form	*Ed* Form	*En* Form	*Ing* Form
be	is	was	been	being
begin	begins	began	begun	beginning
break	breaks	broke	broken	breaking
bring	brings	brought	brought	bringing
burst	bursts	burst	burst	bursting
choose	chooses	chose	chosen	choosing
come	comes	came	come	coming
do	does	did	done	doing
drink	drinks	drank	drunk	drinking
eat	eats	ate	eaten	eating
fly	flies	flew	flown	flying
freeze	freezes	froze	frozen	freezing
give	gives	gave	given	giving
know	knows	knew	known	knowing
see	sees	saw	seen	seeing
sing	sings	sang	sung	singing
swim	swims	swam	swum	swimming
take	takes	took	taken	taking
wake	wakes	waked (woke)	waked (woke)	waking
write	writes	wrote	written	writing

Recognizing Irregular Verb Forms

Indicate whether the verbs in italics are in the *ed* form or the *en* form. Remember that the *ed* form does not use a helper, but the *en* form does.

1. Last Sunday I *drove* to my mother's house in my new Mustang.

2. I *have* always *driven* a Ford. _____

3. My neighbor *wrote* a letter to the editor of the *Times*. _____

4. She *has written* on numerous occasions. _____

You may not always be able to tell by sound whether a verb is in standard form or not. If you use and hear nonstandard forms often, they may sound standard to you. To learn the standard forms, practice saying these sentences aloud:

> I *have drunk* eight glasses of water today.
> The children *have begun* their work.
> Both the boys and the girls *have swum* across the pool.
> All the balloons *burst* before the party was over.
> He *walked* to the bus with me last week.
> Buvani *used* to ride the bus.
> She *uses* her own car now.
> He *remembers* to help me in many ways.
> Mary *remembered* my birthday.
> The students *guessed* my age.

The more you practice using standard forms of verbs as you write, the more natural and "correct" they will sound.

In addition to the verbs already listed, one final small group causes trouble in standard English. You will recognize the list as one you no doubt have studied before but may need some additional practice with.

Troublesome Irregular Verbs

Base Form	S Form	Ed Form	En Form	Ing Form
lie	lies	lay	lain	lying
lay	lays	laid	laid	laying
rise	rises	rose	risen	rising
raise	raises	raised	raised	raising
sit	sits	sat	sat	sitting
set	sets	set	set	setting

These verbs are troublesome not only because some of them are irregular but also because the similarity of *lie* and *lay*, *rise* and *raise*, and *sit* and *set* causes them to be easily confused.

The forms of *lie*, *sit*, and *rise* are used when there are no "receivers" of the action; in other words, you don't "lie *something* down" or "sit *something* down." (Nothing receives the action.)

> I *lie* down every day.
> He *lies* near the pool after lunch.
> Yesterday I *lay* on the bed for two hours.
> I have *lain* down every day this week.
> I am *lying* down now.

> I *sit* here often.
> He *sits* here with me.
> I *sat* here yesterday.
> I *have sat* here every day this week.
> I *am sitting* down now.

> To get to school on time, I *rise* at six o'clock in the morning.
> The dough *rises* twice before it is baked.
> To go running, I *rose* at daybreak.
> I *have risen* early every day this week.
> I *am rising* earlier and earlier each morning.

The forms of *lay*, *set*, and *raise* have "receivers" of the action. That is, you "lay *something* down," "set *something* down," or "raise *something* up." (Something receives the action.) The "receiver" of the action can be either the object of an active verb or the subject of the sentence.

> I *lay* my *books* on the kitchen table every day. [books = object of the verb—receiver of the action]
> The *books* are *laid* on the kitchen table. [books = subject—receiver of the action]
> The *bricks* were *laid* in a straight row.
> Ricardo *lays* his *plans* aside when I come to visit him.
> I *laid* my *plans* aside for him.
> I *have laid* my *ring* in the same place every day for some time.
> I *am laying* my *pen* on the desk.

Verb Forms

I *set* my *reports* on the boss's desk each afternoon.
She *sets* her *work* near mine.
Her *work is set* near mine.
I *set* my *material* on the desk yesterday.
The photographer *has set flowers* on the table.
I *am setting flowers* on the table.

I *raise vegetables* to share with my neighbors.
My grandmother *raises petunias* every year.
I *raised* the *curtain* yesterday.
Carl Marshak *has raised* an interesting *question* about the election.
We *are raising tomatoes* for all our friends.
Fruits and vegetables are being raised.

Exceptions to the "receiver" rule exist. Standard English makes use of *set* in these kinds of phrases:

The sun *sets* every day.
We *set* out on a journey.
It takes three hours for the concrete to *set*.

Using Troublesome Verbs

Fill in each blank with the appropriate form of the verb in parenthesis.

1. (to lay)   Mother _____ her briefcase on the desk every evening when she gets home from work.

2. (to lie)   Then she gets a drink of milk and _____ down on the sofa.

3. (to sit)   While I _____ by the window, she naps.

4. (to set)   I _____ my watch so that I can wake her.

5. (to rise) When she awakes, she stretches, yawns, and _____ to her full height.

6. (to raise)   She _____ the window and yells to my younger brother.

Check Yourself

Rewrite each sentence, selecting an appropriate standard form of the verb in parenthesis.

1. Almost every day I (to write) in my journal.

2. Each day in class we (to discuss) ideas from our journals.

3. Today we (to be) ready for a new assignment.

4. The teacher (to read) our journal entries weekly.

5. She (to stress) the value of writing practice.

6. Last week she (to talk) about a revising strategy.

7. Yesterday we (to rewrite) our essays in class.

Verb Forms

8. Several times the instructor has (to take) us to the writing center.

___

9. Have you (to be) to the center this week?

___

10. I am (to send) a copy of my first essay to my aunt.

___

11. We were (to collect) stories about our community.

___

12. Students were (to lie) on the grass enjoying the warm sunshine.

___

13. Ben (to lay) his books on a nearby bench.

___

14. To get some sun, I will (to lie) outside for several hours.

___

15. (To set) the plant near the window, will you please?

___

16. Each evening he enjoys (to sit) outside and watching the sun set over the lake.

___

17. Just as the sun (to set), it turns a brilliant orange.

18. Earlier in the day we (to set) up a picnic area next to the marina.

19. This morning we (to rise) early to watch the members of the Yacht Club race their boats.

20. As they got into starting position a few hundred yards from shore, they (to raise) their sails.

Editing Practice

1. On a separate sheet of paper, write the appropriate standard form for the verbs that are numbered and underlined in this student essay. Be sure to add appropriate helping verbs where needed.

Let Those Skeletons Dance
by Aneatha Mack

According to George Bernard Shaw, if you can't get rid of the family skeleton, you may as well make it dance. In other words, what was done in the past cannot be changed, so you might as well accept and make the best of it.

A few years back, when I was about fourteen, my grandmother (1) teach me the truth of this statement. Late one afternoon she and I were in the den. I was busy working on a crossword puzzle, and my grandmother was making one of her colorful patchwork quilts. Suddenly there was a knock on the door, and I went to answer it. When I (2) open the door, there stood a somewhat large-looking lady, appearing to be in her mid-fifties. She (3) be wearing a brown tweed coat with a matching hat and gloves. She said, (4) "I looking for Roxie Mack; (5) do she live here?" I answered, "Yes, she does; please come in and have a seat, and I'll get her for you." Next I (6) ask her, "What's your name?" She (7) reply, "My name is Vera Simmons." I went back down the hall and into the den. I told my grandmother that a lady by the name of Vera Simmons (8) sitting in the living room waiting to see her. My grandmother (9) jump up and quickly (10) set her quilt aside. I asked her who this woman was, and she (11) say that she was her sister. I asked, "What sister?" I thought I had met all her sisters and brothers, but not once had I ever seen this lady before or ever heard anyone say a word about her. My grandmother did not stop to answer me; she (12) hurry into the living room and embraced the lady. After the introduction was over, they both (13) taken a seat and began reminiscing about the old days. I went back into the den, wondering how this lady could possibly be my grandmother's sister and asking myself where she (14) been all this time.

After the lady had left, I immediately began asking my grandmother how this lady could be her sister. She (15) tell me that Vera was actually her half-sister; she and Vera had the same father. I asked if my great-grandmother (16) knowed about this. She said, "Of course she did; Vera (17) use to come to our house and play with us, and sometimes she would spend the weekend too." From this experience I (18) decide that none but a mule denies his family.

2. For practice in using troublesome verbs (such as *lie* and *lay*), underline the correct verb forms in the following student paragraph.

Sometimes for a short time you may become a stranger to your wife. Maybe one night you kiss good night and you both (1: *lie, lay*) there, each wanting to be held, each wanting to be loved, but neither taking the initiative; you just (2: *lie, lay*) there, unsatisfied, before drifting into an uneasy sleep. The second night you still want to be held, but now an invisible wall has (3: *raised, risen*) between you. You kiss good night and she rolls over, her back to you. You reach out and (4: *lie, lay*) your hand on her shoulder and feel the tension there. All clues say, "(5: *Lie, Lay*) down and leave me alone." The third night you barely brush lips as you kiss good night and fall asleep, back to back. The fourth night you come home and the tension has turned into longing. The words pass, unsaid by each: "Hey, I've missed you." The baby has been (6: *lain, laid*) in her crib early, and with the excitement of new lovers, you (7: *sit, set*) down to a romantic candlelit dinner you've prepared together from leftovers in the refrigerator. Later that evening you jump into bed, each the aggressor. After making passionate love, you (8: *lie, lay*) awake, drinking hot tea and playing backgammon into the wee hours while your favorite records play softly on the bedroom stereo. You talk and talk and talk, each willingly sacrificing hours of sleep to make up for the days of lost love. All too soon the morning sun will (9: *rise, raise*) to find you just drifting off to sleep.

For Further Practice

Select a piece of writing you did earlier in the semester, and proofread it to see if your verbs are in standard form. If you find any nonstandard forms, ask yourself if the standard form would be more appropriate. For review, look back at the material in this section. Then correct your errors.

SUBJECT-VERB AGREEMENT

You are on your way toward mastering standard English grammar once you have a general understanding of verb forms. In the preceding section you learned that these include the base form, the *s* form, the *ed* form, the *en* form, and the *ing* form.

Base Form	S Form	*Ed* Form	*En* Form	*Ing* Form
walk	walks	walked	walked	walking
take	takes	took	taken	taking

The purpose of this section is to help you develop additional mastery in the use of the base and *s* forms.

The base form is used with the personal pronouns *I*, *you*, *we*, and *they*; with plural nouns, such as *boys*; and with plural combinations, such as *he and I*.

I walk.   I take.
You walk. You take.
We walk.   We take.
They walk. They take.
Boys walk. Boys take.
He and I walk. He and I take.

The *s* form is used with the pronouns *he*, *she*, and *it*; with singular nouns, such as *boy*; and with other singular words such as *one* and *everyone*.

He walks.   He takes.
She walks. She takes.
It walks.   It takes.
The boy walks. The boy takes.
Everyone walks. Everyone takes.

Singular and Plural Subjects

When plural subjects are used with plural verbs (the base form) and when singular subjects are used with singular verbs (the *s* form), we say that the subjects and verbs *agree* in number. Conversely, if a plural subject is used with a singular verb or if a singular subject is used with a plural verb, we say that the subject and verb *do not agree*, and this lack of agreement is considered a grammatical error in standard English.

Note: Generally nouns that don't end in *s* take verbs that do, and generally nouns that do end in *s* take verbs that don't. For a list of nouns that do not end in *s*, see page 274.

canary sing*s*   monkey climb*s*
canarie*s* sing   monkey*s* climb

To train your ear for subject-verb agreement, match a subject from the first column with a verb from the second column by drawing a connecting line so that the subjects and verbs agree. Then practice saying these combinations aloud.

ballerinas   cooks
chef   dance
cat   shop
student   meows
buyers   laugh
friends   share
children   learns
he   try
it   paints
they   falls

Choosing Verbs for Singular and Plural Subjects

Underline the verb that agrees with the subject.

1. Tabatha (*wants, want*) to study genealogy.

2. She (*hopes, hope*) to find her roots.

3. Her brothers (*thinks, think*) she is wasting her time.

4. They (*says, say*) their ancestors (*is, are*) just a bunch of dead people.

Compound Subjects

When two or more subjects are joined by *and*, they form a *compound subject*. The compound subject is usually plural and, therefore, needs a plural verb.

A warehouse and an old factory *were* torn down.

There is, however, an exception to this rule: When two subjects joined by *and* form a single unit or refer to the same person or place, the compound subject is considered singular and takes a singular verb.

Peanut butter and jelly *is* my favorite filling for a sandwich. (*Peanut butter and jelly* forms one unit.)
My good friend and teacher *is* Ms. Jones. (*Good friend and teacher* refers to one person.)

Choosing Verbs for Compound Subjects

Underline the verb that agrees with the subject.

1. The eight-track player and even the turntable (*seems, seem*) somewhat obsolete.
2. The cassette and the compact disk (*appears, appear*) to be replacing vinyl records.
3. Fruit and cereal (*is, are*) my favorite breakfast.
4. The shop and storehouse (*stands, stand*) behind the garage.

Alternative Subjects

When two subjects are joined by *or* or *nor*, they are called *alternative subjects*, and the verb agrees with the nearer subject.

Neither the club members nor the president *knows* **the rule.** (The singular subject *president* is closer to the verb; therefore, the verb must be singular.)

Neither the president nor the club members *know* **the answer.** (The plural subject *club members* is closer to the verb; therefore, the verb must be plural.)

Choosing Verbs for Alternative Subjects

Underline the verb that agrees with the subject.

1. Neither the secretary nor the treasurer (*is, are*) present.

2. Either the president or the vice president (*has, have*) asked us to hold this meeting.

3. Neither the club sponsor nor the committee chairs (*knows, know*) why.

Words between the Subject and the Verb

When any phrase comes between the subject and the verb, you may find it harder to make your subjects and verbs agree. But the rule still applies: Use singular verbs with singular subjects and plural verbs with plural subjects.

The *rain* on the windows *looks* beautiful to me.
The *napkins* on the table *match* perfectly.
One of the girls *knows* my sister.
The *woman* in the blue suit talking to the salespeople *is* the department manager.

Choosing a Verb When Words Are between the Subject and the Verb

Underline the verb that agrees with the subject.

1. A frosty morning during the winter months (*gives*, *give*) me a good feeling.
2. The warm days in February (*reminds*, *remind*) me that spring is coming.

Check Yourself

Underline the correct verb in each sentence.

1. Jonathan (*hopes*, *hope*) to make some friends on campus.
2. Nadia (*has*, *have*) chosen her roommate, and they are living in a new apartment.
3. Her mother (*thinks*, *think*) that the rent is too high.
4. A washer and a dryer (*comes*, *come*) with the apartment.
5. A weight room and a clubroom (*is*, *are*) added features.
6. Her apartment manager and next-door neighbor (*is*, *are*) Mrs. Steinberg.
7. Either the owner or the manager (*is*, *are*) proposing an increase in the rent.
8. Neither the manager's assistant nor the residents (*supports*, *support*) the increase.
9. The owner, as well as the manager, (*insists*, *insist*) that the services will be upgraded.
10. The groundskeeper, along with the maintenance staff, (*says*, *say*) that upkeep is expensive.

11. The swimming pool behind the apartments (*has, have*) to be cleaned daily during the summer months.
12. Several pieces of equipment in the weight room (*needs, need*) to be repaired.
13. Any resident who refuses to pay the activity fee (*is, are*) not allowed to participate.
14. The apartments that (*has, have*) been damaged by tenants cannot be rented easily.
15. There (*is, are*) a new apartment complex opening this summer.
16. Here (*is, are*) some brochures describing the extras it will offer.

Editing Practice

Underline the correct verb forms in the following student essay, written by Julia Moore.

For years teenage pregnancy (1: *has, have*) been a major social concern across the country. We all probably (2: *knows, know*) someone who has become pregnant while in high school, or even junior high. Or perhaps someone reading this paper has experienced teen pregnancy firsthand. When we hear that a girl is pregnant, the following questions (3: *comes, come*) to mind. What decision will she make about the baby? What kind of role will the father play in that decision? If she (4: *decides, decide*) to keep the baby, how will she cope as a young mother while still trying to get an education and grow up herself?

When a teenager (5: *discovers, discover*) that she is pregnant, she is asked, "What are you going to do?" Often she does not have a great deal of time to make major decisions that will affect the rest of her life. There (6: *is, are*) varied options available to her, none of which (7: *is, are*) ideal. One option is to have an abortion. Another option is to carry the baby full-term and then place it for adoption. Two other options (8: *is, are*) intertwined—she can marry the father and they can try to raise the baby, or she can opt to keep the baby and try to support it on her own or with somebody else's help. Let's concentrate on the problems associated with the last two options.

When a young couple (9: *is, are*) faced with parenthood, the future lives of at least three people are involved. The prospective father may care about the unborn child but realize that he does not love the child's mother enough to have a successful marriage. Or the couple may decide that because of their ages, it would not be practical for either of them to try to raise the baby. Some teenage boys are simply uncaring and (10: *tells, tell*) the young mothers-to-be, "I don't care what you do. It's your problem, not mine."

If the teenage mother (11: *decides, decide*) to keep the baby but (12: *has, have*) no one to turn to for help, in addition to trying to support herself and the baby, she is faced with the added burden of finding her place in society. On the inside (13: *is, are*) a carefree teenager trying to get out. But that teenager is bound by something larger than she can imagine. She is forced into the adult world long before she is ready for adult responsibilities. Adults (14: *does, do*) not want her to enter their world before she is mature enough any more than she wants to be in it. The world of the teenage mother can be one of confusion and sadness. And we (15: *has, have*) not even touched on the countless problems the child who is born under uncertain circumstances will be forced to grow up with.

One of the biggest challenges facing society today (16: *is, are*) how to prevent such situations from occurring in the future. We as parents would like to think that our teenage children are not sexually active, but the statistics (17:

proves, prove) otherwise. Parents and schools (18: *needs, need*) to convince teenage girls and boys of the problems a teenage pregnancy can bring. The young people of today (19: *needs, need*) adequate sex education. The most effective way to prevent the problem of teenage pregnancy in the future (20: *is, are*) to begin communicating at an early age with our children today—at home and in the schools. A teenage pregnancy can turn the best of times into the worst of times.

For Further Practice

Select a piece of writing you did earlier in the semester, and proofread it to be sure that all your subjects and verbs agree. If you find any errors, try to identify the problem by looking back at the material in this section. Then correct your errors.

PRONOUNS

A *noun* names a person, place, or thing. For example, *Susan, Chicago, computer, softness,* and *equality* are all nouns. *Pronouns* are used as noun substitutes and allow us to refer to a topic repeatedly without having to repeat the noun each time. The noun that a pronoun replaces is known as its *antecedent.* Consider the following example:

I wrote to Susan and invited her to come to New York on Wednesday.

In this case, *her* stands for Susan; *her* is the pronoun and *Susan* is the antecedent. You would not say, "I wrote to Susan and invited Susan to come to New York on Wednesday." Nor should you say, "I wrote to her" without first indicating that you are referring to Susan. Using standard English, neither would you say, "I wrote to Susan and invited she to come to New York on Wednesday."

By understanding and applying a few key principles related to these examples, you can master standard usage of pronoun reference and pronoun form and thereby write more clearly.

Pronoun Reference

A pronoun should refer to a specific noun (or a group of words functioning as a noun) included in the same sentence or to one specifically identified in an earlier sentence. Once again, this noun is called the pronoun's *antecedent*.

Sometimes the meaning of a sentence is not completely clear because an antecedent is missing altogether:

> UNCLEAR REFERENCE:
> On the television program "Crisis in the Workplace" they said that TV has turned America into a nation of nonreaders. They may be right.

Who is *they* referring to? Without a clearly stated antecedent, we can't be sure. Note that with the addition of the noun *panelists*, which serves as an antecedent for the pronoun, the meaning is clarified:

> CLEAR REFERENCE:
> Panelists on the television program "Crisis in the Workplace" said that TV has turned America into a nation of nonreaders. They may be right.

Sometimes a sentence is unclear, not because the antecedent for a pronoun is missing, but because more than one possible antecedent is present, as in the following example:

> UNCLEAR REFERENCE:
> George left the lecture early and played a video game. It gave him a headache.

What gave George a headache, the lecture or the video game? In this case, the pronoun *it* could refer to either noun, and the reader is left to decide. One way to correct such an error in pronoun reference is to eliminate the pronoun completely.

CLEAR REFERENCE:
The lecture gave George a headache, so he left early and played a video game.

Making Pronoun Reference Clear

Correct any problems with pronoun reference that you find in these sentences.

1. James gave the dog part of a sandwich. He didn't like it.

_____

_____

2. Alvin danced with Simone, which was fun.

_____

_____

3. Some years ago Marlon Brando refused to accept the Oscar in protest of the treatment of native Americans. It increased our awareness.

_____

_____

Using Standard Pronoun Forms: Case, Number, Gender, and Person

In an example used earlier, we noted that it would be incorrect to say, "I wrote to Susan and invited she to come to New York on Wednesday." This is known as an error in pronoun case. We will look at this type of problem next and then turn to other common problems in the use of pronoun *number*, *gender*, and *person*.

Pronouns

The following chart shows the standard forms of some of the pronouns used most often.

	Subject Case	Object Case
First Person		
Singular	I	me
Plural	we	us
Second Person		
Singular	you	you
Plural	you	you
Third Person		
Singular	he, she, it	him, her, it
Plural	they	them

First, look at the subject-case pronouns *I, we, you, she, he, it,* and *they.* These pronouns can be used as the *subject* of a verb. The subject is the person, place, or thing that performs the action named by that verb.

STANDARD:
Helena gave the poodle a shampoo.
She gave the poodle a shampoo.
Arizona has hot weather most of the year.
It has hot weather most of the year.

You would not say the following:

NONSTANDARD:
Her gave the poodle a shampoo.
Me and him went to Arizona last Christmas.
Him and me went to Arizona last Christmas.

When do you use the object-case pronouns *me, us, you, him, her, it,* and *them* correctly? These pronouns can be used as the *object* of an active verb. The object is a person, place, or thing that receives or experiences the action named by the verb.

STANDARD:
Please give me some of that pizza.
Sluggo beat him and me in the contest.

NONSTANDARD:
Please give I some of that pizza.
Sluggo beat he and I in the contest.

Object-case pronouns are also used to replace a noun that is the object of a preposition. Prepositions are words that show relationships between a noun or pronoun and the rest of the sentence. Here are some of the most common ones:

about	before	by	to
above	below	for	toward
across	beneath	of	under
after	beside	on	upon
among	between	over	with
at	beyond		

The object of a preposition almost always comes directly after the preposition.

STANDARD:
I sat down beside her.
I sat down beside Nancy and her.

NONSTANDARD:
I sat down beside she.
I sat down beside Nancy and she.

Using Standard Case Forms

Underline the correct case of the pronouns of standard English in the following sentences.

1. My friend and (*I, me*) enjoy reading African-American literature.

2. (*She, her*) and (*I, me*) especially like to read novels.

3. Toni Morrison is one of my favorite novelists. (*She*, *her*) and Alice Walker are contemporary writers.

4. Just between you and (*I*, *me*), I find Ralph Ellison's *Invisible Man* a bit strange.

5. All of (*they*, *them*) write interesting stories.

Choosing the Correct Number and Gender

If you look back at the pronoun chart on page 243, you will notice that some forms are singular and others are plural. Just as subjects and verbs must agree in number, so must pronouns agree in number with their antecedents. The rule is simple: use plural pronouns to replace plural nouns (antecedents), and use singular pronouns to replace singular nouns (antecedents). In standard English, you would write the following:

Helena washed *her* poodle.
Helena and Alex washed *their* poodles.

Generally this aspect of pronoun usage, known as *pronoun/antecedent agreement*, will give you no trouble. The only difficulty you may have is when using a special group of singular words, shown here:

anybody	neither
anyone	nobody
anything	none
each	no one
either	one
everybody	somebody
everyone	someone

Since these words are singular, use singular pronouns to replace them.

STANDARD:
One of the men sold *his* own camera.
Everyone should bring *his or her* own lunch.

Notice in the second sentence that *his or her* is used. The use of *his* alone would suggest that no females are in the group.

Similarly, to avoid what is known as *sexist language*, you would say, "The *student* is expected to do *his or her* best." You may prefer to use the plural noun *students* and the plural personal pronoun *their*. Or you can eliminate the pronoun altogether.

STANDARD:
The *students* are expected to do *their* best.
The *student* is expected to do excellent work.

Using Standard Number and Gender of Pronouns

Underline the standard pronoun forms in the following sentences.

1. A writer should write about what (*he, he or she, they*) knows.

2. One doesn't always do what (*he, he or she, they*) should.

Choosing the Correct Person

Finally, in addition to choosing the correct case, number, and gender of your pronouns, you will also need to choose the correct person, whether first, second, or third form. Again, look at the chart on page 243. The main point to remember here is that you need to be consistent. For example, if your antecedent is third person, the pronoun that replaces it should also be third person, for the sake of consistency.

STANDARD:
When *students* study ahead for their exams, *they* usually make good grades.

NONSTANDARD:
When *students* study ahead for their exams, *you* usually make good grades.

Pronouns

Using the Standard Person of Pronouns

Underline the standard pronoun forms in the following sentences.

1. Ernest Gaines, the author of *A Gathering of Old Men*, spoke to a group of beginning fiction writers. *(They, You)* were enthralled by what he said.
2. He explained how he struggled to make good grades in English when he was a college freshman. *(He was, You were)* not sure how to write essays.

Check Yourself

Underline the standard forms of pronouns in the following sentences.

1. My sister and *(I, me)* are proud of our Indian heritage.
2. When I went to East Texas to attend a family reunion, *(we, us)* met Tecumseh Lycurgas Joseph Ross, whose grandfather was a great Indian chief and who goes by the nickname "T.L.J."
3. *(He, Him)* and his wife brought some Indian frybread.
4. T. L. J. brought with *(he, him)* some arrowheads and an old bow.
5. Everyone asked *(he, him)* to explain the markings on the bow.
6. Several women wore beaded moccasins and colorful shawls *(she, they)* had made.
7. T. L. J. asked us to refer to Indians as Native Americans. *(You, We)* certainly will respect his wish.

> **Editing Practice**

In the following student-written essay, underline the appropriate standard pronouns.

A Day on Grandpa's Farm
by Steve Witte

The day on my grandfather's farm started for (1: *I, me*) when my grandmother shouted from the kitchen, "Steve, your breakfast is ready." My eyes popped open but shut immediately after I had glanced at the clock on the dresser and noticed that it was only 4 A.M. Between you and (2: *I, me*), it was closer to time for midnight snacks. However, the fragrance of coffee and sausage and biscuits started drifting up to my room. Sticking one foot out from under the six thick blankets on the bed to see how cold it was, I decided to get my clothes on as fast as I could and get downstairs before Grandpa ate everything all by himself. After dressing, I headed for the kitchen table, where Grandma had platters of eggs, salt pork, homemade biscuits, and gravy waiting for Grandpa and (3: *I, me*). Those were the biggest biscuits I'd ever seen. As full as a tick, I started back upstairs when Grandpa grabbed me and said, "Boy, we're burning daylight. It's time for (4: *you and I, you and me*) to go to work.

Outside it was damp and cool, but as we would soon see, the day would warm up fast. First we went to the hen house to gather eggs. Soon I learned there were two good reasons why a city boy like (5: *I, me*) shouldn't go into a chicken coop: the nauseating smell and the awful feeling between my toes. I lifted each sleepy hen and found (6: *her, their*) eggs. Then Grandpa sent me back to the house to wash my feet and put on some shoes.

Next it was time to tend the hogs. Grandpa and (7: *I, me*) picked up three sacks of feed, mixed the feed with some milk, and poured the mixture he called slop into the feeding troughs. Meanwhile the mama sow had pushed one little pig between the fence and (8: *she, her*), the boar had wedged one little pig under (9: *he, him*), and all the pigs were squealing.

That afternoon Grandpa and (10: *I, me*) plowed Grandma's garden for (11: *she, her*). It was a hot, dusty job, and by the end of the afternoon blisters covered my hands. Finally I stumbled to the house and collapsed under a big oak tree in the back yard. About that time Grandma called out, "Your dinner is ready." After filling up on fried chicken, fresh vegetables, and hot apple pie, I turned the window fan on and headed for bed, knowing that before long Grandpa would be standing over me and uttering those encouraging words, "Get up, boy; we're burning daylight."

For Further Practice

Select a piece of writing you did earlier in the semester, and proofread it to be sure that all your pronouns are in standard form, applying what you have learned. If you find any errors, try to identify the problem by looking back at the material in this section. Then correct your errors.

PUNCTUATION

Though you may think of punctuation as little more than a nuisance you would prefer to ignore, it's actually a tool that can serve you well in your writing if you know how to use it effectively. It allows you to be a kind of traffic cop for your readers, giving signals, telling the reader when to pause, where to turn, and when to stop. Best of all, there are a relatively limited number of fairly simple rules to learn in order to use punctuation for good effect. You can write with more confidence as you use punctuation to show relationships between ideas and to emphasize ideas.

In the past some writers have sprinkled punctuation marks all over their work with about as much thought or restraint as one might use when salting french fries. Today, however, it's considered more appropriate to aim for a less cluttered punctuation style, using only the necessary marks, just as doctors today are advising us not to overuse salt.

End Marks: Period, Question Mark, Exclamation Point

Three marks can indicate the end of a sentence.

❑ Use a *period* to end a statement or a command.

Linda Chavez has a nice smile.
Please leave the room.

❑ Use a *question mark* to end a direct question.

Are you ready to talk?

❑ Use an *exclamation point* to end an emphatic statement.

How right you are!

Using End Marks

Put the appropriate mark (period, question mark, or exclamation point) at the end of each sentence.

1. Skiing is a popular sport
2. Start enjoying some sport today
3. Is break dancing considered a sport
4. What demanding sports skiing and break dancing are

Turn Mark: Semicolon

❏ Use a semicolon to turn from one main idea within a sentence to another.

Barney won a million dollars; the whole family went wild.

❏ Use the semicolon between two related main ideas that are joined by a logical connective such as *however*, *nevertheless*, or *therefore*.

Barney had to give some of the money to Uncle Sam; however, there was plenty left for his family to spend.

Note: The semicolon is not an end mark, like a period. The semicolon indicates a connection between ideas, whereas the period indicates a separation of ideas. (For additional information on using the semicolon, see page 202.)

Using the Semicolon

Use the semicolon in the appropriate places in the following sentences.

1. In cities much of the land space is covered with concrete therefore, parks and landscaping near office buildings are especially important.
2. In winter the sidewalks are sheets of ice they can be dangerous for the elderly.

Pause Mark: Comma

The comma is the punctuation mark with the largest number of uses and is probably also the one most often misused. Generally, it marks the end of a unit of thought within a sentence where the reader should pause. As you study the rules presented here, try reading the examples aloud. Notice how often the comma marks a place where it seems natural for your mind to pause.

Use commas to separate two complete thoughts within the same sentence when they are joined by a coordinating conjunction (*and*, *but*, *for*, *or*, *nor*). (For additional information on using coordinating conjunctions, see page 208.)

> The stock market crashed on Monday, but it began to recover on Tuesday.

Using Commas to Separate Two Complete Thoughts

Put commas where needed.

1. Construction workers are subjected to noise constantly and some of them become completely deaf.
2. They are encouraged to wear earplugs but many of them ignore the advice.

Use a comma to set off introductory material in a sentence. The introductory material may be just a word:

Suddenly, the world seemed to stop.

The introductory material may be a short phrase:

To tell the truth, I don't have my wallet with me.

The introductory material may be a long phrase or a subordinate clause:

> After several years of helping the poor, Sister Mary gave up in despair.
> Although Sister Mary is a kind and loving person, she has her limits.

Note: A *clause* has a subject and verb, but a *phrase* does not.

Using Commas after Introductory Material

Put commas where needed.

1. When the workers are finished the building will be ready for occupancy.
2. In fact it should be ready within two weeks.

Use commas to set off "interrupters." An interrupter may be a word, a short phrase, a long phrase, or a clause that cuts into the middle of a sentence.

I try to communicate well. At times, however, I am misunderstood.

The ex-model seems destined, in spite of all her bad reviews, for major box-office success.

Women, who have traditionally come out poorly in divorce cases, are beginning to get fairer treatment.

Note, however, that not every clause that comes in the middle of the sentence should be set off by commas. Sometimes a clause is needed to identify the person, place, or thing being discussed. In this case, what looks like an interrupter may not really be interrupting; it may be necessary to the sentence's meaning:

The man who threatened to break my arm was only joking.

Here, the clause *who threatened to break my arm* is necessary to show which man is being discussed; it does not really interrupt the sentence and thus should not be set off with commas. (For additional information on restrictive and nonrestrictive modifiers, see pages 210–211.)

Using Commas to Set Off Interrupters

Put commas where needed.

1. Replacing slabs of concrete it seems is an endless job.
2. Potholes even in streets built fairly recently are found all over the city.
3. Engineers who design our bridges try to eliminate all structural defects.

4. The Golden Gate Bridge which spans over a mile is a wonder of the modern world.
5. The man who designed it came from a small town in Michigan.

Use commas to separate items in a series. A series is composed of three or more items; an item may be a word or a group of words. Note that each item in the series must be the same part of speech, or must be grammatically parallel.

He collects tapes, records, and compact disks.

The route for the race took us over city streets, onto freeways, and out to country roads.

Using Commas to Separate Items in a Series

Put commas where needed.

1. Jackhammers car horns steam shovels and subway trains give the city its noisy sound.
2. Drivers blast their horns in the early morning at lunchtime and in the evening rush hour.

When Not to Use a Comma

❑ Do not use a comma to separate a subject from its verb. What looks like introductory material may really be the complete subject.

INCORRECT:
A play written by Tennessee Williams, is sure to be interesting.
CORRECT:
A play written by Tennessee Williams is sure to be interesting.

Punctuation

❏ Do not use a comma to separate a verb from the rest of the predicate.

INCORRECT:
I believe, that you should be congratulated.
CORRECT:
I believe that you should be congratulated.

❏ Do not place a comma between two complete thoughts unless they are connected by a coordinating conjunction (*and, but, for, or, nor*). Doing so would create a comma splice. (For more information on comma splices, see pages 204–207.)

COMMA SPLICE:
Sonja loved the house, however, Charlie cleaned it.
CORRECTION:
Sonja loved the house; however, Charlie cleaned it.

Correcting the Overuse of Commas

Put an *X* through all commas that are not needed.

1. Construction workers led by Manny, always respect his authority.
2. He says, that he is just a common man.

Colon

❏ Use a colon after a complete sentence that precedes a list.

In order to hang wallpaper, I need these supplies: razor knife, scissors, sponge, pan, and plumb rule.

❏ Use a colon to draw two sentences together when the sentence after the colon explains the first one.

There is one simple rule: Do your best.

Using Colons

Put the colon where it is needed in the following sentences.

1. My favorite writers include the following Gwendolyn Brooks, Robert Frost, Emily Dickinson, and D. H. Lawrence.
2. The Golden Rule is clear do unto others as you would have them do unto you.

Quotation Marks

Use quotation marks around a direct quotation.

Benjamin Franklin said, "Fish and visitors smell after three days."

The rules for using other marks with quotation marks are clear: Use commas and periods inside quotation marks. Use colons and semicolons outside. Use question marks and exclamation marks inside if the quoted material is a question or exclamation, outside if it is not.

"There was never a good war," Franklin said, "or a bad peace."

Franklin said, "There was never a good war or a bad peace"; he also said, "A penny saved is a penny earned."

The teacher asked, "Should we have the test this week?" (The quoted part is a question.)

Did the teacher say, "We will have the test this week"? (The quoted part is not a question.)

Use quotation marks around the titles of short works.

I read T. S. Eliot's "The Love Song of J. Alfred Prufrock."

"Don't Be Cruel" is one of Elvis Presley's biggest hits.

Using Quotation Marks

Put quotation marks where they are needed in the following sentences.

1. One of his most sympathetic critics said, If D. H. Lawrence's attitude toward sex were adopted, then two things would disappear, the love lyric and the smoking-room story.
2. And this, I think, is true, responded Lawrence.
3. Did Lawrence say, One suffers what one writes?
4. Concerning England, Lawrence exclaimed, This is only a tomb!
5. The librarian recommended that we read Lawrence's short story The Prussian Officer.

Check Yourself

Place punctuation marks—periods, question marks, exclamation points, semicolons, commas, colons, and quotation marks—where they are needed in the following sentences. Put an *X* through any unnecessary commas.

1. Last summer I visited New York City
2. My mother advised me, Take this trip now while the weather is good
3. Have you ever been there
4. What an exciting experience to be in New York
5. I have read *The New Yorker* for years
6. I wanted to see the main tourist attractions therefore I took a bus tour.
7. Near the Bronx Zoo I saw a vendor selling sandwiches he had a cart parked on the sidewalk.
8. He put mustard onions and catsup on every hot dog he sold.
9. He sold a sandwich he called the "Monte Cristo" which had corned beef mustard dill pickles and Swiss cheese on it.
10. He was selling the sandwiches in the morning but by noon his cart was empty.

11. The hot dogs, smelled good.
12. The kind vendor needed, no marketing tips to sell his wares.
13. In any case he knew the art of selling.
14. As he pushed his cart along the sidewalk tourists crowded around.
15. The guy who bought the most hot dogs worked in an office building across the street from the zoo
16. He said to the vendor Old man, put plenty of mustard on those dogs.
17. The vendor a local legend has been in the same area of the park for years.
18. When I walked, up to the vendor, I noticed that a sign on his cart had a misspelled word. The sign read as follows sandwitches for sale
19. Thinking I would help him with his spelling, I said, Did you know that *sandwiches* is spelled without a *t*
20. Acting like he didn't hear me he motioned me closer and said, Hot dogs pretzels and peanuts—what will you have?
21. The food smelled so good that I couldn't resist then I repeated my spelling lesson, and he whispered so no one else could hear, You'd be surprised how many sandwiches I've sold with that misspelled word.

Editing Practice

Insert the needed punctuation in the following student essay.

Role Change
by Bill Rice

The war of role change struck my house about ten years ago. That's when my wife Betty decided to chuck the apron give the diapers away and seek to realize the dream of becoming a professional career woman. Because I wanted peace and harmony to stay in the family she got my blessings immediately. Besides I was confident her outside career wouldn't last long. Little did I know that this single act would make such radical changes in our lives and shake the very foundation of our marriage and personal relationship.

After eight years of experiencing jobs in many different fields of employment Betty finally found her niche she got a job at a local television station in outside sales. Her career took off in a way mine never had and she started bringing home more money than we had imagined possible. But instead of it being a time of pleasure and carefree spending for us it became a time of competitive war. My male ego was bruised and I had the feeling I had lost my prominent position as breadwinner of the family. My role as the lord and master of our household was being undermined and I had no idea how to deal with the challenge.

Even though I truly admired Betty and wanted her to succeed I unconsciously tried to sabotage all her efforts. I was feeling very insecure because she no longer had to depend on me for financial support. Being the wise person she was Betty recognized my negative attitude and tried to include me in all the social functions connected with her job in sales but being the stubborn person I am I dragged my feet and indulged in self-pity at every possible opportunity. Soon her patience grew thin and we started having running battles and verbal confrontations on a daily basis. Life was miserable for the entire family.

Fortunately before too much time passed we recognized that changes had to be made on both sides. After many hours of talking to each other and not at each other we got a better view of each other's perspective. I finally realized that her past statements about wanting to be more than a coal miner's daughter or just a housewife was a goal she had set for herself and really needed to achieve for her own sake. Betty's self-esteem was reaching an all-time high while mine was in the pits. With this new insight our problems didn't automatically go away but at least we weren't aiming at an intruder in the dark. We were beginning to resolve our real differences and not just selfish gripes.

For many weeks our relationship was touch and go but we eventually made the transition and gained a lot of respect and admiration for each other as individuals as well as lovers. As I look back to those troubled times I now realize I was spending all my efforts focusing on the negative aspects of her working and not recognizing the positive opportunities she was providing both of us. When we finally started building on the advantages of our two-career family and mutually seeking solutions to the problems life was happier for everyone.

> **For Additional Practice**

Select a piece of writing you did earlier in the semester, and proofread it to be sure that your punctuation is correct. If you find any errors, try to identify the problem by looking back at the material in this section. Then correct your errors.

CAPITALIZATION

Like punctuation, capitalization is a graphic means of directing your readers' attention. In general, capital letters are used to call attention to a particular item, such as the first word of a sentence or a person's name. The material that follows should serve as a quick review since you are no doubt familiar with most of the rules already. But because they are so familiar, it's especially important to observe them as you write. Otherwise, your readers may focus on your failure to use conventional marks rather than on the point you are trying to make.

Capitalize the first word of every sentence, including sentences in direct quotations.

>   **I love you.**
>   **My friends said, "We love you."**

> **Capitalizing the First Word of a Sentence**

Add capital letters where needed.

1. men with diverse backgrounds and skills have led our nation.
2. the professor asked, "do you know anything about our leaders?"

Capitalize the names of persons and their titles and the first person pronoun *I*.

I
Jesse Jackson   Mr. Stuart
Yolanda Wilson, Ph.D. Dr. Wilson

Capitalizing Names of Persons, Titles, and the Pronoun *I*

Add capital letters where needed.

1. i know that ronald reagan was once a movie star.
2. Did you know that ronald reagan, star of *Bedtime for Bonzo*, later became president reagan?

Capitalize the names of specific places.

Orchard Lake Road
Superstition Highway
Detroit River
Scotsdale High School
Wayne State University

Capitalizing Names of Specific Places

Add capital letters where needed.

1. George Bush owns a home in maine.
2. Lyndon Johnson's old home is near the pedernales river in texas.

Capitalize specific languages and course titles.

English   Spanish   Biology 101

Capitalizing Specific Languages and Titles

Add capital letters where needed.

1. President Johnson spoke spanish as well as english.
2. However, he never took spanish 101; he was too busy with political science 101.

Capitalize specific names. These include names of brands, political parties, institutions, and organizations, including acronyms that stand for organizational names.

    Mazda   Centers for Disease Conrol (CDC)
    Democrat   Sigma Tau Delta

Capitalizing Specific Names

Add capital letters where needed.

1. President Carter was a democrat.
2. President Bush belongs to the republican party.
3. President Johnson studied at southwest texas state university in San Marcos.
4. Has a president ever worked for ibm?

Capitalize the names of months, days, holidays, and celebrations.

    January   Memorial Day
    Wednesday   Fourth of July

Capitalizing Months, Days, and Holidays

Add capital letters where needed.

Capitalization

1. New presidents take office in january.
2. Some years the weather is severe on inauguration day.
3. The date could be moved to the spring, perhaps around easter.

Capitalize specific events or periods in history.

Civil War   **Age of Reason**

Capitalizing Specific Events or Periods in History

Add capital letters where needed.

1. The renaissance marked the end of the dark ages.
2. the battle of iwo jima took place during world war II.

Capitalize the first and last words in titles and all other words except articles (*a*, *an*, and *the*), prepositions, and short conjunctions.

Notes of a Native Son
"Rhapsody in Blue"

Capitalizing Words in Titles

Add capital letters where needed.

1. As a young man John F. Kennedy wrote the book *profiles in courage*.
2. Louisiana's governor Jimmie Davis wrote the song "you are my sunshine."

Capitalize words referring to religions, deities, churches, and religious celebrations.

Hinduism	St. Patrick's Catholic Church
Zeus	Life Tabernacle
Christ	Passover
Jehovah	Mass

Capitalizing Religious Words

Add capital letters where needed.

1. John Kennedy was our only catholic president.
2. Jesse Jackson, a candidate for president in 1988, is a baptist preacher.

Check Yourself

Add capital letters where needed.

1. every spring the caucasian members of the parker family and the indians who descended from cynthia ann parker hold a reunion.
2. as a girl cynthia parker was stolen from her family by the indians.
3. at that time she lived at fort parker, texas.
4. her caucasian family members were leaders in this early settlement; dr. parker was the only physician there.
5. cynthia grew up near the river.
6. americans love holidays, especially the fourth of july.
7. the band usually plays "stars and stripes forever" and "america the beautiful."
8. two religious holidays that fall in december are christmas and hanukkah.

Capitalization

Editing Practice

The following newspaper article, written by Bill Deener for the *Dallas Morning News*, appears without capital letters. Indicate where a capital letter is needed by writing the appropriate capital over the lowercase letter.

when jerome walked into saint thomas the apostle episcopal church three years ago, he asked only that the priest give him a proper burial.

jerome was dying of aids.

his face was covered with the purplish lesions of a rare cancer. . . . he had no other place to go, said the rev. ted karpf, rector of the north dallas church.

karpf dutifully began to care for jerome and encouraged him to attend st. thomas. but when jerome started attending church, the fear of acquired immune deficiency syndrome (aids) began to fester within the 180 members of the congregation. by september 1985 only about 50 people were attending mass.

"it was sort of like the worst fear i've ever had came true—suppose someone gave church, and nobody came. well, nobody much came," karpf said.

some of the parishioners said they would stay if karpf would ask jerome and the gay members of the church to leave.

"all jerome had asked for was compassion and support. he asked that we go with him on his journey," karpf said. "and i could only keep the covenant with him in the same way i keep that covenant with the other members."

"it never occurred to me that there was any reason not to care for him. i was scandalized that anybody could tell another human being, 'no, we are not going to take care of you,' but it happened."

karpf, 39, who had come to st. thomas from a fort worth church in August 1984, had envisioned from the outset that the church would serve those who really had no church. six other episcopal churches are within a four-mile radius of st. thomas church at 6525 inwood road.

the park cities [neighborhood] is just east of the church, love field is to the west, and oak lawn to the southeast, but st. thomas really isn't in any of those neighborhoods.

"another neighborhood church didn't seem to be needed," karpf said. "it didn't need to be a black church or a mexican church or a park cities yuppie church."

karpf advertised the church in the *dallas observer*—a cultural arts newspaper whose readers are primarily in their 20's and 30's—in hopes of attracting those with what he called a "fairly open world view" and those who weren't already identified with another church.

the strategy worked. membership climbed from 80 people to 180 within a year of karpf's arrival.

but by june 1985, word began to spread among parishioners that jerome had aids and that there were other homosexuals attending church who might spread the disease. the fact that they were all taking communion from the same chalice concerned some parishioners.

karpf, who is married with two young children, called the national centers for disease control in atlanta, georgia, to determine if his congregation was at risk. aids experts at the cdc assured him that the disease was not spread casually and that no aids cases had been spread by people sharing a drinking cup.

to reassure church members, karpf, who was always the last to drink from the communion chalice, would face the congregation instead of having his back to them, as is the usual practice. his wife, kay, who was pregnant at the time, and their 3-year-old daughter also drank from the chalice. . . .

gradually word spread among the oak lawn gay community that homosexuals were welcome at st. thomas.

the elderly along inwood road also began to hear about this brash young preacher who wanted to be their advocate; they came too.

blacks and hispanics heard that karpf's church was built on tolerance and inclusion, not exclusion. they joined as well.

less than two years later, the congregation is about 40 percent homosexual; 20 percent are over age 65; 10 percent are black; and about 30 percent are recovering alcoholics. the church, says karpf, has been reborn, this time with a social vision of commitment.

with membership approaching 200, it has become a center of civic activism and the meeting place for a variety of neighborhood and political groups. one night recently a group of republicans met in one wing of the church while a group of democrats met in another. an alcoholics anonymous group meets there, and most of the aids programs in dallas meet there. . . .

parishioners said the church has opened their eyes to the fact that death is real and they must come to terms with it.

"life becomes more meaningful because of those people being here," said ruth woodward, one of the members. "that person being here with us is precious."

when asked if she had any fear of contracting aids, ms. woodward said, "there is nothing i will do at church that is going to give me aids." . . .

karpf said he doesn't dwell on the aids issue in his sermons. he never mentions aids during mass. instead, he deals with issues such as poverty. his ministry, he said, is based on new testament doctrines. . . .

"everybody that i know who is infected with this disease has said to me, each in his own way, 'i am under the judgment of my own death,'" he said. "what else needs to be said?"

a favorite message of karpf's is that "we are all condemned under the eyes of god to be loved."

For Additional Practice

Select a piece of writing you did earlier in the semester, and proofread it to be sure that your capitalization is correct. If you find any errors, try to identify the problem by looking back at the material in this section. Then correct your errors.

SPELLING

Unfortunately, writers are sometimes judged on the basis of their spelling ability. As a matter of fact, some very talented writers are poor spellers, and some writers have good spelling as their only claim to fame. Still, spelling is an important skill to develop, and this section will help you do so.

Here are four steps:

1. Decide to improve.
2. Recognize the pitfalls.
3. Learn some spelling remedies.
4. Practice faithfully on your own.

Spelling Demons

Here is a list of common words that are often misspelled.

accidentally	all right	apparent
accommodate	amateur	appearance
acquaintance	analyze	article
adolescence	apologize	athlete

Spelling

attendance	disastrous	precede
audience	discipline	preferred
beautiful	discussion	prejudiced
becoming	efficient	principle
believe	embarrass	psychology
benefit	environment	pursue
breathe	equipment	receive
business	especially	recommend
carried	exaggerate	seize
category	existence	separate
cemetery	experience	similar
changeable	familiar	succeed
comfortable	grammar	sufficient
coming	guarantee	transferred
committee	guidance	unnecessary
condemn	height	surprise
convenience	interest	tragedy
criticize	knowledge	truly
deceive	leisure	usual
definitely	loneliness	valuable
dependent	miniature	villain
description	noticeable	weather
despair	occasion	whether
desperate	parallel	writing
difference	paralyze	
dilemma	peculiar	
disappoint	possession	

Spelling Hints

Following are three hints for using your senses to help with spelling.

1. *Listen to how words sound.* Though it is true that many words in our language are not spelled the way they sound, paying attention to the sound of words can prevent some misspellings. For example, if you say "denist," you are likely to spell it that way. Hear the *t* in *dentist* as you say the word.

Here are some other words to listen to. (Italicized letters indicate troublespots to pay special attention to.)

F*ebru*ary   envir*o*nment
disas*trous*   mini*a*ture
at*h*lete   su*r*prise
com*fo*rtable   conv*e*nience

2. *Look at words carefully*, especially those that don't sound like they are spelled. A good example of a word that needs to be seen, either literally or in the mind's eye, is *foreign*. While writing the word out, file a mental picture of it in your brain, and as you do so, associate the image of the written word with someone who is foreign.

   Other words to look at and associate with their meanings are these:

   *p*neumonia   analy*z*e
   *k*nife   psy*ch*ology
   o*cc*asion   a*cc*o*mm*odate
   W*ednes*day

3. *Feel the words as you write.* One way is to write the words in the air. Try the word *category*. Trace the letters in the air. Feel each letter as you form it. Or try writing the words in large letters on a chalkboard. Work very slowly. As you put effort into forming the letters, feel them as you write.

   Or try the method of writing a word, *category*, for example, twenty times. Your fifth-grade teacher probably had you do this, and you thought it was punishment. The purpose was to have you feel the words over and over until the correct spelling was a part of you. Be sure to concentrate on the correct spelling and the meaning of the word as you write it repeatedly.

Rules of Thumb

Rules can become more trouble than they are worth. But a few rules of thumb are useful.

1. Use *i* before *e* except after *c* or when sounded as *a*, as in n*ei*ghbor or w*ei*gh.

believe	receive
relieve	deceive
belief	deceit
siege	

EXCEPTIONS:

either	leisure
neither	science
foreign	height
seize	efficient

2. With words ending in silent *e*, drop the *e* before a suffix (a group of letters that comes after a root) beginning with a vowel and keep it before a suffix beginning with a consonant.

use + *i*ng = using
use + *a*ble = usable
use + *f*ul = useful
use + *l*ess = useless

EXCEPTIONS:
argue + ment = argument
judge + ment = judgment
true + ly = truly
notice + able = noticeable
change + able = changeable

There are always exceptions. Try learning the exceptions by looking at and feeling the words.

3. When adding a suffix to a word, double the final consonant if the suffix begins with a vowel and the word has one syllable or is accented on the last syllable.

rot + ing = rotting
sit + ing = sitting
control + ed = controlled
refer + ed = referred
offer + ed = offered (The accent is not on the last syllable of the root, so the *r* is not doubled.)

4. Add a prefix (a group of letters that comes before a root) to the *whole* root word.

un + necessary = unnecessary
co + operate = cooperate
mis + spell = misspell
grand + daughter = granddaughter
dis + appear = disappear
im + mature = immature
il + legal = illegal

Memory Devices

A memory device is simply word association. You make up some phrase or word that will help you remember the spelling. Sometimes these phrases are silly, and you might not even want other people to know what they are. But the secret is that they work!

A useful list of popular memory devices follows. (You may want to make up some of your own.)

all right	My answers are not all wrong; they are *all right*.
attendance	*At ten* we shall go to the *dance*.
calendar	The *DAR* [Daughters of the American Revolution] are fond of their place on the calen*dar*.
capitol	The capit*o*l has a d*o*me.
committee	It was a co*mmittee* of six, with two *m*'s, two *t*'s, and two *e*'s.
familiar	A *liar* should be fam*iliar* with his lies.
separate	There is *a rat* in sep*a*r*at*e!
stationery	Station*e*ry is for l*e*tters.
pursue	a *purse pur*sued may mean wealth.
principal	When princip*a*l means m*a*in, it is spelled with an *a*. The m*a*in person in the school is the princip*a*l. The m*a*in dancer of a dance company is the princip*a*l of the com-

pany. The m*a*in street is the princip*a*l street in the town. The m*a*in amount of money before interest is added is the princip*a*l.

Noun Plurals

Most nouns form their plurals simply by adding *s*.

boy	boys	pen	pens
girl	girls	window	windows
hand	hands	tree	trees

There are some exceptions, however. When a word ends in *s, z, x, ch,* or *sh,* add *es* to form the plural.

box   boxes
buzz   buzzes
bus   buses
church   churches
dish   dishes

When a word ends in *y* preceded by a consonant, change the *y* to *i* and add *es*.

baby   babies
lady   ladies
city   cities
library   libraries
story   stories

When a word ends in *y* preceded by a vowel, simply add *s*.

key   keys
day   days
attorney   attorneys

Add *s* to most words ending in *o*.

piano	pianos
memo	memos
banjo	banjos
Eskimo	Eskimos

Note: Some words ending in *o* require *es*.

hero	heroes
tomato	tomatoes
potato	potatoes
veto	vetoes

Some plurals don't end in *s*.

freshman	freshmen
woman	women
man	men
child	children
goose	geese
mouse	mice
ox	oxen
tooth	teeth

Noun Possessives

Add *'s* to form the possessive of singular nouns.

instructor	instructor's
book	book's
Geraldine	Geraldine's

Add *'s* to form the possessive of plural nouns that do not end in *s*.

freshmen	freshmen's
mice	mice's

Add *s'* to form the possessive of plural nouns ending in *s*.

instructors	instructors'
books	books'

Look-alikes and Sound-alikes

Words are often misspelled because they look like or sound like another word with a different meaning. The following is a list of commonly confused words.

accept: to receive, to welcome, to say yes
except: excluding

affect: to influence (verb)
effect: result (noun)

aloud: out loud
allowed: permitted

altar: a place for worship (noun)
alter: to change (verb)

bare: without clothes, naked
bear: to carry

cite: to summon, to quote
site: a place
sight: a view

course: a direction, a series of classes
coarse: rough, vulgar

desert: a dry region
dessert: the last part of the meal, often something sweet

forth: to go forward
fourth: after third in a series

led: past tense of *lead*
lead: a metal

passed: went by (verb)
past: before the present time (noun or adjective)

peace: harmony, tranquillity
piece: a portion

principal: main, chief; invested funds
principle: rule

quiet: free of noise
quite: entirely, completely

sole: bottom of the foot; fish
soul: spirit

to: a preposition
too: excessive; also
two: a number

weather: atmospheric conditions
whether: if

Some pronouns and contractions also look or sound alike.

your: possessive form of *you*

you're: contraction of *you are*

its: possessive form of *it*

it's: contraction of *it is*

whose: possessive form of *who*

who's: contraction of *who is*

their: possessive form of *they*

they're: contraction of *they are*

Editing Practice

Correct the spelling errors in the student journal entry that follows. Use the dictionary to check on words that you aren't sure about and that don't appear in the spelling list.

I'm taking mathmatics on the forth floor of Bronson Hall; its the last day of the sumester, and the bell rings. Everbody runs and jummps on the elavator. There must be fifteen people in their. Its packed. Someone manages to push the buton with an elbow. We start going down. The elevator stops on the third floor. The doors open, and waiting to go down are two students. They take one look at the mass of humanaty inside and decide to ketch the next ride. The elevator continus on it's way but is stoped at the second floor. The doors slide open and reveal three huge football players, each one at least six feet four inches tall and weighing at least 250 pounds. They look at all the bodies cramed inside, grin, turn around, and back into the elevator. Bodys are now flattened against the wall; breatheing becomes dificult. The elevator drops a full three inchs as their wieght settles. The doors close and the air is stifleing. A couple in the back miraculusly still continue to talk. I feel sorry for the little chick squeazed into the far corner who looks like she's to shy to say a word even under normal circomstances. Finally we get to the first floor and I feel that I'll faint before I step out into the open aire.

For Additional Practice

Select a piece of writing you did earlier in the semester, and proofread it to be sure that you have spelled all your words correctly. If you find any errors, try to identify the problem by looking back at the material in this section. Then correct your errors.

Index

Abstract idea, 107
Accept/except, 274
Advice to writers, Mark Twain's, 89
Affect/effect, 274
Agreement
   pronoun-antecedent, 245–247
   subject-verb, 233–237
Aim of text, 3
Allowed/aloud, 274
Altar/alter, 275
Alternative subjects, 235–236
Ancestral Voices, 89–90
Angelou, Maya, 38, 39–43
Antecedent, 241
   agreement with pronoun, 245–247
   definition of, 240
Anxiety, writing, 5–6
Apostrophe, 276
Arguing (*See* Logical appeal)
Arrangement (*See* Organization)
Assignments
   additional reading, 10–11, 37, 63, 90, 130, 166, 188
   additional writing, 10, 37, 62, 89, 130, 166, 188
   reading (*See* Readings)
   writing
      cultural/family essay, 75–84
      essay using sources, 144–162
      introductory letter to instructor, 3–4
      job application letter, 178–186
      journal, 52–53
      opinion essay, 119–127
      paragraph, class newsletter, 26–30
      personal narrative essay, 53–59
      résumé, 185–187
Attitudes toward writing, overcoming negative, 5–7
Audience
   for business correspondence, 175, 177
   for class newsletter, 27, 30
   for cultural/family essay, 89
   emotional appeal to, 160
   enhancing credibility, 161–162
   for essay using sources, 143–144, 147–148, 156–157, 159–160
   for job application letter and résumé, 180–181, 183
   for journal, 52
   logical appeal to, 160–161
   for opinion essay, 120
   for personal narrative essay, 56

Back to Bachimba (Lopez), 64, 65–69
Bare/bear, 275
Bear/bare, 275
Brainstorming, 144–145, 153, 155
Business writing
   conventions in, 174–178
   job application letters, 178–185
   résumé, 185–187

Capitalization, 260–264
Checklist(s), revision
   for cultural/family essay, 83
   for essay using sources, 158–159
   for job application letter, 183–185
   for opinion essay, 125–127
   for personal narrative essay, 56
Chronological order, 81, 83

Cite/site/sight, 275
Clarity, 175 (*See also* Evaluating evidence)
Class newsletter assignment, 26
   audience for, 27
   drafting, 28–29
   planning, 27–28
   revising, 29–30
   sample, 30–32
Clause, definition of, 252
Climactic order, 81, 83
Clustering (*See* Mental map)
Coarse/course, 275
Coherence (*See* Related parts)
Colon, 255–256
   use of, with quotation marks, 256
Combining ideas, 208–211
Comma, 251
   correcting
      comma splice with, 206–207
      overuse of, 255
      run-on sentence with, 203
   after introductory material, 210, 252–253
   nonuse of, 254–255
   to separate complete thought, 252
   to separate items in series, 254
   to set off interrupters, 253–254
   use of, with quotation marks, 256
Comma splice, 199–201
   correcting
      with comma and coordinating conjunction, 206–207
      with period, 204–205
      with semicolon and logical connective, 205–206
      with subordinator, 207
   definition of, 199
Commonly confused
   words, 274–276
   verbs, 225–227
Completeness
   of information, 83
   of sentences, 191

Compound subjects, 235
Comprehension, 46–50 (*See also* Reading comprehension)
Conciseness, 176–177
Conclusion (end)
   of cultural/family essay, 82, 84–85, 88
   discussion and examples, 29–32, 56, 58, 59, 61, 82, 84–85, 88, 125, 129, 157–158, 164, 181–184
   of essay using sources, 157–158
   of job application letter, 181–184
   of opinion essay, 125, 129
   of paragraphs in newsletter, 29–32
   of personal narrative essay, 56, 58–59, 61
   plan and purpose, 39, 56, 125, 127, 157–158, 181
Conjunction
   coordinating, 202, 203, 206, 208, 251–252
   correcting comma splice with, 206–207
   correcting run-on sentence with, 203
   subordinate, 203, 207, 210–211
Connectives, logical, 201, 209
Contractions, 276
Conventions in professional writing, 174–178
Coordination, 208–209
Correctness, 175
Course/coarse, 275
Courtesy, 177
Creating
   as aspect of planning, 22
   for assignments
      cultural/family essay, 75–78
      essay using sources, 155
         instructor, 3
      job application letter and résumé, 178–179
      journal, 52–53
      newsletter paragraph, 27
      opinion essay, 121–123
      personal narrative essay, 53–55
   methods
      brainstorming, 145, 153
      freewriting, 121–122

journal writing, 52–55
　　　questioning, 27, 55, 76–77, 121–123
　　　shifting point of view, 3–4, 55
　　　staircase method of freewriting, 122–123
　　　use of conflict, 53–54
　　　use of experiences stored in memory, 3,
　　　　52–55, 119–123, 178–180
　　　use of observation, 52–53, 119–123
　　　use of sources, 145
Credibility, 161–162
Critical thinking, 106–119
Cultural/family essay assignment
　　choosing interview subject, 75–76
　　conducting interview, 76–79
　　creative thinking for, 75
　　prereading, 65
　　revising draft on, 84
　　sample, 81–82, 84–88
　　sample interview for, 78–81
　　sharing draft on, 83–84
　　writing rough draft for, 81–82

Days, capitalizing names of, 262
Description, 54, 56
　　(*See also* Sensory language)
Desert/dessert, 275
Details (*See* Sensory language, Support)
Development, adequate (*See* Support)
Diagramming
　　main points, 124–125
　　tree, 154–155
Dialect, 72–73
Diction, 274–276
Direct quotations, 149
Discovery (*See* Creating)
Documentation (*See* Sources, identification of)
Draft(s)
　　of class newsletter, 28–29
　　of cultural/family essay, 81–83
　　of essay using sources, 156–158
　　evaluation of, 24, 29, 58–59, 83–84, 126,
　　　158–159, 183

　　of job application letter, 180–182
　　of opinion essay, 126
　　of personal narrative essay, 56–58
　　refining, 24, 30, 59, 84, 126, 162–164, 183,
　　　185
　　revising, 29–30, 59, 84, 126–127, 158–162,
　　　183–185
　　reworking, 24, 29–30, 59, 84, 126, 159–162,
　　　183, 185
Drafting
　　in reading, 48–49
　　in writing, 23–24

Editing (*See* Revising, Reworking, Refining)
Editorial Research Reports, 145
Effect/affect, 274
Emotional appeal, 160
End marks, 250
Errors (*See* Correctness)
Essay
　　cultural/family (*See* Cultural/family essay assignment)
　　developing journal entry into, 53–61
　　formal (*See* Essay using sources and Opinion essay assignments)
　　informal (*See* Cultural/family essay and Personal narrative assignments)
　　introduction, body, and conclusion, plan and purpose for, 157–158
　　opinion (*See* Opinion essay assignment)
　　personal (*See* Personal narrative assignment)
　　using sources (*See* Essay using sources)
Essay using sources, 144
　　bare-bones outline for organizing, 154
　　collecting information, 148–150
　　developing thesis statement, 151–153
　　drafting essay, 156–157
　　evaluating draft, 158–159
　　exploring sources, 145–146
　　mental map for organizing, 154, 155–156
　　organizing material, 146–156
　　prereading, 131–132

refining draft, 162–164
reworking draft, 159–162
selecting topic, 144–145
summarizing problem, 146–148
tree diagram for organizing, 154–155
Evaluating
as aspect of revising, 24, 29
evidence, 111
main point and subpoints of, 125
opinions of others, 95–96
samples of student writing
cultural/family essay, 83–85
essay using sources, 162
introductory letter to instructor, 3–4
job application letter, 183
opinion essay, 125
paragraphs, newsletter, 32–36
personal narrative essay, 125
Evidence
definition of, 107
evaluating, 111
types of, 107–109
using, 107–109
Examples, opinion supported with, 108
Except/accept, 274
Exclamation point, 250
use of, with quotation marks, 256

Facts, opinion supported with, 107
Family Story (Fisher), 74
Feedback, sample
group, 83–84
instructor, 183
tutor, 58–59
Final draft(s) (*See* Draft(s))
Focus (*See* Staircase method of freewriting)
Focused freewriting (*See* Staircase method of freewriting)
Formal writing (*See* Essay from sources, Job application letter, Opinion essay, and Résumé assignments)
Forth/fourth, 275

Fragments, 194–195
Frankl, Viktor, 131, 133–139
Freewriting, 121–122
discussing, 122
questioning, 122–123
staircase method of, 122, 123

Goals
career, 178
of chapters, 1, 15, 38, 64, 93, 131, 167
Goal setting
as aspect of planning, 22
for course, 8–9
evaluating and refining, 165, 187–188
for newsletter, 27
See also Purpose
Grammar rules, 191
Group work
assignments (*See* Class newsletter, *Ancestral Voices*)
building vocabulary, 142
discussing freewriting and main point and subpoints, 122, 125
interviewing class members, 26
sharing draft(s) and getting feedback, 58–59, 83–84

Habits, self-defeating, in writing, 7
History, capitalizing events or periods in, 263
Holidays, capitalizing names of, 262
Homonyms (*See* look-alikes/sound-alikes)

I, capitalizing, 261
"I" attitude, 177
I Know Why the Caged Bird Sings (Angelou), 38, 39–43
Illustrations, opinion supported with, 108–109
Imagination Helps Communication (Royal Bank of Canada), 170–172
Incomplete sentences (*See* Sentence fragments)
Independent clause (*See* Sentence, definition of)
Informal writing (*See* Class newsletter, Cultural/

family essay, Introductory letter to instructor, Personal narrative assignment)
Interrupters, using commas to set off, 253–254
Interview
  conducting, 26–27, 75–78
Introduction (lead)
  as minidrama, 160
  discussion and examples, 28–32, 56–58, 60, 82, 84–85, 88, 125, 128, 156–157, 160, 162, 181–184
  of cultural/family essay, 82, 84–85, 88
  of essay using sources, 157–160
  of job application letter, 181–184
  of opinion essay, 125, 129
  of paragraphs in newsletter, 28–32
  of personal narrative essay, 56, 58–59, 61
  plan and purpose, 28, 56, 125, 127, 156–160, 181
Introductory letter to the instructor, assignment, 3–4
Introductory material, using commas after, 210, 252–253
Invention (*See* Creating)
Its/it's, 275

Job application letter assignment, 178
  assessing your strengths, 178–179
  drafting your letter, 181–182
  getting feedback on your draft, 183
  preparing to draft, 180–181
  revising your draft, 183–185
  setting career goals, 178
  writing a "nutshell" biography, 179
Journal
  developing essay from entry in, 53–61
  keeping, 52–53
  questioning entries, 55
  recording memories in, 53–55
Journalists' questions, 27, 76–77, 123

Key words
  in organizational plan, 124–125, 155–156
  in topic sentence, 28–29
Knowledge
  of grammar, 191
  sources of, 119
  of writing process, 6
  See also Memories and Reading comprehension

Language
  capitalizing names of, 262
  sensory, 43–44, 83
  standard versus nonstandard English, 72–73
Lay/lie, 225–230
Lead/led, 275
Letter(s) (*See* Introductory letter to instructor and Job application letter assignments)
Let Those Skeletons Dance (Mack), 230–232
Lie/lay, 225–230
Logic, faulty, 161
Logical appeal, 160–161
Logical connectives, 201, 205, 209
  correcting comma splice with, 205–206
Lopez, Enrique "Hank," 64, 65–69

Main
  paragraph(s), body, 126, 157, 181
  idea of essay, 124–127, 151–157
  idea of paragraph, 28–29, 124–126, 157–158
Main idea statement, 28
Man's Search for Meaning (Frankl), 131, 133–139
Mechanical errors (*See* Correctness)
Memories
  answering questions about, 55
  asking questions about, 55
  recording, in journal, 53–55
  as resource in writing, 53–54
Memorable writing (*See* Sensory language)
Mental map, in essay using sources, 154, 155–156
Modifiers, 216 (*See* Sensory language, Nonrestrictive clause, and Restrictive clause)

Months, capitalizing names of, 262

Names, capitalizing specific, 262
Negative writing attitudes, strategies for overcoming, 5–7
New York Times Index, 145
Nonrestrictive clause, 211
Nonstandard English, 72
Noun
   definition of, 240
   spelling plurals of, 273–274
   spelling of possessives, 274

Opinion
   appropriately supported, 111
   inappropriately supported, 111
   definition of, 107
   supporting
      with examples, 108
      with facts, 107
      with illustrations, 108
      with statistics, 108
      with testimony of authority, 108
Opinion essay assignment, 119
   conclusion in, 125
   creating bare-bones outline, 125–126
   diagramming subpoints and points, 124–125
   discussing freewriting, 122
   finding evidence, 126
   finding main point and key subpoints in, 124
   freewriting, 121–122
   getting feedback in, 125
   introduction in, 125
   prereading, 95–96, 100–101
   questioning freewriting, 122
   revising rough draft, 126–127
   sample, 127–129
   sharing draft, 126
   staircase method of freewriting, 122, 123
   topics for, 120–121
   writing rough draft, 126

Organization
   as aspect of planning, 22
   bare-bones outline in, 125–126, 154
   chronological or time order in, 81, 83
   climactic order in, 81, 83
   diagram in, 124–125
   mental map in, 154, 155–156
   spatial order in, 81, 83
   tree diagram in, 154–155
Order (*See* Organization)
Organizational plan
   for cultural/family essay, 81
   for essay using sources, 154–158
   for job application letter, 181
   for opinion essay, 124–126
   for paragraph in newsletter, 27–29
   for personal narrative essay, 56
Outline, barebones, 125–126, 154
   for essay using sources, 154
   for opinion essay, 125–126

Paragraph, principles of writing, 28–29
Parallelism, 254
Paraphrasing, in essay using sources, 148
Passed/past, 275
Peace/piece, 275
Peck, M. Scott, 15, 16–19
Period, 250
   correcting comma splice with, 204–205
   correcting run-on sentence with, 201–202
   use of, with quotation marks, 256
Personal experience, as writing resource, 52
Personal narrative assignment
   revising draft, 59
   sample, 60–61
   sharing draft, 58–59
   writing rough draft, 56–58
Personal summary of chapters, 9–10, 36, 62, 88, 129, 164–165, 187
Personal writing (*See* Class newsletter, Cultural/family essay, Introductory letter to the instructor, Journal, Personal narrative assignments)

Persuasion
   and enhancement of credibility, 161–162
   use of emotional appeal for, 160
   use of logical appeal for, 160–161
Phrase, definition of, 252
Piece/peace, 275
Plagiarism, 149
Plan (*See* Organizational plan)
Planning
   in reading, 47–48
   in writing, 21–23
   See also Organizational plan
Plural forms, 217, 219, 221, 233–236, 245, 273–274
Point of view, 93
   Shifting point of view, as creating, 3–4, 55
Possessives, noun, spelling of, 274
Power of the Positive Woman (Schlafly), 101–103
Practice, importance of, in writing, 21
Predicate(s), 192
   definition of, 192
   identifying, 193–194
Prereading questions, 12–16, 38–39, 65, 95–96, 100–101, 131–132, 170–174
Principal/principle, 275
Problem-solving process, writing as, 15–37
Process (*See* Reading process; Writing, process of)
Professional writing, conventions of, 174–178
Pronouns, 240–247
   agreement with antecedent, 245–246
   consistency of, 81
   definition of, 240
   objective-case, 243–244
   reference, 241–242
   relative, 210–211
   subject-case, 243
   using standard forms, 242–244
      case, 244–245
      gender, 245–246
      number, 245–246
      person, 247
Proofreading (*See* Evaluating, Refining)
Public writing (*See* Essay using sources, Job Application letter, Opinion essay, Résumé assignments)
Punctuation, 249–250
   colon, 255–256
   comma, 203, 206–207, 210, 252–256
   end marks, 250
   quotation marks, 256–257
   semicolon, 251
Purpose
   of introduction(s), 156–157
   of writing assignments
      class newsletter, 26
      cultural/family essay, 75, 89
      essay using sources, 144, 147
      job application letter and résumé, 181
      journal writing, 52–55
      opinion essay, 119, 120
      personal narrative essay, 55
   See also Goals

Question (*See* Journalists' questions)
Questioning
   as a method of creating, 6, 7, 27, 55, 76, 77, 93, 121, 122–123
   to find main point, 124
   to evaluate (*See* Checklist(s), revision)
Question mark, 250
   use of, with quotation marks, 256
Quiet/quite, 275
Quotation marks, 256–257
   for direct quotations, 256
   for titles of short works, 256
Quotations, use of direct in essay using sources, 149

Raise/rise, 225–230
Reader's Guide to Periodical Literature, 145
Reading comprehension, 46–50
   questions, 19–21, 43–46, 69–71, 98–100, 103–106, 113, 115, 139–143, 172–174
Reading process, 46–50
   comprehension (*See* Comprehension)
   drafting, 48–49

planning in, 47–48
prereading in (*See* Prereading)
revising, 49–50
Readings, 16–19, 39–43, 65–69, 96–98, 101–103, 133–139, 170–172
Readings, additional (*See* Assignments, additional reading)
Reasons for writing
(*See* Assignments, writing)
Refining, in revision, 24, 30, 59, 84, 126, 162, 183, 185
Related parts of paragraph and essay, 29, 127
Relative pronouns, 210–211
Religious words, capitalizing, 264
Restrictive clause, 210–211
Résumé assignment, 185–187
Revising
  class newsletter, 29–30
  cultural/family essay, 84
  essay using sources, 158–162
  evaluation in, 24, 29, 58–59, 83–84, 126, 158–159, 183
  job application letter, 183–185
  opinion essay, 126–127
  personal narrative essay, 59
  in reading, 49–50
  refining, 24, 30, 59, 84, 126, 162, 183, 185
  reworking in, 24, 29–30, 59, 84, 126, 159–162, 183, 185
  in writing, 24
Reworking, in revising, 24, 29–30, 59, 84, 126, 159–162, 183, 185
Rise/raise, 225–230
Road Less Traveled (Peck), 15, 16–19
Rough draft(s) (*See* Draft(s))
Rules, 191, 270–272
Run-on sentences, 199–201
  correcting
    with comma and coordinating conjunction, 203
    with period, 201–202
    with semicolon, 202
    with subordinator, 203–204
  definition of, 199

Samples of student writing (Parts One and Two of text), 4–5, 28–32, 54–61, 78–90, 120–122, 124–125, 128–129, 146–147, 155–156, 160–164, 178–182, 184, 186
Schlafly, Phyllis, 95, 101–103
Self-discipline, importance of, in writing, 21
Semicolon, 209
  correcting comma splice with, 205–206
  correcting run-on sentence with, 202
  to correct two related main ideas, 251
  use of, with quotation marks, 256
Sensory language, 43–44, 83
Sentence, 192
  capitalizing first word of, 260–261
  completeness, 191
  definition of, 200
  joining fragments to, 196
  subjects and predicates in, 192–194
  topic, 28–29
  See also Run-on sentences
Sentence fragments, 194–195
  correcting, 195–196
  joining to sentences, 196
Series, commas in, 254
Set/sit, 225–230
Sexist language, 246
Sight/cite/site, 275
Significance, 54–56, 119, 124, 152
Singular forms, 218, 219, 221, 233–236, 245
Sit/set, 225–230
Social Sciences Index, 145
Sole/soul, 275
Sources
  exploration of, 145–146
  identification of, 150, 151
  sample in essay using sources, 162–164
Spatial order, 81, 83
Spelling, 268
  common words often misspelled, 268–269
  hints for, 269–270
  look-alikes and sound-alikes, 274–276
  memory devices for, 272–273
  noun plurals, 273–274

rules of thumb for, 270–272
Staircase method of freewriting, 122, 123
Standard English, 72
Statistics, opinion supported with, 108
Steinem, Gloria, 94, 95, 96–98
Student writing (*See* Samples of student writing)
Subject(s), 192
   agreement with verb, 233–237
   alternative, 235–236
   compound, 235
   definition of, 192
   identifying, 193–194
   plural, 233–234
   singular, 233–234
Subordination, 209–211
Subordinators, 203–204, 207, 210–211
   correcting comma splice with, 207
   correcting the run-on with, 203–204
Suffixes, 271
Summarizing, in research paper, 146–148
Support, 28, 107, 111, 126, 156–158, 181

Tense (*See* Time of verbs)
Testimony, opinion supported by, 108
Their/they're, 275
Thesis statement, 124–126, 151–153
They're/their, 275
Time of verbs
   order, 81, 83
Title of essay, 158
Titles
   capitalizing words in, 262, 263–264
   use of quotation marks for short works, 256–257
Topic
   focus and depth, 122, 158
   selecting, 3, 27, 53, 75–77, 119–120, 144–146, 152
Topic sentence, 28–29, 124–126, 157–158
To/too/two, 275
Transitions (*See* Conjunction and Connectives, logical)
Tree diagram, in research paper, 154–155

Two/to/too, 275

Unified point of view, 127
Unity, 83 (*See also* Paragraph, principles for writing)

Van Thyn, Rose, 142, 143
Verbs, 216–217
   agreement with subject, 233–237
   base form, 217–218
   ed form, 218–219
   en form, 219–221
   ing form, 221–222
   irregular, 223–227
   regular, 222–223
   s form, 218
   tense, or time (*See* Verbs, base form, *s* form, *ed* form, *en* form)
   using troublesome, 227–228
Vocabulary, 142

Wallis, Claudia, 108
Weather/whether, 275
Whose/who's, 275
Words and Change (Steinem), 96–98
Writer's block, 2
Writing
   attitudes about, 5–7
   class newsletter, 26–32
   conventions, 174–178
   drafting in, 23–24
   planning in, 21–23
   as problem-solving process, 6, 15–37
   process of, 21–24
   related to career field, 167–169
   revising, 24
   setting goals for, 8–9
   (*See also* Samples of student writing)
Writing skills, importance of, 167
   See also Assignments, writing

"You" attitude, 177
Your/you're, 275